APPAREL ENTREPRENEURSHIP

How to Start & Run
a Successful Apparel Brand

Ana & Klas Kristiansson

**APPAREL
ENTREPRENEURSHIP**

Table Of Contents

Introduction

Welcome to the Second Edition of Apparel Entrepreneurship: How To Start A Successful Apparel Brand.

This book is for apparel entrepreneurs who are about to start or have already started their brand. It's the perfect read for anyone wanting to take their brand, products and business to the next level.

If you want to learn how to run an apparel business efficiently, get your brand noticed, avoid costly mistakes, tap into industry experience, and align your business with your highest values, this book is for you.

Background

We've been working in the apparel industry for years and have been involved in numerous apparel startups around the globe. Despite the fact that we had the education and industry experience, though, starting our first brand was a challenge. There were clear gaps in our competencies, and we struggled to find the information we needed. This is why we created Apparel Entrepreneurship—a one-stop place for apparel entrepreneurs.

The reason we're so passionate about helping startups is that we've successfully started and run two own brands and now have the experience, knowledge, and resources we wished we had when first starting out. In this book, we're going to share all this with you. It's time to give back.

In 2016, we launched Sportswear Inc., an educational online platform to help entrepreneurs start and run a sportswear brand. With a passion for apparel and brand building, we shared our experience and knowledge about apparel design and product development, branding, entrepreneurship, sourcing, merchandising, product sustainability implementation, concept, and sales presentation. In 2018, the platform evolved to Apparel Entrepreneurship, to include all apparel entrepreneurs, not only sportswear brands.

Modern education

Our educational systems typically involve going to school for a few years, earning your diplomas, and then starting work. This is all great if you're aiming for regular employment. But if you want to start your own brand, you'll likely be seriously lacking in industry experience.

With Apparel Entrepreneurship, we approach learning the modern way. It's not a regular school. It's for *everyone*—all ages, all backgrounds. You can learn from wherever you're based, at any time. It is of course based online, where you purchased this book—and all for a fraction of the price and time of a traditional school.

Apparel Entrepreneurship provides the education and experience, together with hands-on tools and steps to action. The platform gives you the information you need and tells you how to *implement* it in your business.

You don't want to make mistakes that'll not only prove costly but will also waste your valuable time. Educate yourself on *your* terms.

Mission, vision and goal

Our mission is to help apparel entrepreneurs all over the world, irrespective of their background, to launch, run, and grow successful and meaningful apparel brands.

Our vision is to reduce environmental harm in the apparel industry through education, inspiration, and motivation for better entrepreneurship.

Our goal is to be the No. 1 educational source and community for starting, launching, and running apparel brands.

Who is this book for?

We're entrepreneurs, just like you, and today we've achieved the freedom lifestyle we dreamt of for years. We know what it feels like to be in full control of our time and business. With this book, we want to help *you* achieve *your* dreams, live the life you want, accomplish creative freedom, and utilize this freedom to do what you love.

Our typical readers fall into one of these three categories:

1. Action-driven, ambitious beginner

Whether you want to start a new apparel brand, or you have an existing business and want to expand into apparel, this book will help you get started the right way.

Is your dream to have your own apparel brand with a brick-and-mortar store, or be totally virtual? Whether you're a designer, entrepreneur, store owner, or totally new to the apparel industry, this book will make sure you get started and up and running the right way.

2. Action-oriented apparel-industry novice

Already working in the apparel industry and want to launch your own brand? Perhaps you've worked in the business but have knowledge gaps in specific areas. In this book, you'll learn the full process, from A to Z, gaining extensive knowledge that will enable you to take full ownership, with an in-depth understanding of all of the business areas involved in a brand.

3. Established apparel-brand owner

Already running a (mostly) successful business? Ready to take things to the next level? If you have an existing apparel brand and want to expand your collection, deepen your knowledge, improve areas of your business where there are competence gaps, and grow your business, this book is for you.

Which clothing sectors does it cover?

In the book, we talk about apparel and functional clothing. Our book is applicable for sportswear, streetwear, tech wear, activewear, urban wear, workwear, and apparel where function and fit are important.

How to read it

You can read the book from start to finish—we suggest this approach if you're new to the apparel industry, as it'll give you a good understanding of the parts involved. Or you can read it by starting with the chapters that are most relevant to you at this point.

You can use the next chapter as a checklist and high-level project plan for your apparel business. Make notes and tick off the boxes as you go along.

Want to learn more and speed up the process?

If you need templates, accountability, support, networking, help with finding manufacturers and suppliers, we suggest you take a look at the Apparel Entrepreneurship Member Zone.

It's your essential resource for the training, advice, and support you need to plan, create and grow a profitable and successful apparel brand.

What's in the member zone?

- Search and find manufacturers in our database with 500+ companies.
- Search and find fabric suppliers in our database with 40+ companies.
- Download templates, cheat sheets, and checklists.
- Participate in live Q&A video calls.
- Follow the step-by-step guide. We give you a structure and take you through the process of starting and running an apparel brand.
- Learn about the time schedule for starting your apparel brand in 30 weeks.
- Read and watch our guides, articles, videos, and how-tos about apparel entrepreneurship. From idea to launch—and beyond.
- Read, communicate and find answers in the supported community forum. Connect with us as well as with peers around the globe who are in a similar place to you.

Read more at ApparelEntrepreneurship.com

Checklist

How to use it

Use these three pages as a checklist for running your apparel brand.

This is a live document for you to keep track of your progress.

Step 1. Entrepreneurship
- ☑ Think through the 23 questions to ask yourself before starting an apparel brand.
- ☑ Make a plan for how you'll do this.
- ☑ Make room in your life for an apparel business—e.g., create a physical space for your work.

Step 2. Administration
- ❑ Register business.
- ❑ Founder's agreement.
- ❑ Set up bookkeeping.
- ❑ Open bank account.
- ❑ Reserve domain name and social media accounts.
- ❑ Arrange insurance.
- ❑ File for trademark.

Step 3. Idea and Customer Need
- ❑ Figure out the customer need and the problem your product solves.
- ❑ Answer the question: What's so special about your product?
- ❑ Collect as much information about your product as you can.
- ❑ Make sure your product is different and stands out. If there are similar products, how can you make yours better?

Step 4. Market Scan
- ❑ Perform a thorough market scan. Get to know the market.
- ❑ Examine the price ranges in your market.
- ❑ Find out who your competition is.
- ❑ Find out what quality your competitors offer and at what price level.
- ❑ Determine the unique selling points and values that will differentiate your brand from others.

Step 5. Business Plan
❏ Answer all the questions in the business plan. This is the groundwork for your business.
❏ Clarify WHY you're starting your brand. What do you want to achieve?
❏ Determine your values.
❏ Do NOT continue before you're done with the two points above. These will guide you along the way and make every decision clearer from now on.

Step 6. Branding
❏ Create a brief for your brand.
❏ Create a mood board.
❏ Determine your story.
❏ Create a graphical profile (colors, fonts).
❏ Create a logotype.
❏ Determine your visual expression.
❏ Write communication texts.
❏ Make sure it all matches your products.
❏ Create branding packaging (labels, hangtags and packaging).

Step 7. Money
❏Create a budget for the next 3 years.
❏Secure funding.
❏ Facilitate cash flow.

Step 8. Team
❏ Decide who is going to do each of the 17 roles.
❏ Where do you need help? How are you going to get it?

Step 9. Define the Collection
❏ Determine the styles you're going to make.
❏ Decide if it's both men's and women's.
❏ Decide the colors/variations per style.
❏ Decide the sizes you want the styles in.
❏ Determine who your customers will be.
❏ Determine price/style and a total collection price structure.

Step 10. The Design
❏ Design all styles in the collection.
❏ Decide the materials (fabrics and accessories).
❏ Make sure there's a red thread in the collection. Make it consistent.
❏ Determine the type of fit you want for each style.

❏ Produce tech packs, BOMs and measurement lists for all styles.
❏ Order branding package.

Step 11. Sourcing
❏ Contact factories. Decide upon a match.
❏ Contact material suppliers. Ask for samples.
❏ Decide material.
❏ Order material for prototypes.

Step 12. Pattern and Prototype
❏ Create patterns.
❏ Create prototypes.
❏ Fit and adjust for each style. Communicate comments to sample-makers.
❏ Adjust and create samples until satisfied. Finish with SMS (salesman sample).
❏ Create graded patterns.

Step 13. Pricing
❏ Calculate the garment price. Does the margin match your business strategy?
❏ Review all the posts in the budget. What can you adjust?

Step 14. Production
❏ Confirm delivery deadlines with suppliers.
❏ Order all materials.
❏ Approve size-set samples and preproduction samples.
❏ Order manufacturing. Cut, sew, and trim.

Step 15. Sustainability
❏ Decide on a sustainability strategy—what will you focus on?
❏ Incorporate sustainability in your brand values.
❏ Decide on USP for your brand.
❏ Decide on collection and styles sustainability design rules.
❏ Make garment-standards list.
❏ Decide on supplier standards.
❏ Decide on manufacturer standards.
❏ Decide on material criteria.
❏ Make a garment life-span plan.
❏ Decide on recyclability standards.
❏ Make a responsible logistics setup/plan.
❏ Create a packaging and presentation plan.
❏ Make product-care standards.

Step 16. Sales Period
❏ Ask for and receive orders. Be clear about what you offer.
❏ Make a buyers contact list.
❏ Organize your sales kit.
❏ Present your collection to buyers.
❏ Ask for and receive orders.
❏ Make a merchandising plan.
❏ Create an online strategy.

Step 17. Order
❏ Perform customer background check.
❏ Get signed orders.

Step 18. Shipping
❏ Research and find logistics partners.
❏ Arrange shipping from the factory to your warehouse.
❏ Arrange shipping to your end customers.

Step 19. Marketing
❏ Get your story together.
❏ Create customer profiles.
❏ Communicate your story and values in everything you do.
❏ Start your marketing activities as early as you can.

Step 20. Customer Care
❏ Implement a customer-service plan and strategy.
❏ Listen to your customers!
❏ Register and use the feedback to improve your business.

Step 21. After The Launch
❏ Reflect on your business.
❏ Update your strategy.
❏ Update your collection.

1.
Entrepreneurship

1.1 Twenty-Three Questions To Ask Yourself Before Starting An Apparel Brand

Running your own business isn't a 9-to-5 job. It's not the hours you spend in the office that matter—what matters is what you *produce*. You're your own boss and *you* need to make it all happen. You'll live and breathe your brand, working 24/7. It'll require you to put in the work and follow through on your dream. Are you cut out for this or not? Is it really what you want?

You'll be your own boss—no one will be there to make sure you put in the work and stick to your deadlines. Focus on your dream, your vision and mission of the brand, and don't let anyone or anything get in your way.

Here are some questions that will help you determine whether you're cut out for this or not:

1. Why do you want to start an apparel brand?

Starting an apparel brand takes commitment, time, and money. You'll be eating, breathing, and living your brand. Research, ask around, talk to people who've started a brand to see what they've gone through. Is that something you want? Try to envision what it's like to have an apparel business. The more you know, the better you can prepare. Be realistic—you need to be really ready when you start.

2. Do you have what it takes? Do you have passion, ambition, and determination?

Without passion, to truly love what you do, you'll not have the mental power to grind away. You need to really, really WANT this—not just talk about it with your friends because it's cool to be an entrepreneur. Ask yourself the above questions multiple times, before you start.

3. Do you take action when you have an idea or are you just a dreamer?

It takes some serious action to start a brand—to DO, to execute on every little step involved. If you know that you're usually a dreamer, find an accountability friend or group. They'll help you stick to your schedule. Everybody has ideas. The differentiator is: those who succeed *execute* on their ideas.

4. Does decision-making come quick and easy to you?

When you start out, unless you do it with a partner, you're usually the one making decisions. There will be tons of things to make decisions about, and if you can't make up your mind pretty quickly about what you want, things will be delayed and you'll fall behind. And usually, it doesn't really matter if you choose one way or the other—the important thing is that you pick something and go with it.

5. Are you good at planning and organizing?

We're not saying you need to be extreme about it, but as mentioned above, there will be so much going on that you'll need to keep track of things. A good idea would be to start from the beginning by implementing systems and processes.

6. How will starting a brand affect your family and friends?

Starting out will consume your time, energy, focus, and money. It could be a good idea to talk to the closest people to you about how this will affect them. If they know what you're going through, it'll be easier for them to support you and understand your situation. Who knows, some of them might even want to help out. But in the end, it's about you and it's your decision.

7. How well do you cope with stress and long working hours?

Undoubtedly there will be more to do than you'll have time for. Planning is key. If you don't take care of yourself by eating properly and getting enough sleep, you'll not have the energy to work.

Stressing out because you have too much to do won't help. The only thing that helps is to actually do what you have on your To-Do List. Focus on the important things—those that will actually move your brand forward—and drop the dumb stuff.

8. Are you okay working by yourself or do you need a partner?

Most of the successful designers/entrepreneurs out there have a partner or mentor. Someone who will complement you and your competencies. Working with a partner means you can always discuss issues with each other. How do you want to do it? Before getting a partner, you need to ask yourself what your strengths and weaknesses are and what areas you need to develop. That way you will be clearer in terms of what you need from the other person.

9. Do you have the self-discipline needed?

When it's time to grind and hustle, it's time to grind and hustle. You'll have to put in the work to later reap the success. There are tons of tools out there to keep you away from all the distractions. Make sure you know what sucks out your time and seek tools to prevent it.

10. Do you have an interest in the field you want to position your brand in?

Depending on what category you want to place your brand in, you'll need to have a personal interest in what you do. Without the interest, you'll have a hard time motivating yourself to do the work. If the interest is there you'll be your own customer and you'll know what you need and want.

11. Who is your ideal customer?

When you know exactly who your customer is, you'll know, in all areas of your business, what decisions you need to make.

12. Do you have something unique to offer?

There are tons and tons of brands out there. What makes yours stand out from the crowd? The fewer competitors you'll have, the better.

13. What problem does your product/brand solve?

The response, "People will always need clothes," is not a good one. Go deep! What is the customer need for your products and brand? What will get easier for your customers once your products are available?

14. What does your product do for your customers?

Is it helping them in any way? Is it helping them perform better? Is it making them feel a certain way?

15. Have you done thorough market research in order to find your niche?

When you know the market, you also know where there's a gap. If you can fill that gap, you're in business.

16. Have you spoken to potential customers to see if there's a need for your intended brand/product?

If no one wants your products, you'll never have a business.

17. What price segment will your brand fall into?

This is directly related to the values and positioning of your brand. If you're aiming for mass market, then the price and product should reflect exactly that, otherwise those customers will not buy your products because they'll be too expensive. Keep in mind also that the cheaper the products, the lower the margin you'll get. And if you end up with a small margin you'll need to sell many more times the amount to reach the funds needed to keep your business going.

18. Who will be your three main competitors?

Knowing your competitors' offers is important for you. When you know their offers and price points, you know what you need to put out there in order to differentiate yourself. Don't risk being No. 2 or No. 3. You'll know what NOT to do, because they already offer that. It can also be good to see how easy it's been for them to attract customers. Is there a big need for the type of product?

**The harder you work, the more luck you get.
Keep on grinding!**

Make your own luck!

---

19. Why should customers buy your products instead of your competitors'?

With your answer to the above question, you can easily make a product offer that stands out. What else in your business plan is different? If too many things are similar, go over it again until you stand out.

20. What type of legal structure will your business have?

Study the different forms and see which one suits you best. Corporation, partnership, or sole proprietorship?

21. How much money do you need and where will you get it, to get started?

This depends on how big you want to start out. Will you start with a small collection with a couple of styles or will you go for the big bang? Whichever you pick, you'll need much more than you've calculated. Talk to the bank or your family. Are investors, angels or Kickstarter an option?

22. How will you handle financial insecurity?

Do you have a family who are dependent on you? Do you have enough saved money to keep you going for a while without any income? Remember, product-development cycles are typically a year long.

23. Do you have the experience needed? If not, what external help do you need? Who do you want in your team?

Make an evaluation of your competencies, to determine what you have and what areas you need help with. Check your network for people who can help you out. What exactly do you need to get you where you want to be?

Some tough questions here—so, great job! With the answers from the above questions, you're well prepared to move on.

1.2 Read This Before Starting Your Apparel Brand

Reset your expectations

You have a great idea and a vision of what you want to do with your brand. You're ready to kick off your project and get started with your apparel business. You probably have a picture in your mind of how it'll go—and it's for sure good to have a clear vision and goal. If you haven't been in the game before, it's difficult to know what to expect. It's going to be the best journey of your life—but in order to make it less stressful, we suggest you take a look at your expectations. Disappointment usually comes from too-high expectations. Right before you make your business plan, think through what your expectations are.

Here are five areas where you may need to reset them:

It takes time

Developing a new product from scratch to perfection takes time—and this is particularly true for apparel. Sure, if you had all of your resources gathered in one place, it could move pretty fast, but in reality this is not often the case. It's all about setting your expectations correctly. The entire startup phase doesn't necessarily need to take a long time. The product-development phase, on the other hand, can be time-consuming; for example, you need to define the collection before you design it; you need to design it before making a tech pack; you need to have a tech pack before you can make the pattern, and so on. All these steps require first that you find someone to actually perform them, and then account for the time needed to accomplish them. Since one is a prerequisite of the other, a delay in one step will delay your entire plan.

It's a winding road

It's not uncommon for a fabric order to take eight weeks. Before the order, you need to decide on it and find the manufacturer. But all of this is nothing to worry about—it is just part of the process. It's important, however, that you have realistic expectations from the start—this will avoid stress along the way. Developing a new product takes time, and sometimes it's two steps forward and one step back. Things happen along the way—a fabric doesn't work, your collaboration with a manufacturer goes south, or you notice that you've been infringing a patent. Typically, the work on a new collection starts one to one and a half years before it reaches customers. Just stay focused on what you want to achieve, don't worry, don't play the blame game—and make sure to enjoy the ride. If you don't like problem-solving, then product development isn't for you.

Product Development = Problem-Solving

It's all about the people

It's also very much about people. Even if one person takes on several roles, there will be a group of working people to coordinate. People communicate in different ways, and it's up to you as the founder to make sure there's some sort of project management. Find people you like to work with and who share your way of doing things, and this part will be much easier. As always when there are many people involved in projects, there's a risk of miscommunication. If you find out along the way that the relationship doesn't work with someone in particular, save yourself energy and make adjustments accordingly.

When working with third-party suppliers like factories, it's important to talk to them about your expectations. Get in writing what you expect the factory to deliver, as well as what they should expect from you. Things will go wrong along the way, and if it does it's always your fault. Don't blame others. It's up to *you* to double-check, triple-check, pick up the phone, send that email, check that things are actually done, etc. *You* are in charge.

Money, money, money

Okay, we'll say it right off the bat: Plan for no income for the first two years. Since the production cycle is fairly long, it also takes a while before you can start actually selling your products. And even longer before you sell enough to make a profit big enough to make a living. Depending on how skilled you are and how many good friends you have who're willing to work for free, there will be quite a few situations where you'll need to spend money up front. Stay on top of your budget and in control of your money management. If you have large orders, making a large production batch can cost more than you have. In this case you can look at a temporary loan to bridge the gap between paying the manufacturer and delivering the orders. You can also negotiate for your customers to pay parts up front.

How large is your margin for each garment? Let's say you have a product that retails for €/$40. The product cost €/$30 to make, and your margin is €/$10. How many do you need to sell in order to cover your costs? How many do you have to sell in order to make a living out of it and scale up your business? When you know how many sales you have to make, you know that the number of people you have to reach is much greater than that. And that takes us to the next topic.

Reaching the customer

The fact you've opened an online store doesn't mean customers will start to pour in and buy your products. There's a load of work needed on the marketing and sales side. Especially if your clothes are in a crowded segment. Even selling to retail stores can be cumbersome and requires hard sales work.

This isn't meant to be discouraging and stop you from realizing your dream of starting an apparel brand. However, in our experience, more often than not people underestimate the work, time, and money needed to accomplish their goals. So, mix up your dream scenario with a bit of reality and get started with your project.

1.3 Achieving Work-Life Balance

Being an entrepreneur and running your own apparel business means there's always something to work on. No matter how much you work, you're never really done. At the same time, there could be other things in your life that you want or need to do. Maybe you have a family you want to spend time with, or maybe you just have to catch the morning surf. The stress level is different from person to person. Don't leave the day-to-day work-life balance to chance. Plan on living a balanced life with some of the tips below.

To-Do Lists

Make a habit of writing down things you need to do. If you're using software such as Asana, you can note it down as soon as the idea comes up. If not, end the day by noting down the tasks you need to address the following day. Having a list of all the things that need doing makes it easy for you to prioritize your work and plan how to move forward. A positive effect of having a to-do list containing all your tasks is that it helps you to feel relaxed—both when you're working and when you're not. You don't have to constantly think about what you need to do or what you should have done. Have you missed anything? You know it's all on the list. You don't have to think about it when you're doing other things, and it'll be there in front of you when you're ready to attack it.

Prioritize

You'll probably have more tasks on your list than you can handle at the moment. This leaves you to prioritize your work. Does one task depend on another task? Then make sure you address that other task first. There may be some fun tasks and some less-fun ones. The important thing is to ask yourself what effect they're going to have on your business. Prioritize accordingly. Do things that matter, that have an impact, and that enable you to advance. It's not about how much time you spend working—it is about what you actually do and how efficient you are.

Delegate

You don't have to do it all by yourself. There could even be someone better than you for that task. You can't be really efficient trying to do it all. Maybe you're a control freak and don't like letting someone else do it for you. Let the 80 percent rule guide you: If you think someone else can do it 80 percent as good as you, let them do it.

The On/Off Switch

Put all your attention and energy into what you're currently working on. Don't look at your email or start doing other things at the same time. No one can do two things well simultaneously. You may be good at alternating between different tasks, but you're not actually *doing* them at the same time. A track coach once gave some valuable advice. He said there's no point in being nervous and tense long before a race—it will only drain your energy, leaving you exhausted when the race starts. At the same time, when the race is about to start, you shouldn't go around thinking of your practice or things you're doing afterwards. You need to put all of your attention and focus on the race in hand. He said to imagine you had a built-in on/off switch. Don't worry about the race before it starts, but when it's time, you push the "on" switch for full attention. The lesson is to focus *fully* on what you're doing. It makes it much better in all senses.

Stay Zen

There will always be a load of things to do. As an entrepreneur, you'll never be done—there will always be more you can do and things you can improve. Keep calm and don't stress about it, though. Accept that it's that way. The more productive work you put in, the quicker and better you advance. But at the same time, it's a waste if you can't sustain it in the long run. Don't fool yourself and think that there's only a load on your plate at the moment and that there will be less up ahead. No—you have to find a good work balance where you feel it's fun and enjoyable at the same time as you're advancing. Do you find it difficult to let go of work? Why don't you schedule some free time? Just as you plan for a meeting, you can put some "free time" stuff in your calendar, too: Tuesday, 11:00-12:00 a.m.—Bike ride!

Have Fun

One of the advantages of running your own business is that you get to work with what you love. The idea is to have fun and enjoy what you're doing. Even when you have your own brand, though, there can be tasks that are not that fun to do. The solution? Make them fun. Find ways of making the tasks more enjoyable. It can be as simple as choosing a new location for the day, borrowing your friend's dog to accompany you to the studio, buying nice pencils and notebooks, or putting on an inspirational podcast.

Health

You're in the game for the long run so make sure you can handle it. Sleep well, eat healthily, and exercise. The success of your business goes hand in hand with your well-being: you can't be lazy when it comes to your health and still have the energy to perform at work. Take a look at Arianna Huffington's TED Talk about the importance of sleep. When it comes to food, read up and do what you think is best for you and your beliefs. And working hard is no excuse for not exercising. It's always possible to squeeze in some exercise: ride your bike to work, do some push-ups, run during your lunch break, take a walking meeting, etc. You'll feel stronger and energized.

So, decide how you want your life to be. Take control of your situation and implement a strategy that makes sure you sustain it over the long run. You want to keep doing what you love.

1.4 Become Your Own Boss

We've been entrepreneurs for around ten years now. Here and there, we've entered into traditional employment, but each time we were drawn back to the freedom of entrepreneurship. Once you get a taste of it, it's really tough to do anything else. So, what's so appealing about running your own business? First of all, we know it's not for everyone. Ask yourself the 23 questions in chapter 1.1 to see if you're cut out for it or not. For us, the following are the main reasons someone enjoys being their own boss.

Work with what you love

You're an entrepreneur because you have a great idea and a burning interest. You get to spend your days working with exactly what you love. You work because you find it rewarding, stimulating, fun, and exciting. Money is not the main reason. You don't want to work in a boring job just because you want that paycheck at the end of the month. Some people do. If *you* do, ask yourself how much it's worth if it means killing your dreams.

Work-life balance

You set your own schedule, meaning you get a better balance between work and other activities. Do you want to exercise in the morning or at lunchtime? Want to pick up the kids early from school? No problem— you don't have to ask anyone else's permission. And because what you do is so much fun, it's not difficult to work evening hours to make up for lost time. With today's technology it's easier than ever to work from wherever you are. Your everyday life and work will intertwine and one doesn't need to stop the other.

Pick your work buddies

Ever worked with an annoying colleague or customer? Don't like your boss? Well, being your *own* boss means you get to pick who you work with. Evidently you can choose your employees and outsourced workforce. But you can also decide if you want to work with specific partners and clients. If you don't click with another person or don't agree with their way of doing things, then don't work with them. Save yourself energy and surround yourself with people you like.

You get the rewards

Ever worked hard on projects, just for someone else to reap the fruits? If you want an extraordinary life, it's hard to achieve on a mediocre salary. Running your own successful business means that all that hard work will pay off—for *you*, not someone else.

No corporate games

You don't need to get involved in the corporate games and politics of large enterprises. Nothing you do is for show. You don't have to show up at a certain time just because that's what you're supposed to do. No —everything you do is for your own business's sake. You know what needs to be done. Don't see any sense in that report? Then don't do it. If you prefer working in your underwear from your couch, then go ahead and do it—and don't mind what anyone else thinks.

Run it the way you want to

You get to set your work culture, processes, and the way things are done. You do things in a certain manner because you're convinced that's the best and most efficient way to move forward. No more long and pointless meetings.

Pick the location

You can determine where you want to work from. Do you want to set up a home office, or a studio within cycling distance? Then you should do that. If you want to work remotely in a coffee shop for the day, or up in the mountains for a week, you do that. Choose the location that's the most inspiring and efficient for you to do your work from. No more cubicles or boring office buildings. Those will strangle your inspiration and motivation.

Do the above reasons sound appealing to you? Then it's time to take some action. Welcome to the next chapter of your awesome life.

No one is going to stand up and hand you
a plate of progress in life.
You must make progress by your own sheer will,
discipline, and efforts every day.

–Brendon Burchard

1.5 Ten Valuable Tips For Running Your Business

–By Ana

1. Always do your best

While still in college, I did three internships. I tried to pick diverse companies so as to spread my learning and *really* see what it was like in the industry. As is the case with most internships, I did some really basic, boring stuff. But I tried to do my best, every day. Before I graduated from college, two of my internships offered me a job. My first job was as a design assistant. There too I had to do some very basic things but I was eager to get going and learned fast. Soon I started to design for real. And even today, not all the styles I design are fun—some are even really boring entry-price-point stuff—but it doesn't matter. They're all equally important to the customer who buys that product. What's important is my respect for and responsibility toward the end consumer who is going to wear that piece. I don't want to disappoint him or her. And I want to be able to say of all my designs: "I'm proud of what I did."

33

2. Never settle or get comfortable

I have jumped from company to company—the longest I've been with a company has been almost four years. You could argue that that's a bad thing, or do as I do: see all the positive things this has given me. By switching companies, you learn a load of new things in a short period of time, and it keeps you on your toes. Of course one of the major perks of doing this is the salary increases. You also accumulate knowledge about doing things in many different ways—then you just pick the one way you like and that suits you best. Your network grows, and you'll forever have great contacts. I don't even need to say this, but you NEED to do a good job; the industry is a small pond and people and companies will soon find out if you're a jerk—and you'll never ever have a job again. So, back to getting comfortable: you can't. You need to step up your game with every project you join. Push yourself out of your comfort zone and take risks. That way you'll grow enormously, both as a person and as a creative.

3. Always trust your gut feeling

No matter what you design, your signature will always be on it and you need to stand behind it 100 percent. There'll always be some pieces that are less fun and interesting for you to design, but the important thing is to give it your all—even when you're not screaming "Yay!" about it. In meetings you always have a choice: to give in and give up, or stand behind your design and argue for it. If you feel strongly about something —a product, an idea, a decision—you need to speak up and let everyone know your opinion. You'll not always be able to get every decision to go the way you want it, but at least you've spoken your mind, and people— and you yourself—know where you stand.

4. There are no excuses

Deadlines are deadlines and you know what needs to be done and by what time. There's never a good excuse for not delivering what you're supposed to deliver. If you need to stay up all night the night before, well, then, shame on you for procrastinating—but you do what you gotta to do! As with everything, your colleagues are expecting you to be a professional and do your job. If you miss a deadline, their trust in you'll be broken. You'll usually know beforehand—at least a couple of days— whether you're going to be able to deliver on time, and if you can't, you need to communicate that you'll be late. That's perfectly acceptable— and you won't waste people's time.

> Working hard for something we don't care about is called stress.
> Working hard for something we love is called passion.
>
> *—Simon Sinek*

5. Be friendly with everyone—even the jerks

As I mentioned above, this industry is small, and personal chemistry is tricky. You never know who is buddy-buddy with whom, so the best course of action is to be friendly with everyone. I'm not saying you need to be a bootlicker; just stay neutral with the jerks—you may well end up working on a joint project in the future.

6. Look outside your field for inspiration

It's all too easy to get inspiration from your own field. The problem with this is that everybody watches what everybody else is doing, and it all kind of ends up looking the same. Sometimes the deadlines are tight, and you haven't been on any inspirational trips, and you need to be done tomorrow. But, I promise you, you'll be so much more inspired and your work will be so much more original if you force yourself to look for inspiration in other fields.

7. Trust the process and say *Yes*

If you feel you don't really have the skills to tackle a project at a particular moment, it's fine to say *Yes* and figure it out along the way. You'll force yourself to learn and solve the problem—and in the end you'll have learned something new and will have pushed yourself. It might be really scary but you'll be fine. So, say *yes* to unexpected opportunities.

8. Enjoy the fun and the great people

In the outdoor-apparel world, most people are outdoorsy and pretty relaxed. Being a designer is fantastic. It's so diverse—no day is the same, and no collection is like the previous one. Working with the latest technologies is incredibly inspiring. Traveling around the world to different suppliers and factories is fantastic and I never seem to get tired of it. So, while you're at it, enjoy it and thank yourself for choosing this field—you get paid to be creative and to travel the world. That's pretty sweet.

9. Ask for what you want!

Yes, it's kind of simple—yet so many people don't even know what they want, let alone that they can *ask* for what they want. The only bad thing that can happen is that you get a *no*. The other 50 percent can turn into something amazing. So, think about what you want and ask for it.

10. Be you!

There's only one of you in the whole world. One amazing, fantastic, and incredible YOU. No one else is like you so why pretend to be someone else, copy someone else's work, or even want to be like someone else? Think about what makes you unique. You are your own brand, so bring those fantastic features to the surface. No matter what, in any situation, stay true to yourself, your values and beliefs, and be your awesome self. I know they say you're supposed to "fake it till you make it"—but why not, instead, put what's best in you out there and *use* it, rather than fake it?

Persistency is what wins in the end.
It never gets easier; you just get better.

1.6 Entrepreneurship Tasks

1. Think through the 23 questions to ask yourself before starting an apparel brand.

2. Make a plan for how you'll do this.

3. Make room in your life for an apparel business—e.g., create a physical space for your work.

2.
Administration

2.1 Business Startup Checklist

Business name, domain name, trademark, bank account... There are a few things to set up when you launch your business. Use this startup checklist to make sure you tick everything off and set off on the right foot.

Thorough market research

The first thing to do on your checklist is a deep market scan. Who else is doing what you intend to do? Take a look at the players who are doing something similar to your idea. Just get on top of what the market looks like. How are other brands coping? What possibilities are out there? And what can you offer? Knowing the market will force you to push yourself and make something extraordinary of your idea.

Write a business plan

A business plan can be perceived as pretty boring, but it's something you should get started with right away. A business plan consists of your answers to all those tough questions about your project. It puts a focus on what you need to do. You need to think about all aspects, but there's no need to overwork it. Nobody knows the future, and a plan is based on an educated guess about what is going to happen. However, a ship without a course will end up anywhere—or in the middle of nowhere.

Come up with the business name

The name of your business is an important part of your brand. Think it through and make sure it's suitable in all markets you'll address. The name can be anything you want and like. Do you want your customers to understand what you do directly from seeing your brand name? How will it stand out in an online search? Is it similar to a trademark? Do you want it to stand out in a directory?

Create a logo and graphical profile

Come up with the logo early on. When you get started with product development, you'll need it—e.g., hangtags and embroidery. The graphical profile with colors, fonts, and layouts will bring brand-identity cohesion to everything you do, from email signatures to apparel labels.

Make an initial budget

This is actually included in the business plan, but we want to lift it out. You should have an idea about how you'll make ends meet. Make sure you have a realistic plan and the funds needed to push it through. Maybe you don't know the exact cost for certain things, but you can always guesstimate to see if the numbers add up.

Raise initial funding

If you don't have the money yourself, ask family, friends, and acquaintances to help you out. If you take on investors, you normally have to give away a larger chunk of your company when involving them early on. Could crowdfunding be an option for you?

Look for partners

What are you good at? Which skills do you need to improve? Look for people you can work with, who complement your competencies and make up a strong team.

Seek out advisors

Sit down and make a list of all the people who could help you in different areas with your business. Who do you know with a proven track record of running a business? Pick up the phone and give them a call. Ask them for the help you need.

Create a founders' agreement

Do you have cofounders? Draw up an agreement about the share each person owns in the business, expectations, roles, and what will happen in the case of disagreements. It's better to draw up such a contract when you're the best of friends. Then, if that metaphorical shit does hit the fan, you don't have to end up in lengthy discussions since everything is super clear in your agreement.

File for trademark

Trademarking has two primary purposes. The first is to protect your brand so no one interferes with your business efforts. The second is to make sure you don't step on somebody else's toes. When you apply for a trademark, the trademark organization will conduct a search to make sure of this.

Reserve domain name and social media accounts

Buy a domain name that matches your brand's needs. Once you have the domain, you can set up your email addresses and at the same time register the social media accounts you want to use.

Register the business

Register your legal entity to the appropriate authorities in your country —typically, the Companies Registration Office and the Tax Agency.

Set up bookkeeping

The Accounting Act will tell you what you need to do in this area. Are you old-school, preferring a ledger? Can you find an online tool? Or will you outsource it?

Open a bank account

Contact a bank that you trust and open an operating account so you can get paid.

Arrange insurance

It's a really good idea to get company insurance. Typically, this will cover you for liability, legal costs, interruption, and theft.

Launch

Okay, now you've set up the basic stuff and you're ready to kick off your business. This is where the fun starts! It's time to leave the dreaming stage and enter execution mode. Don't overthink things—just keep working on your business. You'll make mistakes along the way, but that's part of the game. Don't give up—keep moving.

> Luck is not a business model.
>
> *–Anthony Bourdain*

2.2 Protect Your Brand And Products

There are a few ways you can protect your brand and products from getting copied or violated. You need to be aware of these rights for the sake of your own brand, but also to make sure you don't infringe someone else's brand. Having the right protection in place can boost customer confidence, attract potential investors, and improve your brand's overall value.

Intellectual property

Intellectual property or IP is, according to WIPO, creations of the mind, such as inventions; literary and artistic works; designs; and symbols, names and images used in commerce.

Trademark

A trademark is a recognizable sign, design, or expression which identifies your products and sets them apart from those of others. You typically want a trademark for your brand name and logo. In order to receive a trademark, you need to apply to an intellectual property organization. You apply separately for each market or country you want the protection in. Every country has its own organization, such as the

USPTO (the United States Patent and Trademark Office) in the US. There are also a few organizations that cover larger areas, through which you can apply for protection in several countries at once, such as EUIPO (the European Union Intellectual Property Office) in the EO, and the WIPO (The World Intellectual Property Organization), covering over 100 countries.

A trademark application takes time so you should get started as early as possible. You want to ensure your logo is protected before making labels and marketing material. You apply for a trademark in certain categories or classes. Make sure you apply under each of the classes your products—current as well as upcoming—fall into. There's an extra application fee for every class you want the protection in. Normally, a trademark lasts for ten years, and then you need to renew your application.

You want the trademark protection for two major reasons. The first is so that your brand is protected and no one tries to steal your thunder. The second is to make sure YOU don't impinge on someone else's brand. You don't want to be sued because your brand turns out to be too similar to an existing one.

With a trademark, you can pursue legal action when someone intentionally or unintentionally uses a similar logo or name for a similar product.

Copyright

Copyright is a right that grants a creator of original work to determine how it can be used by others. The exact legislation for how copyright works varies from region to region. Sometimes copyrights are granted by public law, in which case they're considered regional rights. This means that copyrights granted by the law of a certain state do not extend beyond the territory of that specific jurisdiction. Many countries have made agreements with other countries regarding how to act in cross-border situations and when national rights collide. Typically, the public law duration of a copyright expires 50 to 100 years after the creator dies, depending on the jurisdiction.

Generally speaking, you don't apply for copyright protection; you automatically have copyright protection when you're the creator of original work. However, in some countries, certain formalities are necessary before the copyright protection becomes valid. Copyright protects only the original expression of ideas, not the underlying ideas themselves.

Our experience is that you should not focus on copyright protection. If a competitor copies you and makes even just a minor tweak, then your copyright is not valid. So, instead, focus on your product development and make sure you'll be the first one out on the market with your products anyway.

Registered design

A registered design protects the way a product looks. A registered design is a monopoly for a design when applied to an article and is granted under the laws of the country the registered design is filed in.

The registered design allows the owner of that design to grant access to, or exclude others from, making, selling, offering for sale or hire the design protected by the registered design. The exact monopoly the design covers is contained in the drawings in the registered design.

A registered design is, just as a trademark, valid for a certain period of time. After that period you need to renew it, including paying the renewal fee. If the registered design protection is not renewed, other people are free to use your design.

Patents

Can you patent a clothing design? Yes, you can. It also means that your competitors can patent a design. Clothing companies will often patent a unique design to prevent other companies from imitating it. This is a major reason for you to constantly stay up-to-date with your market and the products in it. It's not unusual for clothing companies to mass-produce a product, unaware that they're using someone else's patent. This results in them having to either scrap the entire production batch or pay a license or settlement fee. In any case, it gets expensive.

You can patent a unique clothing design with a design patent, or a unique function with a utility patent. Registration of a clothing design for a patent is more difficult than obtaining a trademark or registered design. You need to show evidence that your design or function is unique and can be classified as an invention. You're claiming invention of the unique look of the clothing, not the clothing itself.

If you hold design patent rights, you can sell or license them to another clothing company.

Fighting legal battles is a drain on your time, money and energy. Often, the best way to handle these kinds of issues is just to make sure you're innovative, first out in the market with your designs, and constantly changing. If someone's copying you, they won't be the original and will already be behind when you launch a newly updated collection.

Doubt, Clarity, Growth

Doubt increases with inaction.
Clarity reveals itself in momentum.
Growth comes from progress.
For all these reasons, BEGIN.

–Brendon Burchard

2.3 Toolkit

Running an apparel business will require a set of tools, of which some you'll use every day, and some will be very project-specific. When it comes to your working tools, we suggest to always go for quality. Precision and detail are key, and you want perfect results. Buy tools that have a purpose for your business and that you absolutely need and like. You should feel joy, inspiration, and motivation when you use them.

At the start, you'll need a specific set to facilitate your projects—after that, your tool list will grow with you and your business.
Think long term when acquiring your tools and material. Get the right tool for the right job.

Decide where you won't compromise on quality and where you could make some "sacrifices."

Below are four lists of tools based on where you are in the process:

Design-phase tools

- Computer
- Software —Adobe Suite

- Camera
- Printer/Scanner
- Pinboard
- Board pins
- Ruler
- Graphite pencils
- Eraser
- Mechanical pencils
- Designer markers
- Colored pencils
- Marker Paper
- Sketchbook
- Scissors—paper and fabric—big and small

Product fitting and commenting phase tools

- Dress form—good to have, not a must
- Tape measure
- Pins
- Safety pins
- Muslin
- Chalk or fabric pencil/marker
- Style tape
- Stitch ripper
- See-thru ruler
- Fabric scissors

Good to have

- Sewing machine
- Muslin
- Fabrics
- Threads
- Trims
- Dotted paper
- Hip and French curve for redrawing shapes on protos or patterns

To work properly with garments, you do need a bit of space. Samples will be coming in that need to be fitted, reviewed, and commented, and you might want to sew some protos of your own or work on detail mockups.

> But remember: Tools do not a craftsman make.

Studio tools

- Large table
- Garment rail
- Mirror
- Industrial sewing machine
- Steam press or steam iron

> Do not wait; the time will never be "just right."
> Start where you stand, and work with whatever tools
> you may have at your command,
> and better tools will be found as you go along.
>
> *–George Herbert*

2.4 Administration Tasks

1. Register business

2. Founder's agreement

3. Set up bookkeeping

4. Open bank account

5. Reserve domain name and social media accounts

6. Arrange insurance

7. File for trademark

3.
Idea &
Customer Need

3.1 Exciting Idea, Burning Interest And Customer Need

Starting an apparel brand requires a load of hard work, but it'll be the best ride you've ever had. It's vital that you have a burning interest for what you do if you're going to be able to cope all the way. You'll need to keep that strong gut feeling you have about your idea alive, so don't get pulled down by friends and family members who try and talk you out of it.

That exciting idea usually starts with: "Why doesn't this exist? I wish I had this type of garment. I need to have..." Try to solve common problems and figure out the customer need. Without a need, no one will buy your product. Either you do a certain sport/activity and you can't find the product you want with specific features or look, or you just want something that is YOU.

The apparel business is very crowded and you could argue that everything you may wish for is already on the market. Fortunately, apparel is a human necessity and there will always be a need for it. If you feel your brand/product is needed, GO FOR IT!

Pick up a pen and sheet of paper and start writing down words that you relate to your idea. Print out inspirational pictures and collect magazine tear-outs—then put them on the wall so you can clearly see a connection between your choices. Get out and travel so you can really *sense* that feeling you want to have in your brand. Collect as much information about your future brand/product as you can—the clearer the better. Also try and narrow down all the information—the simpler the better. If you can find ONE picture that says it all about your brand (the feeling, the customer, and the type of product), BRAVO! Keep it simple!

So, to sum up this section: TRUST YOUR INSTINCT! Get your idea out of your head and put it IN FRONT OF YOU so you can see it clearly and simplify.

> What makes you different or weird—that's your strength.
>
> *–Meryl Streep*

3.2 Idea And Customer-Need Tasks

1. Figure out the customer need and the problem your product solves.

2. Answer the question: What's so special about your product?

3. Collect as much information about your product as you can.

4. Make sure your product is different and stands out. If there are similar products, how can you make yours better?

4.
Market Scan

4.1 Do Something Different

So, you're full of enthusiasm for idea and you've pretty much figured out what you'd like to do. The products you're thinking about are styles *you* would wish to wear—but will someone else want your stuff too? Is there a need for your clothing? Is there a gap in the market?

Go downtown and have a look in the stores. See what's there—and also try and see what *isn't*. Scan the Internet for similar brands, because there will be similar brands. If there aren't, then you should ask yourself WHY.

The most important factor here is you need to differentiate yourself from what already exists. You don't want to be the "No. 2" brand—it'll never survive the market. Find your niche, so you can articulate clearly why YOUR brand is different and what customers will get from you that they can't find anywhere else. Stand out and be the wow-maker.

If someone is already doing what you intend to do, bummer, you'll always be No. 2. It'll be an uphill struggle and you risk being seen as just a copycat.

Also look at price ranges and what you get for your money. What price range do you want your products to be in? This information will be important when it comes to deciding your designs, materials, and making of your styles. More on this topic later.

Have your ideal customer in mind and seek out stores you want your brand to be in. What other brands are in there? Where your ideal customer is—that's where you and your brand/product should be too.

> Everyone is not your customer.
>
> –Seth Godin

BESPOKE

HAUTE COUTURE

LUXURY

DESIGNER

HIGH END

MID LEVEL - HIGH STREET

MASS MARKET

LOW PRICE - HIGH VOLUMES

4.2 Market Levels

The clothing industry is segmented into seven market levels. These levels categorize brands in different brackets according to distinct price points, quality, craftsmanship, and service levels. Different levels require different skills, marketing strategies, pricing strategies, product development, and production planning. Designers need to pick one level and position themselves through their product offerings, prices, quality, and target customer. Once you've positioned your brand in one of these market levels, it'll be very hard to switch to another level. Your brand's positioning will also depend on your intent for your collection, and what type of products you're aiming to design and produce— sportswear, activewear, formalwear, etc. It's critical you know who you're designing for! When you know exactly who your target customer is, everything else will fall into place.

With today's online, direct-to-consumer models, the entire market-level structure can get a bit confusing. The lines have become blurred, and direct-to-consumer markets have flipped pricing/quality and product-offering strategies on their heads.

Below is a guide to facilitate your understanding of the traditional market and price structure. The prices are intended as a rough guide for each price bracket, and can of course differ.

1. Bespoke
2. Haute couture
3. Luxury
4. Designer
5. High-end
6. Mid-level high street
7. Mass market—fast fashion

1. Bespoke/Made to measure

Tailor-made suits and shirts are very popular in the menswear sector. Think of the traditional English bespoke tailors. These types of products are custom-made to the customer's requirements. He/she chooses the design, trims, and materials, and the product is made exactly to the customer's body measurements. This model is very time-consuming and will require several fittings with the customer before the product is perfect. The customer pays a relatively high price for the product.

2. Haute couture

Haute couture, which translates from French as "high fashion," refers to handmade, custom garments of extremely high quality, for private customers. Usually no more than ten pieces are made of one style. These are not bulk-produced products, and since they're handmade, haute couture garments are very expensive, starting at €/$10,000. These are garments for special occasions—you can think of them more as works of art than clothing.

Haute couture brands can only become part of the Chambre Syndicale de la Couture Parisienne in Paris, France, upon selection, and are required to adhere to very strict rules in order to preserve the craft.

Brands: Chanel, Dior, Jean-Paul Gaultier, Maison Margiela, Elie Saab

3. Luxury

This segment is highly exclusive, focusing on creativity and experimental high-quality garments. Products come in limited availability. Luxury brands usually present a mixture of day and evening wear, ranging from casual to formal depending on the collection theme and designer inspiration. Luxury products are fairly high-priced, between €/$300-€/$9,000 and up.

Brands: Dior, Chanel, Hermes, Burberry, Fendi

4. Designer

The designer ready-to-wear market level is characterized by a high level of innovation, trendsetting styles, and high quality. It's all about the designer's expression and ideas. Product prices fall around €/$150-€/$1000 and up. Garments generally cover a wider range of categories—day, evening, work, and special events.

Brands: Alexander Wang, Phillip Lim

5. High-End

The high-end product segment focuses on a couple of trends and has its specific target customer. The quality of the products tends to be fairly high, but materials and trims are a bit cheaper than those used in designer products. These products are intended and designed to reach a broader audience. Price points fall in the range of €/$50-€/$500 and up.

Brands: Acne, Lacoste, A.P.C

6. Mid-level high street

This segment connects high-end to mass-market. A significant number of brands compete in this segment. Prices are more affordable than in the high-end sector and generally products are of a slightly higher quality than the mass-market brands. The products are intended for daily use. Styles in the mid-level high street segment are mass produced, hence the affordable prices. Prices €/$20-€/$200 and up.

Brands: COS, J.Crew

7. Mass market—Fast fashion

This is a very crowded market level, with brands that sell huge volumes. Prices are low, quality is so-so, and the products are intended to appeal to the masses—people who want to keep on trend at a low price.

Mostly products for daily use. Expected price points: €/$10-€/$100 and up.

Brands: H&M, Zara, Topshop

4.3 Market-Scan Tasks

1. Perform a thorough market scan. Get to know the market.

2. Examine the price ranges in your market.

3. Find out who your competition is.

4. Find out what quality your competitors offer and at what price level.

5. Determine what unique selling points and values will differentiate your brand from others.

5.
Business Plan

5.1 Answer The Tough Questions

Before you start your brand, you need to know where you're going and what your plan is. Don't drag it out for a whole year—the market could change or someone else might have the same idea as you and get to market before you. The business plan should be a fun part of the creative process. What you put in it will form the basis that you'll rely on for the near future. The process is as important as the outcome—because once you're done, it'll be obvious what your strengths and weaknesses are; it'll help you see the problems you can hopefully avoid.

It's an effective way to force yourself to answer the tough questions:

Who is your customer?

What is your niche?

What is your brand's "raison d'être"?

How much money do you need to get going and operating, etc.?

This is a great process to go through if you need to present your idea to investors and show that you've thought your business through. Even if you intend to run your business without external funding, it's good to do a loose business plan, as it'll help you see what your focus is and will keep the entire team on the same page. You'll all have the same clear reference. Of course you'll learn things along the way, and of course you'll change your mind, but the main plan is set—you know what you need to do. Without a plan, how would you know where to go?

Having a solid plan, and actually knowing what to do and doing those things, will make or break your success.

Losers have goals.
Winners have systems.

–Scott Adams

Without a plan, how would you know where to go?

If you're a visual person, add a load of pictures and sketches to your business plan. Make it inspirational if you want to—no need for the boring Word document version. Just make sure it covers all the information you need, to have a clear vision and goal. When the rough times come and you doubt yourself—and these times *will* come once in a while—you'll have something to go back to and remind yourself of what the point of this whole thing is. It'll help you stay on track.

BUT—and here comes the big but—keep it light! A super-duper detailed plan won't make sense (unless you're pitching to investors). Once you encounter, for example, a change in the market, your plan is going to go out the window. You need to stay loose on your toes, have your fingers on the market/customer pulse and be ready to shift and change if you need to. Who said you can't change along the way?

Have fun with it. Make it in PowerPoint or your own format.

4 things to keep in mind

1. Always do it yourself.
2. Include a budget with monthly cash flow for the first two years.
3. The process is more important than the final document.
4. Show it to experts for business advice.

**Strategic planning is worthless—
unless there is first a strategic vision.**

–John Naisbitt

5.2 Business-Plan Questions

Include these questions in your business plan and answer them. Take your time and answer them thoroughly.

Mission statement

Make a clear statement indicating why you're in business.

Executive summary

A summary of what you're going to do and how you're going to do it.

1. Company

1.1 General
Company name, address, etc.

1.2 Activity
What are you going to do?
1.3 Partners
Who are the business partners?

1.3.1 Partner 1
Partner 1's CV.

1.3.2 Partner 2
Partner 2's CV.

1.4 Team and organization
Who is involved to make your business happen?

2. Business concept

2.1 Background
Where did the idea come from?

2.2 Business idea
Describe your business idea.

2.3 Vision
What's the bigger picture?
What are you trying to accomplish?
Where do you want to take your business?

2.4 Goals
Describe your goals, both short-term and long-term. Divide the sections into stages relevant to your business—e.g., divide your goals into two steps: 1-3 years and 4-10 years.

2.4.1 Short-term goals—1-3 years
Describe what you want to accomplish with your business short-term.

2.4.2 Long-term goals—4-10 years
Describe what you want to accomplish with your business long-term.

3. Product

3.1 Product definition
Describe your service or product. Make a mood board!

3.2 Products today
Which service or product will you start out with?

3.3 Products tomorrow
How will you develop your service or product range?

3.4 Why should the customer buy this product?
(You're—rightfully—biased, so you'll be able to come up with a long list here!)

3.5 Why should the customer NOT buy this product?
(Play devil's advocate and list possible reasons customers won't buy your product.)

4. The customer

4.1 Target customer
Who is your customer? Try to pin it down as much as possible.

4.2 Customer description
Describe your customer. What is she doing? What does he like? What are her interests?

5. Market

5.1 Market location
Where is your main market?

5.2 Market today
What does the market look like?

5.3 Competition
5.3.1 Largest competitors
List your competitors.

5.3.2 Competitors' strengths
What are your competitors' strengths?

5.3.3 The company's strengths
List your strengths.

6. Marketing and sales

6.1 Reaching the customer
How will you reach your customer?
6.2 Marketing and sales activities
What are the activities that will sell your product?

7. Material and premises

7.1 Need for premises
What are your needs in terms of space and location?

7.2 Need for tools and material
What tools and material do you need, to get started?

8. SWOT analysis

Strengths
List your strengths.

Weaknesses
List your weaknesses.

Opportunities
List your opportunities.

Threats
List your threats.

9. Budget

Make a budget. How will your numbers add up? Make it for at least a couple of years.

10. Business model

This is perhaps the most important aspect of your business plan: How exactly will you generate income?

5.3 Five Ways To Make A Profit

You want your business to evolve and be successful so that you to keep doing what you love. Of course you want to make a profit, but that doesn't happen on its own. Look over your processes, at each and every step along the way, to envision how you want it all to unfold. Plan for profit from the beginning and don't leave the numbers to chance. The first step is to plan for it.

Consider these five steps when making your plan:

1. Target

What do you want to achieve? We encourage you to put in some time and effort and to work hard on your business plan, as the first thing you do. Ask yourself why you're doing this and what you're aiming for. Set clear targets, and then make a plan as to how you will get there.

2. Make a budget

Running an apparel business involves spending a considerable sum of money in the startup phase before you get any revenue. Typical areas in which you'll spend your cash are studio rent, office supply, computer, phone, Internet connection, website, advertising, photos, branding, marketing, sales, salaries/consultant fees, and of course product development. Before you start spending, make a detailed budget plan, have a look at financing options for your business, and have a potential plan B in case "stuff happens."

> It doesn't take a great entrepreneur to spend a load of money.

3. Use costing sheets

To help you keep track of all of the costs associated with each product design/development, you can use a costing sheet. This is a list of all the costs embedded in one garment—everything from fabrics to trims, making, labels, and packaging.

4. Margin

The margin is what keeps you in business. It should give you enough money for you to reinvest in your business, and for you and your employees to live off. The budget and costing sheets will help you calculate your margin so that you can stay in business. To ensure the right margin, you have to look at your pricing strategies. Read more in our Pricing Strategies chapter.

> Price your product to make a profit no matter what.

If you price low with the intention of raising prices later, you risk having to find a whole new customer base and positioning for the brand.

5. Keep the costs down

If you have little capital, opt for bootstrapping: do as much as possible yourself and find smart ways to start up with less money. The downside of bootstrapping can be that the launch takes more time, or you can have a tough time making your business grow at a satisfactory pace.

It doesn't take a great entrepreneur to spend a load of money. It's much more difficult to be profitable from the start, but this should be your aim. See to it that your margin covers your costs, including overheads. Prepare a realistic budget to help you achieve your goals. Product-development cycles are long—with a clear plan you won't lose yourself and your money along the way. You'll need the profit to reinvest in your collection and to manage larger demands and production. It's all doable, but you need to stay in control.

Price your products so that you have the option for both direct-to-consumer and wholesale strategies.

> **Profit for a company is like oxygen for a person.**
> **If you don't have enough of it, you're out of the game.**
> **But if you think your life is about breathing,**
> **you're really missing something.**
>
> *–Peter Drucker*

5.4 How Much Does It Cost To Start An Apparel Brand?

You've got the ideas and your motivation is flowing. You've asked yourself all the tough questions and you're convinced this is the best idea since the wheel. Now it's time to figure out how much it'll cost to get up and running with this fantastic project. Let's start by listing all the things you'll need in order to run your business. This can of course be very individual since we're all at different places in our lives.

Of course, to make it more precise, we'd need to know the specifics of your brand, such as the size and type of your collection, marketing and sales strategy, etc. So what we'll do here is look at the different areas in which you'll need to spend some money. Your starting-up costs will of course depend on whether you plan to do it yourself, get a friendly soul to help you for a low fee, or plan to outsource it.

Let's take a look at 11 different areas where you'll need to spend your cash:

1. Business administration

You have to register your company, open a bank account, do bookkeeping, register trademark, get insurance, etc.

2. Branding

If you can't do it yourself, you'll need help with your logo, graphical profile, labels, hangtags, etc.

3. Designer

The designer will take your ideas and turn them into your collection. She/he will help you create sketches, designs, tech packs, and communicate with the factory. The designer will also be involved in choosing fabrics, trims, and accessories as well as in fitting later on.

4. Pattern-maker

You need someone to create your patterns. For each style, you need a separate pattern, and the length of time it'll take to make it depends on the complexity of the design. The process can be faster if there's any repetition from other styles in the collection.

5. Material sourcing

Typically you need to travel to a fabric trade show to find the fabrics you like. There'll be travel and accommodation costs. In addition to fabrics, you need to find accessories and trims for your garments.

6. Materials

Once you've found your materials, you actually need to buy them. First you need to buy small quantities for your sample collection, and then you'll need to buy a load more for the bulk production.

7. Samples

When product developing, you'll need samples to measure, fit, and adjust. Typically you'll need two to three samples per style and they're usually double the normal production price.

8. Photography

When you've finally got your sales samples, you'll need to take some good photos of them.

9. Web

How will you build your online presence? At the very least you'll need a simple Web page, but it's pretty likely you'll also need a webshop. Costs incurred here include building and hosting the site. You can set up social media accounts yourself.

10. Marketing and sales

You've made great stuff—now you have to let your customers know about it. Time for marketing and sales. This could be anything from running online ads to hiring a traveling salesperson to show your samples to potential buyers. Maybe you want to print a product catalogue or do a trade show?

11. Production

Production costs include the actual making of the products, the materials, transport, and also the travel involved for product development. It's essential that you visit the factory at least once to talk about the production of your styles.

Write down all of the above areas on a sheet of paper. Under each topic write down what you want and can do by yourself. Then think about people you know who could help out and whether there's any possibility of a friendly price. For the rest, you can contact freelancers and agencies to help you achieve your goals. Once that's done, you'll get a fairly good picture of how much your endeavor will cost you. Finally, take the amount you came to and triple it. *Now* you're closer to the reality.

5.5 Business-Plan Tasks

1. Answer all the questions in the business plan. This is the groundwork for your business.

2. Clarify WHY you're starting your brand. What do you want to achieve?

3. Determine your values.

4. Do NOT continue before you're done with the points above. These will guide you along the way and make every decision clearer from now on.

6.
Branding

6.1 Eleven Questions To Help You Create Your Brand Identity

Branding is the process of building a product image based on associations, feelings, lifestyle, and identity that's projected by a label.

The competition is tough out there. Just look at all the brands that exist on the market. Business owners recognize that brand-name awareness and brand loyalty are the driving forces behind repeat purchases. They therefore work to improve their brand image by:

- Identifying the product attributes demanded by the market.
- Broadening a brand's assortment by gender and across multiple product categories.
- Effectively delivering and promoting the product.
- Effectively controlling the product scope and distribution channels.
- Maintaining consistency in terms of brand value in the eyes of the consumer.
- Implementing customer inclusivity from the start.
- Incorporating business values and creating a strong brand culture.

> A brand for a company is like a reputation for a person.
> You earn reputation by trying to do hard things well.
>
> *–Jeff Bezos*

The most successful brands of the 2000s have evolved into lifestyle brands. Lifestyle brands go beyond specific apparel product identification to include many areas of everyday living, from sheets and dishes to furniture and wood. Think Polo Ralph Lauren. So, how do you create a brand identity?

Answer these questions and they'll guide you to your brand identity:

1. What are you doing?

What does your business do? Summarize what your business is about. Explain it like an elevator pitch—short and sweet.

2. What problem do you solve for your customers?

Why is your product needed and how can it facilitate daily living for the customer? Describe the problem you're trying to solve and how your product solves it.

3. Who are your main competitors?

What do you like about their brand identity and what do you want to do differently? Learn from them and make sure you're not just copying them.

4. What about your product sets you apart from your competitors'?

Why should customers buy your product instead of your competitors'? There must be some unique selling point.

5. What's your story?

Storytelling connects your customers with your brand. What can you relate about your product, background, and business?

6. Can you give five words that describe your company?

Use adjectives or any words to describe your company—simply. This brings focus to your brand.

7. Can you describe your ideal customer?

Use five words that describe your client. Do you have any market research that you can add?

8. Can you name three brands that inspire you?

Describe what it is that you like about these brands. How do they make you feel? It doesn't necessarily have to be a clothing brand.

9. Can you mention three brands that you think are weak?

What is it that you don't like about these brands? What do you associate with these brands?

10. Can you describe your brand's desired look and feel?

Using only a few words, can you explain feelings and associations you want your brand to identify with?

11. What is the primary message you want to present to your customer?

How do you want your customer to feel every time they're in contact with your product?

Answering these 11 questions will give you a good foundation upon which to create your brand identity. Enlist help from someone who's good in the brand-identity field. Not only will they be able to help you with the actual identity; they'll also make sure you avoid any similarity with existing labels or unwanted associations. When creating your brand, remember to tie it closely together with the product.

The brand and product have to deliver the same message and feelings to customers. Make sure it all sticks out. Make a brand that gets noticed.

What does your brand stand for?
What would the world miss if your company disappeared?
What is the role of your company in people's lives?

It's dumb to make things no one wants or cares for. Make fewer, amazing products that help people in one way or another and that people absolutely love.
Stand for something!

6.2 Naming Your Apparel Brand

The importance of your brand name

Your brand name is an important part of your business and overall brand image. When you choose the right name, your customers immediately identify with your value proposition. If you choose the wrong name, your customers have no idea what your business stands for or what it does.

The importance of your brand name has to do with human psychology. As human beings, we evaluate information quickly and make snap judgments. We usually make up our minds in just a few seconds, and then it takes much longer to change that first impression. Choosing a great brand name is not easy—we know that. We can't tell you what name to pick for your business, but we can help you with some pointers to get you going.

Brand, trade and domain names

Here, we're mainly going to talk about brand name. Your trade name doesn't have to be the same as your brand name, even if that would be advantageous. Your trade name is used when you're conducting business operations, such as ordering fabrics. It's the name you use when incorporating your business. If it's the same or similar to your brand name, you'll avoid confusion. Your domain should preferably be your brand name with a domain ending, such as .com. If your brand name is already taken as a domain name by someone else, you need to be creative and find a free domain name that incorporates your brand name somehow.

Get the creative process started

The foundation of your brand is based on your core values. Start by asking yourself WHY you're running your apparel brand, and from that, work on your values. Continue to work on identifying your business identity: brainstorm ideas, perform market research, consider self-evaluation processes, and so on.

Google and study images that show up for different words. Can they inspire you? Think of synonyms for words that evoke value. Merge words and create new ones. Put letters together that sound cool but don't mean anything (yet). Put up Post-its on the wall with names on them to get a better overview and to spot synergies. Sleep on it and continue the process. Let the process take time. You'll feel it when you've found the right name.

There are many aspects to a great name. Here are some of them:

Emotions
When we know we're dealing with human nature, a good idea is to consider the emotions your brand triggers. What associations pop up in your head upon hearing the brand name?

Availability
First off, you want to know that your name isn't already taken. The best way to do this is to google your target country's main trademark association. They typically have brand-name databases that you can search. This is a quick way to see if your name is free or not. Make sure it's free, since you don't want to get involved in trademark infringement. Once decided, you want to register your name for a trademark to protect the goodwill and reputation of your business from competitors.
Secondly, you want to check that the domain name is free. To do this, you can visit, for example, bluehost.com and use their tool on the first page. There you can see which domain endings are free for your name and which are taken. You can also type the name you want directly into

the address field on your browser to see if it's already taken. If the domain is taken you can ask to buy it from the owner, but the easiest way is to tweak your domain name a bit and see if that's free. Be creative and change up your desired name. It's great to have local domain endings—e.g., .de, .co.uk, and so on—especially if those are your target markets. If you're going global, try to get the .com version of your name.

Thirdly, search online to see if someone else is using your name.

A great and fun tool for brainstorming domain names is BustAName, where you can enter your initial keyword ideas and automatically get domain-name suggestions. You can also get your domain name at Bluehost.

SEO
You'll need to think about SEO, search engine optimization, when starting a website. Try to pick a name that stands out and that's not too popular. Let's say you have a brand and domain name that includes "New York"—it'll be really tough for you to end up in the top search results on the search engines. You'll compete with all the (already established) sites talking about New York, including hotels, travel, fashion, and more. So, google your brand name a bit before deciding what to go with, and see what people will find when searching for you.

Simplicity
If you tell someone your brand name, they should directly understand it. Make it easily pronounced, or your brand will sound different depending on your customers' interpretations—which will make your marketing much more difficult.
Make it easy to spell. After hearing your brand name, you want your customers to find your brand easily when searching for it.

Uniqueness
A memorable, unique name will ensure your customers immediately think of you when they see or hear it. Make sure it sticks out. Make a brand that gets noticed. *Own* your brand!

Timelessness
Don't look too much at current trends and what's popular right now. Trends pass, and the risk is that the coolness of your brand passes too.

You want your name to work for you even in the future. What future plans do you have? Do you want to expand your product range? And if so, would your name still be suitable?

Relevance

Make your name relevant to your business-brand identity. The brand, product, and name have to deliver the same message and feelings to customers.

Appropriateness

When you google the name, you don't want any weird shit popping up. You don't want your name to mean something foul in another language —unless you really want to bum on that market. Maybe you're smiling now, but we've seen this happen...

Test your name ideas with your target audience. What do they think about when they hear your name? Try it on a niche online forum and listen to what they have to say. A benefit of starting your social media activities early is that you can test your name on your fans and followers. Let them comment and vote on different suggestions.

Logo

When working with different name ideas, also think about how they could translate into logos. Could it work as a name logo or can it be turned into a symbol?

If you need help with your logo, you can try 99designs. With 99designs you're essentially hosting a contest online where you'll attract a load of great graphic designers who will submit their concepts to you on the website. Then you'll be able to provide feedback, and pick and choose out of many different proposals.

Personal name

Should you use your own name as a brand name? The advantage is that it's probably unique and it can boost your reputation when you're successful. If you want to use your personal name, first ask yourself whether it may be hard to pronounce in your target markets? If things don't go well with your business, you'll be personally affected by negative press. Naming your business after you can potentially mean you lose control over your name—your business may be controlled by someone else in the future, and with it your name.

Visible appeal

Your brand name will be on your labels, your garments, and in your sales and marketing material. Besides being a great brand name, you also want it to be visibly appealing.

Trademark

When you've decided your brand name, you should apply for trademark protection. Once you've registered your trademark, you know it's free to use and you can pursue legal action if someone tries to copy it.

No rules

Okay, now you've got some pointers—but remember that it's *your* brand. There are no clear rules as to what your brand name should be. If you feel strongly about a name, go for it. However, we still recommend you go through some of the steps above to avoid easy mistakes. Your brand is more than a name and a logo. It's a story that will carry your business for a very long time.

The power of the brand name to consumers is a shortcut— it provides a way to simplify things.

–Kevin Keller

6.3 Visualize Your Brand

What is a mood board?

A mood board is a visual summary of inspirational images, objects, material swatches, trims, or product examples that explain the concept and feeling of your brand, collection, or customer—basically a brain dump of whatever you're inspired by.

The inspiration can be a topic, a place, a color scheme, material story, or entirely functional, based on the activity of your customer. You can build your mood board on the computer or on a large piece of hardboard. If you love to touch things and feel the textures, a physical board or wall could be your thing. Try both until you find your favorite way of working.

Why do you need a mood board?

Because it'll make you stay consistent and focused in terms of your brand values. You'll have it "in your face," a daily reminder of where you're going. Before designing your garments, the images and objects on the board will help steer you in the right direction, design-wise.

When you're finished, make an edited digital version. It'll serve as a fantastic communication tool and it'll keep your team on the same page as you.

The mood board is a living document and should be changed with each season because, just like you, your brand will evolve. Regardless of its evolution, though, it should always remain consistent with your values.

**Find ways to ask your customers questions
and build that into what you do,
your brand and its products.**

Build the customer into your brand.

–Emily Weiss

How to make a mood board

The quick and easy way would be to buy highly priced trend-forecasting books. I know that you're smarter than that, though, and that you want to do things YOUR way. Otherwise a big risk is that your stuff will end up looking like somebody else's because you have the same inspiration. Create your own universe, with your values and tastes, and make your own trend forecasting.

Pinterest and Tumblr are fantastic online sources for pictures—or just type your search word into Google and see where that takes you. For more "live" inspiration, go on a trip, visit galleries, exhibitions, the library, and music festivals. Buy fashion, design, and architecture magazines that catch your eye. Your board doesn't necessarily have to only include garment pictures; it can be a modern architectural building, a fine sculpture, a vintage shoe, a breathtaking view, even a conversation.

Write down words that pop up into your head and put them on your board. For some people, words are more inspirational than images.

It's very easy to look at what other brands are doing and to pin pictures of referential garments.

You can also pin material swatches and trims you like. You can make small mock-ups for interesting design solutions. Pin anything that will evoke some sort of feeling. It's a good idea to give your board a title, like a phrase or name. This can be used in your marketing.

No matter how many pics and things you have on your board in the end, *edit*. Stuff that doesn't speak to you that much should be removed from the board. Consistency is key. Too many different things can give a messy impression. With time you'll learn how to curate.

To make sure you're consistent in your head and not only on your board, do a mini presentation of the mood board for a team member or friend. Saying things out loud will force you to think about what makes sense, and what doesn't follow the red thread.

One more very important thing: Have fun! This part, before the product-development phase, is crucial and will dictate the tone of your collection. Give yourself a couple of weeks, don't stress or force it—and trust the process. Take a step back, look at it from afar and open your brain up for the input and flow that it'll give you. Take notes and even sketch if you get spontaneous ideas.

Enjoy. This is one of the best parts about having your own brand.

Give yourself a challenge and DON'T include competitors' products on your board.

6.4 Branding-Package Content

Your Product + Your Voice + Your Vision + Your Visuals
= Your Brand

This is what you need for your package

A small but very important part of product development is the product branding. How and where do you want your customers to see the brand identity? It's the details that make up the whole!

Depending on their strategy, some brands have big logos and some go for the cleaner, sophisticated look. Whichever you choose, the decision should be in line with your concept and the style of the brand.

What is brand identity?

By "brand identity," we mean all the labels, logo embroideries, trims, and hangtags. This is how you show your brand image to your customers.

Why do you need all the labels and hangtags?

Your brand's visual identity is the strongest marketing tool for communicating your philosophy and story to the world.

What do you need?

Brand identity on a garment is applied through the following:

- Printed or embroidered logo somewhere on the outside of the product. Placement and size is up to you, and it should be in line with your brand values and strategy.

- Brand label on the outside of the garment. Depending on the garment and fabrication, a label can be easier to place than embroidery or print. The label size should be in harmony with the garment it will be placed on.

- Neck label or neck print. This label or print indicates the brand the product belongs to. Placement at the back of the neck makes a brand easily visible when a garment is folded or hanging in a store. The size is up to you and should be in line with your brand values and strategy.

- Size label. This indicates the garment size. Placement should be easily accessible for the customer when the garment is folded or hanging. The neck is an easy and logical spot to put the size label or print.

- Care label. A care label is usually placed on the inside of the garment, at the left-side seam. The following information should be stated on the care label: company name and brand logo to extend your brand image, website address, product name, product number, made in..., washing and care instructions (provided by the fabric supplier and dependent on the materials included in the product), material composition (also provided by the fabric supplier), plus some small phrases, information or fun fact, if you want.

How to make it

Labels and hangtags can be sourced through labeling suppliers or directly through your manufacturer. Both parties will need the following information from you in order to create the artwork for your brand-identity kit.

Hangtag:
- Hangtag. Indicate size, shape, color, material quality and structure.
- Logo. Indicate size, color and structure.
- Text (if you want any on the hangtag).
- Webpage.
- Cord. How do you want the hangtag to be attached to the product? Cord, plastic strap, or other material you have in mind for the attachment? How long should it be and how exactly should it be attached to the garment?
- Note that space is needed on the backside of the hangtags for barcode and price label.

Neck label:
- Label itself. Indicate size, shape, material quality and texture.
- Logo. Indicate size, color and texture.

Size label:
- There are standard size labels, printed or woven, in black with white text, or white with black text. Size labels can also be factory-sourced for lower minimums.

Care label:
- Care labels can also easily be factory-sourced. As with size labels, there are standard ones, white with black text or black with white text. Entry-price versions are printed; if you choose to go for nicer quality, you can opt for woven one

Consistency is key!

Labels and hangtags form part and parcel of the whole branding package, and should be in sync with materials, colors, logo placement, fonts used in texts, and the entire vibe. A good idea would be to have a branding package with "rules" on how to use the logo and how to communicate the brand throughout all medias.

> If you don't give the market the story to talk about, they'll define your brand's story for you.
>
> *–David Brier*

6.5 Branding Tasks

1. Create a brief for your brand.

2. Create a mood board.

3. Determine your story.

4. Create a graphic profile (colors, fonts).

5. Create a logotype.

6. Determine your visual expression.

7. Write communication texts.

8. Make sure it all matches your products.

9. Create branding packaging (labels, hangtags, and packaging).

7.
Money

7.1 Seven Ways To Finance Your Brand

As your business grows and your sales increase, the costs for running your business will also increase. Improving old styles and developing new ones will add costs to your budget. This is how it should be if you want to expand your brand and take it to the next level. Most costs involved in running an apparel business are up front—you have to spend the money long before you can sell the styles and generate income. When you sell your line you'll make a profit that you can use to continue working on the next collection. But you'll most certainly come to a point where the sales revenue isn't enough to finance the growth of your company. You'll need to look at ways of financing your business and covering the costs until you make enough revenue to pay it back.

Here we take a look at seven different options for financing your business:

1. Investors

Investors can be business angels, investment companies, or anyone providing cash to finance your business. In return they typically get shares in your company. As your business grows, so does the value of your company—meaning that when you're starting out, your company's value will be low. Taking on investors early on will mean giving away a larger part of your business, compared to taking them on later. Angel investors typically provide lower investment capital to business ideas than venture capitalists do.

An investor typically becomes a member of your board and will be included in decision-making. They invest in your business to get some kind of return, typically a financial one—so expect them to have opinions about the direction your brand will take. With this in mind, you should try to find an investor who can provide expertise and experience to your company. Take a look at their network, background, and previous investments, and make it a win-win partnership.

Pros
- Investors offer mentorship and expertise.
- They effectively monitor the progress of companies in which they've invested, to ensure the sustainability and growth of their investment.

Cons
- Investors usually want a clear exit plan when they've recovered their capital and profits. The timeframe until this exit is not more than seven years, and is often considerably shorter.
- You tend to lose control of your business since you're giving up a large part of it to venture capital investors.

2. Loan

Take a look at different loan options. You could take on a personal loan from someone you know, for example. Typically, personal loans are from family and friends.

Then there's the classic option of going to the bank and asking for a business loan or line of credit. With a line of credit you have a maximum loan limit, with funds you can access when you need them. When approaching a bank or a financial institution, you need to do a bit of preparation and present your case as to why they should grant you a loan. One option is to not ask for a loan in general, but to ask to bridge a specific case. Let's say you have the luxury problem of receiving so many orders that you can't cover the production costs. In this case it may be easier to get a bridge loan to cover the production until you get paid upon delivery to the retailers. You can show the bank your signed orders as proof that payment is forthcoming once production is completed.

Factoring is when a bank provides you a cash advance for a shipped order. You receive a smaller payment, but it allows you to keep producing and maintaining your cash flow.

There are also institutions and organizations that specialize in helping new businesses and offer especially advantageous terms for a loan if you qualify. Sometimes they're willing to provide a part of your funding, but require you to secure an equal part from another source.

No matter how successful your business is, you always need to pay back that loan with interest. You'll have monthly interest to add to your monthly expenses—but you'll remain in full control of your business, which is not the case if you take on investors.

Pros
- You don't give away a part of your business.
- Depending on the loan giver, the interest can be fairly low.

Cons
- You may have to sign a personal guarantee. This means if the worst happens and your company fails, the bank recoups its losses from your personal assets—your house, your property, your investments.
- You have to pay interest.

3. Government programs

Governments usually have different startup programs in place to help support new businesses. You have to meet certain criteria and apply within specified timeframes. Often, these are connected to support programs that provide you with access to mentors, facilities, and other help. You should definitely apply for these programs, since they can add valuable support to your business, but you shouldn't count on them in your initial budget. The application process usually stretches over a long period of time, and if you're not selected, you're back to square one and need to find alternative funding. Look your application at a potential bonus that'll help you speed up your business if you're granted this type of funding.

Pros
- The amount of government funding is usually substantial, giving you a large amount of capital to run your business.

Cons
- The process of scrutiny, approval and eventual release of funds may take a long time due to government bureaucracy

4. Crowdfunding

There are a couple of big crowdfunding platforms out there, with Kickstarter being the most well-known. Crowdfunding means that a load of people contribute rather small sums in exchange for perks, typically preorders of your product. This way you don't have to give away any shares, plus you get orders before you've made the products. It's also a great way of getting some attention and spreading the word about your brand. But don't think the platform itself will do the work for you. You need to put in a load of work to prepare the campaign, and then put in even more work on the marketing side to let people know about your crowdfunding project.

Pros
- You get paid before producing your garments.
- Creates public interest for your business.
- You don't have to give away any part of your business.
- Has the potential to attract venture-capital investment as the business progresses.

Cons
- Involves a lot of work since the competition is fierce.
- No guaranteed success.

5. Savings

Your own savings are a great way to finance your business. This way you remain in full control of your company and there's no interest on any loan. A tip is to record this investment as a loan to the business from the shareholder. That way you can just pay back the loan later when you're making profits.

Pros
- You maintain full control of your business.

- You maintain full ownership of your company.
- No interest to pay back and no other party to consider.
- Since it's 100 percent your own money, you might be more careful about how you spend it, making sure to use it in the most efficient way.

Cons
- You're putting all your eggs in one basket. Could put a strain on your personal life.
- Could affect your backup plan if your business fails.

6. Other Income

Production cycles are fairly long, typically around one year, so it'll take a while before you get any revenue. An option can be to secure other income on the side, separate from your business. You can keep your day job and work on your business during evenings and weekends. Part-time jobs and freelance assignments are also great options that will free up some time when you can work on your business while generating income. The downside with work on the side is that it takes time and focus away from your business and therefore slows it down.

Pros
- You maintain full control of your business.
- You maintain full ownership of your company.
- No interest to pay back and no other party to consider.
- Since it's 100 percent your own money, you may be more careful about how you spend it, making sure to use it in the most efficient way.

Cons
- Means you have to share time and focus between your side job and your apparel business.

7. Competitions

Search for business and apparel competitions in your area. In addition to providing funding, participating in a competition can offer you valuable press coverage.

Pros
* Typically no conditions once you win. There's no board to answer to.
* You gain press coverage.

Cons
* It's a long shot, with a slim chance of winning. You invest a load of time and energy that you could have invested elsewhere in your business to move it forward.

To help you figure out which is the best option for you, go back to your *Why*. Why did you start the brand in the first place and what are you trying to achieve? How fast do you want to achieve it and how much control do you want over your brand? Are you planning to make an exit in five to ten years? Your own strategy will determine which option suits you the best.

If money, planning, and numbers aren't your strong point, then get someone on board who can help you out with this crucial part. It doesn't matter how great your products are if you can't make money out of them and survive until you do.

If you don't know your numbers, you don't know your business.

–Marcus Lemonis

7.2 Where To Spend And Where To Bootstrap

Starting a new apparel brand can be challenging. It's even more challenging to do it with limited funds. However, this is a reality many of us are facing—but you don't want it to stop your plans. So how is your money best spent? What should you pay for and where can you bootstrap? Read our guide to spending and bootstrapping.

Spend

- Inspirational material. This is the start to every collection and product-development process. Feel you need to have it? Get it!

- Designer/product developer. Unless you have design skills, we'd advise you to pay someone who knows design/product development. You'll save a load of time and, in the end, money. The products are your entire business—you shouldn't play around with the design until you've learned how to design.

- Photographer. Pictures will be a major part of your communication to the world. Professional pics do wonders for the products and your brand.

- Accountant. It doesn't matter how small you are in the beginning—you always want to have your books in check. If your brain freezes when you see numbers, pay someone who knows what they're doing.

- Necessary tools: computer, phone, and good Internet connection. These will be your everyday tools. You'll quickly get frustrated if you have a crappy Internet connection or an old/broken phone.

- Adobe Program Suite: Illustrator, Photoshop, and InDesign. If you don't know these programs, book yourself a week away from work and learn them. Google, YouTube, or get online on a webinar. Your whole business is based on these programs: Illustrator for tech packs and line sheets; Photoshop for pictures; and InDesign for layouts like workbooks and leaflets.

- Trips to factories. This is important for several reasons: it's relationship-building, you can product-develop quicker while on site, and you control the manufacturing.

- Visit material fairs. Go to the biggest fabric fairs like Premiere Vision, Texworld, and Performance Days. Be well prepared before you go in order to get the maximum out of your visit. You could also stay an extra day and stroll around town in Paris, New York, or Munich for inspiration. Going to fabric fairs is the quickest and best way to source materials. Grow your network and broaden your fabric selection.

Bootstrap

- Studio. At the beginning, working from home is definitely an option. Make a little office space in your home for the new brand. When you need to increase your team, that's when it's time to find a studio.

- Graphic design and branding. Your logo will be seen everywhere—on your products, website, communication, and social media. Use, for example, a service such as 99designs instead of an expensive agency.

- Website. Spend a couple of evenings on YouTube and learn to make a simple website for your brand. Use free WordPress templates to customize your site.

- Expensive models from agencies. Search for your ideal customer amongst your network of friends, and friends of friends—then use them as models in your photo shoots.

- Ditch the printed lookbook. It's neither environmentally friendly nor cheap. An online lookbook is fine. Buyers and customers view it on your website or you can email it to them.

- Spend time on social media instead of money on PR agencies. When you start out, authenticity, transparency, and personality are much better for your branding.

- Wait before exhibiting at fairs. Exhibiting at a fair costs a lot of money and doesn't always give the best return on investment. Contact and visit your most important customers to build long-lasting relationships.

Beware of little expenses. A small leak will sink a great ship.

–Benjamin Franklin

7.3 Ten Steps To Master Cash Flow

Cash flow is the net amount of cash and equivalents being transferred into and out of a business. As an apparel entrepreneur, you need to keep a close eye on cash flow and make sure it remains positive. Product-development cycles are long and your incoming cash must at all times cover the cash going out. If you don't have enough incoming cash, you'll have difficulties paying suppliers, salaries, rent, etc. Not mastering cash flow is a common reason for going out of business.

What can you do to improve your cash flow?

Read the following ten steps to help you master your cash flow.

1. Plan ahead of time

When starting out, you probably have enough funds in your bank account to keep you going through the startup phase, product development and launch. You can easily feel well-funded and tempted to spend your cash on every opportunity you see. Plan in detail how you'll run your business, and determine where to spend your money and where to save it. Go to the Bootstrapping chapter to get some ideas.

2. Control your sample costs

During the product-development phase, you're making a couple of samples per style. The material, making, pattern, and transport costs will add up to a substantial amount. Go through your alternatives for who's making your samples and patterns. Perhaps a factory is the best option —or maybe you can cut down the amount of samples you make?

3. Use your credit card

Using your credit card when paying certain bills can delay your payment 30 days, which can be enough for you to receive an incoming payment.

4. Set your payment terms

Ask your customers to pay earlier and shorten your payment terms. Can you request 30 days net, or even 20 days net, instead of 60? Send invoices out immediately and you'll receive your payments earlier. Buying time this way helps with your cash flow.

5. Have a buffer

Make sure you always have a financial buffer in case you encounter unexpected costs or a customer is late with a payment.

6. Ask your customers to pay up front

You can ask your customers to pay up front for ordered garments. You can also ask for a partial payment upon order. That way you'll have some incoming cash before production and delivery. Everyone loves an incentive—so perhaps offer your customers a discount for up-front payment.

7. Leasing instead of buying

Leasing supplies and equipment generally ends up costing more than buying, so this may seem counterintuitive. But mastering your cash flow means that you have to pay attention to the money coming in and going out for your daily operations. By leasing rather than buying, you pay in small increments, which improves your cash-flow situation.

8. Conduct credit checks

Conducting a credit check of customers paying by invoice will expose any poor credit ratings. A poor credit rating means there's a significant risk you won't receive your payments in time, which will hurt your cash flow. If you still want to sell to someone with a poor credit rating, you can arrange a high interest rate for late payments.

9. Check your stock and inventory

Maybe you have products in your stock that aren't moving at the same pace as your other products or that don't sell at all? Make an extra effort to get rid of them since they're tying up a load of cash. It can be worth selling them at a discount to improve your cash-flow situation.

10. Increase your prices and lower your expenses

Have you found your perfect price point? Experiment with your pricing to see how high your customers are willing to go. When buying materials and supplies, remember that everything is negotiable. When producing a large number of clothes, every small price component matters. Less money flowing out and more flowing in will help you run your daily operations and increase your profits.

Go through the above ten points and look at every part of your business to make sure you maintain a positive cash flow and stay in business.

If I had to run a company on three measures, those measures would be customer satisfaction, employee satisfaction, and cash flow.

–Jack Welch

7.4 Hidden Costs

As well as monitoring your cash flow, you need to be aware of possible hidden costs. You have your business-plan document and yearly budget to help you control your expenses and running operations. You also need to be aware of costs that are not as obvious and may be unaccounted for. Let's take a look at some expenses that are easily overlooked.

Dead stock

Check your inventory to see which products are slow-selling and which are not selling at all. You've paid for the production of the garments—dead stock means you're losing money on them if they don't sell. Create a strategy to get rid of the existing dead stock and to avoid it in future.

Shipping costs

Samples are sent back and forth to factories; sample and production materials are sent to you as well as to the factory; bulk production needs to be shipped to warehouses and end consumers; e-commerce orders are sent to customers. All this shipping involves costs that easily add up to a substantial amount you need to account for.

Non-paying customers

Conduct credit checks of customers paying by invoice rather than cash. You want to be sure you get paid for your products and services, and if customers are not paying your bills it'll hurt your business.

Discounts

Perhaps you work with discounts to increase your sales; e.g., it's quite common for e-commerce sites to offer clients a discount when they sign up for a newsletter. This may work well for you—but remember to track all your discounts since you're paying for them.

Adjustment costs

When working with product development, there are always details that need to be improved and adjusted. You need to agree with each partner what's included in your collaboration and what's not. After a couple of sample rounds, you may ask a factory to make pattern adjustments. Don't assume they'll do it for free. Expect an invoice for the pattern work or negotiate it.

Tolls

Depending on your location and where your suppliers are, you may have to pay taxes and tolls. Read up on the regulations before conducting business with new partners so that you can calculate and incorporate these costs in your budget.

Returns

Normally, returns will cost you the shipping, the lost revenue, the handling, and the administration. An unexpected increase in returns will take a toll on your profit. Talk to your customers and examine why they're returning your garments. Use that information to create a plan to mitigate this issue in the future.

Surcharges

You may, for different reasons, decide to make a smaller production batch than you intended or received price quotes for. Usually a material supplier or garment manufacturer can make smaller amounts than their MOQs. In these cases you'll be billed a surcharge. These surcharges will eat up your margin. This can be planned for and fit into your strategy, but remember that prices vary depending on order quantity.

Inefficient processes and systems

If you don't have clear processes and systems in place for performing all the tasks in your business, it'll cost you valuable time and hence money. With the right processes in place you'll be more efficient avoid delays, double work, and costly mistakes. If you're a small business, implement processes as if you were a large company. If you're a large company, constantly evaluate and improve your processes.

Currency rates

As an apparel entrepreneur, you'll likely be working with suppliers and customers in other countries. This exposes you to currency rates. Even small fluctuations in currency rates can add nasty costs for you. Pay attention to the currency when placing your orders and adjust your calculations accordingly.

Missed production deadlines

When creating your plan, you usually start by looking at your planned delivery date. You use that date together with known lead times to calculate backwards when you need deadlines for certain tasks. A missed deadline can easily incur added costs for you. An example is if you've planned to transport your garments by ship; a missed deadline could mean you won't have time to transport the garments by ship, and instead have to opt for the more expensive alternative: airplane.

Sample costs

If you have to make more samples than you planned for, you'll also have to pay more than expected. Avoid having to make extra samples by creating detailed, structured tech packs, BOMs, and measurement lists, as well as securing the correct materials and good references. Leave as little as possible to chance.

Factory visits

You should plan for at least one, but preferably more, factory visits during product development. Problems with prototypes, production, or communication will mean you'll have to visit more than expected. These visits usually help to sort out issues, but they'll also cost you in terms of travel expenses.

Sourcing

Sourcing means visiting fairs, factories, suppliers, and representatives. If you're unhappy with a material or collaboration, you'll have to start your sourcing over. This could mean new travel costs, more shipping expenses, etc. It's a good idea to include a buffer in your budget for sourcing so as to avoid suffering elsewhere in your organization.

7.5 Money Tasks

1. Create a budget for at least 18 months

2. Secure funding

3. Facilitate cash flow

8.
The Team

8.1 Who Do You Need On Your Team?

> None of us is as smart as all of us.
>
> *–Japanese proverb*

How are you going to do it?

By this point you'll already have a pretty clear vision of what the brand should be about and who your ideal customer is. Now you just need to figure out how you're going to do it and the size of it all. If you're the creative type, you'll probably focus on the product and everything related to it—but of course the other side needs attention too: the business side.

Who's going to do what?

If you're a designer, find a good business partner—and if you're a businessperson, find a good designer. No one can do it all and neither should you. It's better to focus on your strengths than to do everything half-assed. So, what competencies do you possess and what do you need to outsource? What are you good at and what do you most enjoy doing? If you're not working in the clothing industry, it's time to start making some phone calls and get networking because you need to meet the "right" people. Find a great designer who "speaks the same visual language" and let him/her get going on the design, sourcing, and production. Find that amazing photographer you admire and let him take the pictures. You could do it all by yourself—but it'll take you much longer and you'll for sure make a load of mistakes along the way. Starting a clothing brand will have you wearing many different hats—and that's the beauty of it, too. There are no rights and wrongs in starting a clothing brand—the most important thing is that you stay true to yourself and your vision, you have fun along the way, and you learn from your mistakes.

17 Roles to fill

There are many roles that need to be filled in your business. As a small apparel brand, you can and probably will take on several of them yourself. But ask yourself which roles you can actually fill and which you need to outsource.

So, what are the typical roles you need to fill? Here they are—your dream team:

1. Market researcher
Researches and follows market and color trends. Collects ideas, opinions, consumer-behavior info, likes and dislikes, perceptions and attitudes. Needs to understand client requirements with respect to your products. Coordinates the conversion of data, prepares reports on findings, and interprets them. You want to stay up to date with what's going on so that you don't copy anyone else.

2. Designer
The heart of the business. Don't underestimate the need for a designer on your team. After all, it's all about the products. Stays up to date with markets, creates mood boards, stories, decides colors, designs the collection, creates tech packs, sources material, leads fitting sessions,

approves samples, and visits manufacturers to assure product development.

3. Production manager
The link between your brand and the manufacturer. Coordinates and communicates with all suppliers and manufacturers.

4. Buyer
In charge of getting the materials for your production. Ensures delivery requirements are met. Places all orders to suppliers and manufacturers and makes sure everything arrives and gets delivered on time.

5. Pattern-maker
Creates the garment patterns. A skilled pattern-maker can make all the difference to your end result. For the apparel business especially, you need one who understands the body movement and well-fitting clothes. Can also grade the patterns, if not done at the factory.

6. Quality controller
Oversees quality procedures. You can have someone on the team to do it or an external partner.

7. Sample-maker
Creates the samples. The more technical your styles are, the more skilled the sample-maker needs to be with the sewing machine. Sample-making can also be done at the factory.

8. Sales manager
Makes sure your collection sells. It doesn't matter if you've the best apparel collection in the world if it doesn't sell. No sales = no business.

9. Marketing manager
Makes sure the world knows about your brand and creates a demand for it on the market.

10. Stylist
Creates the brand looks for shows and photo shoots.

11. Financial controller
Keeps track of the money. You want it to grow.

12. CEO
In charge of the overall operations.

13. Tech manager
In charge of IT services, social media accounts, as well as your online presence.

14. Bookkeeper
Makes sure your bookkeeping is up to par.

15. Office manager
Takes care of everything that falls between two stools.

16. Copy /graphic
In charge of creating copy and graphics.

17. Photographer
Takes all those unforgettable photos and videos for your workbooks, Web and marketing material.

It's not a bad thing if you're forced to take on several of the roles yourself. You'll learn about the different trades and understand your business better. You'll become less dependent on others and harder to bullshit. Still need to find help and keep your costs down? Tap into your network and see what skills they possess.

7 reasons you should learn to be a jack of all trades in your business:

1. You'll have full control of all aspects of your business.

2. You'll avoid bullshit and stay on top of all things. You know exactly what needs to be done.

3. Time is money and you're the one moving things forward.

4. No dependency on skills or people. You get things done.

5. You'll know your needs when it comes to projecting, planning, and balancing workload.

6. You'll understand the skills needed when you expand your team.

7. Fun. You'll learn all aspects of your business. This will make you a better entrepreneur and leader.

8.2 The Team Tasks

1. Decide who's going to fill each of the 17 roles.

2. Where do you need help? How are you going to get it?

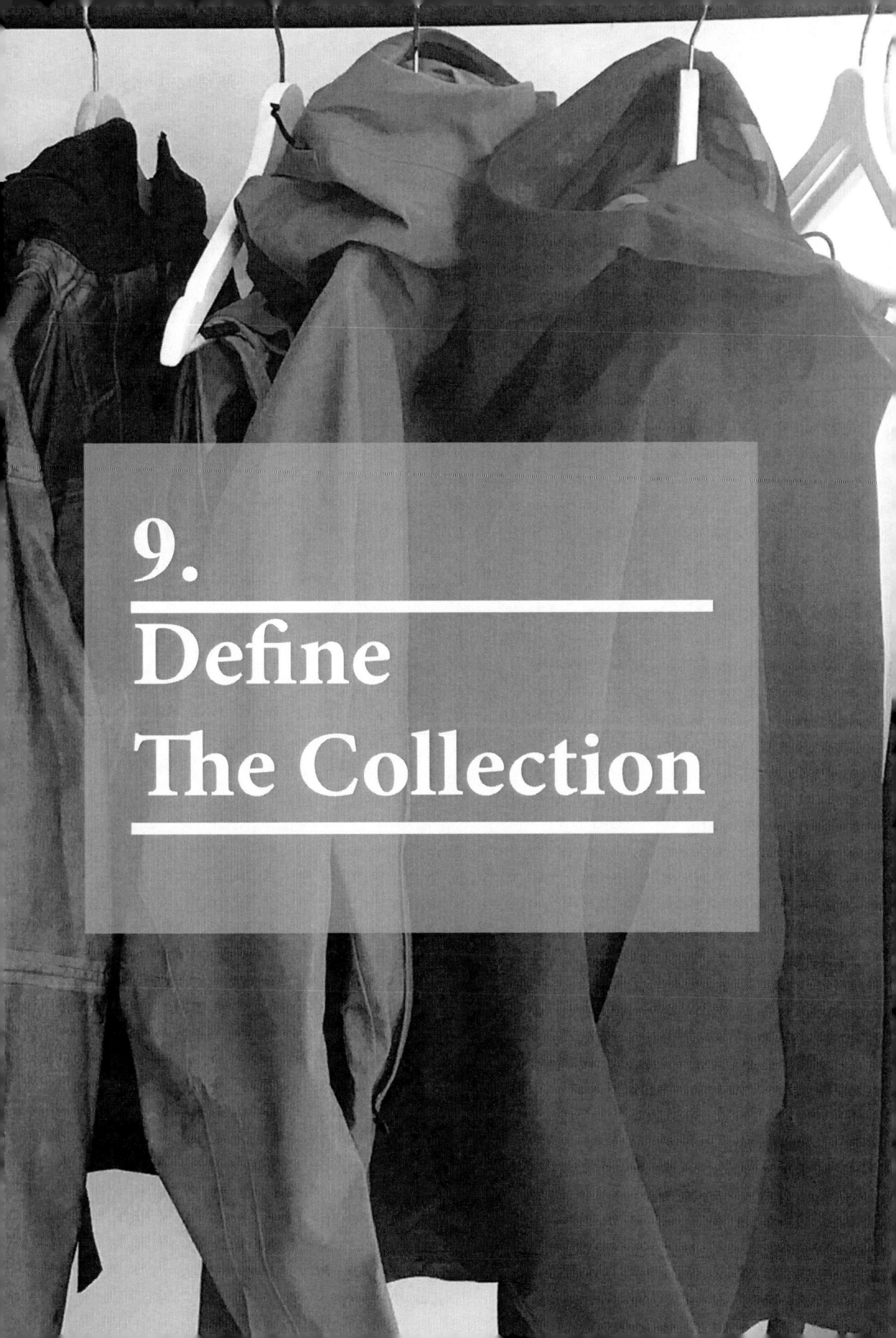

9.
Define
The Collection

9.1 Define Your Collection

It's vital that you stay focused and honed in on your core vision of the brand. Customers generally have *one word* in their minds connected to each brand—e.g., Patagonia = sustainability; H&M = fast fashion, etc. If you want to design jeans, stay on the jeans for a while until the customer gets familiar with your brand—then add on more categories. If the *one word* you like is already taken, make sure yours is different. What do you want your brand and products to stand for? What is your point of view, your identity, and how does that differentiate from those of other designers? When you have that clear, make sure you implement it in every design you do.

Have your specific target customer in mind when you set this up. Who is that person and what does he/she wear? If you already have a "muse," that's great—it means you're all set in terms of knowing your customer.

When you've figured out all the answers to the above, it's time to set the concept, collection, and styles. Will you focus on outdoor stuff, sportswear, or streetwear? Think about the consistency. Should some design features run along all styles?

A good idea is to have a collection structure—both in styles and price level. Too many similar styles at the same price points will confuse customers, and the styles will cannibalize each other in sales. If you're starting out small, you'll only have a small number of styles—which means less headaches. Then add on styles as you grow. You could, for example, make several styles in the same fabric. Fabrics are usually bought in a minimum quantity for a certain price. Just use it up instead of having leftovers in the factory. You'll end up losing a load of money if you have too much leftover material.

It's up to you to decide how trend-sensitive your brand should be. This is connected to what type of customer you want and what your brand identity will be. One way to approach it is to not follow trends but instead make products that last, in all aspects—design-wise and quality-wise. That said, it doesn't mean you can't keep your ear to the ground and feel and take in what's going on in the world.

To sum up, make sure to have a common thread in the collection and make it interesting. The styles should be cohesive and not compete with each other. Stay true to your muse—but the best muse to have is yourself.

Knowing what problem your product solves will be your biggest advantage in the marketplace.

What problem does your business solve? Focus on that!

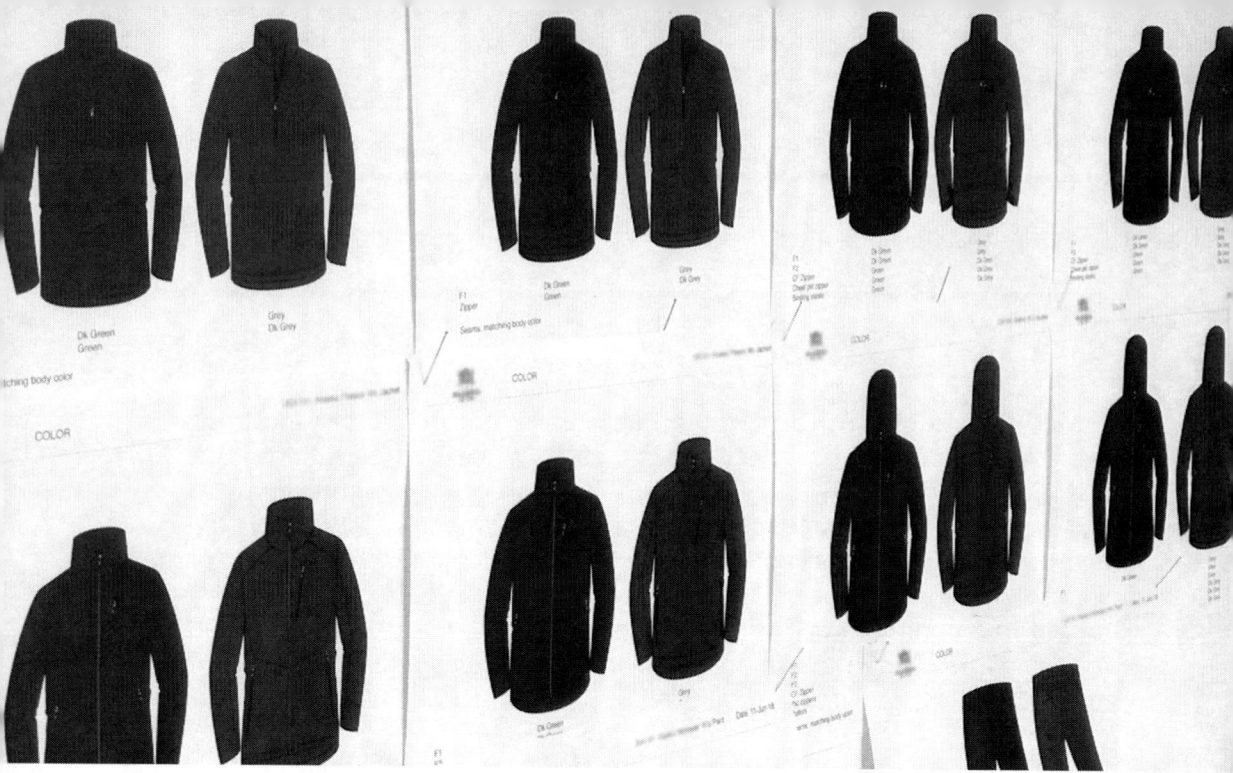

9.2 Product-Range Strategy

Building A Collection

Building a collection requires a delicate balancing act between designing products that incorporate your values as a company and brand, and actually producing garments that sell. The trick here is to fully know who your target customer is, what specific market you want to position yourself in, and what your "muse" wants. Your goal should be to nail both the commercial and creative aspects.

What kind of brand are you?

What will you offer and why?

What are your values?

Figure this out first, before applying the principles below.

What are you going to sell?

When you first decided to start your apparel brand, you had a vision. Either it was a specific product (item brand) or a certain product concept that includes a set of products (collection brand). In the startup phase it's good to clarify this—for yourself, your buyers, and your end customers.

Item brand

If your focus is on one specific product, imagine how this will be placed in a store or displayed on your website/webshop. The same item can be produced in different colors and materials to diversify your offer to your customers.

Do you have enough basic vs on-trend colors?

Will you offer different fits?

Will your product be offered in different materials depending on season?

The benefits of starting with one item are the minimum quantities and the fairly low cash requirement for starting up your business. You'll only need one type of manufacturer; it'll be easier to communicate and easier to get it right from the beginning.

Collection brand

If you choose to go big from the start with a full collection, then here are some things you need to consider:

- Do you have a good diversity of colors?
- Do you have a signature product in the collection?
- Can you build outfits with the items you have?
- Do you have a clear pricing strategy for all items?
- Do you have good diversity in materials?
- Do the styles cannibalize each other? Are they too similar and therefore reduce each other's sales?
- Can you ACTUALLY manufacture all the items in the collection and can you afford it?

Remember you have to pay suppliers and manufacturers about six months in advance. What you present to buyers, you have to manufacture and deliver!

Start with a small collection. When you're an apparel startup and have limited resources this will be your way of gaining solid ground for your brand. Introduce a really unique product, build your brand around that and expand from there. Many of today's big brands started small. They focused on a specific item when they launched their brand and diversified from there. They had already built a community and fan base that wanted their products. Having a niche will be your strength.

Approaching the buyers

When buyers are introduced to new products/brands, the questions that pop up in their heads are:

- What's unique about this product that I don't already have in my store and that I can offer my customers?

- How can I complement my offer with this new product/brand?

In order to be unique, you need to have that special creative vibe in your brand. And if you want to get your business off the ground and stay in business, you also need to be commercial.

Keep the balance between creativity and business.

Create a price structure

Your concept is clear, the design is done—now you need to give the thing a price. How do you go about pricing a product? What pillars should be included in the strategy? Here are a few points to bring into the equation:

- What type of brand are you? Luxury, high-end, midrange, affordable, or entry price?
- What prices do your direct competitors offer for similar products? Do thorough market research so you know how and why to differentiate yourself.
- What materials and quality will your products have?
- Where will your products be manufactured?
- What profit margins do you need to have?
- How much money are you going to make?

Who decides this? Are there any rules? Does the market dictate the pricing? Nope, not really—it all depends on the strategy you want to follow.

Cheaper products can potentially sell more than expensive ones. But if you have certain brand values, selling cheap products could devalue your brand. Once you've decided and set your strategy, make sure you stick to it! The trick is to price your garments in such a way that buyers/customers feel the product is worth its price. Stay on top of the figures. Learn Excel and get yourself comfortable with numbers. Price your products for profit from the start!

Product-range planning

The styles in your collection have different intentions and "raisons d'être." Some styles are your moneymakers with high margins. Some products are designed, developed, and priced to attract consumer interest and make the entire collection come together. These styles are called signature pieces. To wow your audience, there should also be a small percentage of icon pieces in your collection. These are the showstoppers that will get you positive PR and visibility.

Your collection should consist of a selection of products that work together as a group, with a cohesive story, not just random pieces. There should be a variety of silhouettes, colors, materials, and fits; e.g., your tops and bottoms need to tell the same story and have a logical top/bottoms ratio. If you have a jacket assortment, do you have a thin jacket for late summer, a thicker one for fall, and a really warm one for winter? When do you have the different product drops and deliveries per season? The balance of your collection pieces is also very important when it comes to merchandising in stores. Think about and visualize how your products or collection are going to sit in your own store or retail stores.

It's good if every collection includes:
- Your basics. Products for a wider audience, called key pieces. These items can come in many color options and have a high margin.

- Signature pieces. Products that you and your brand are known for, that not many other designers or brands have. These items have a good margin and make your collection interesting.

- Icon pieces and showstoppers. These items enhance your image and are the ones that highlight your collection but they don't tend to sell that much. Most of the time, the margins on these styles can be slightly lower because of the marketing value they bring.

- Accessories. Easy-to-sell products like hats, scarves, and accessories that tie your entire collection together nicely and add that extra touch. Preferably you should have a great margin on these items.

The point with a well-planned collection is to make it interesting for buyers and to give them more buying options, resulting in increased sales. Because you've done such a great job with the collection plan it should be easier and simpler for people to shop from you.

Think about the following questions when you build your range for killer merchandising:

- How will retailers exhibit your products?
- Will the colors merchandise well together and represent your brand in the best way?
- Will it look interesting when it hangs on the wall?
- Do you have popping colors for visual interest?
- How will the customer's eye be drawn to your products?
- When the customer finally finds your garments, will they like the materials, prices, and overall quality?

Okay, there's a load of stuff to think about and each aspect is equally important. Put yourself in your buyer's shoes. Preferably you'll have visited the store beforehand, to determine exactly who their customer is and what other brands the store carries.

After a season or two in a store, you'll be able to analyze the sell-through (what actually sold in the store at full retail price): what sold and why? This information will enable you to design a better collection and actually give your customers a better range of products.

6 final tips

1. Get really clear on how you want to position yourself in the market.
2. Get really clear on who your customer is: end consumer and stores/retailers.
3. Listen to your customers. If a product works, ask why it works; if a product doesn't sell, figure out why and make changes accordingly to rectify that.
4. Use few materials across many styles to cover minimum fabric quantities and to keep the collection cohesive. This will also make your production process easier and cheaper.
5. Do one thing well—you can't be everything to everybody.
6. As we mentioned earlier, there are no set rules for how to structure and price a clothing range. You'll have to test your way through, tweak it season after season till you nail it. But the above tips will definitely help you to achieve that successfully selling range.

9.3 Style-Number Guide

When you're designing your collection, you need to assign style numbers to each design. The style numbers help you identify the specific garment. When you're a small company it's easy for you to keep track of every style and its specifics. But as your brand grows and you add more styles, create carry-over styles, new collections, and new coworkers, you'll need a system for everyone to identify all the different garments.

Professionalism

The style numbers are not only for you and your brand coworkers. They'll help you to better communicate with your retailers, agents, distributors, suppliers, pattern-makers, and everyone else you're working with.

It's better to use style numbers instead of style names when you're communicating with partners, since not everyone speaks the same language and uses the same letters—hence your style names may not make sense to them.

The most important reason to introduce style numbers is for your own logistics and inventory management. You need a system in place that enables you to easily manage the garments in your stock shelves.

Create a system

Start by creating a number system that's consistent and will function for you when you grow and expand your collection. It's your brand, and you can create any number system you want for your garments. There are no set industry rules you have to follow. It's important that you create a well-thought-out system early on, so that you don't have to go back and change everything when product development is in full progress.

Example system

Let's create a number system with the format:

UVWXYYY-ZZZZ
Each letter will have a meaning. For each garment, you'll replace the letter with a number. A garment could have the number:
3132001-9999
In this case, this would mean the brand's first women's tights in black. How? Let us explain the system.

U means gender and has 3 number options:
UVWXYYY-ZZZZ
1. Unisex
2. Man
3. Woman
Example 3132001-9999
Example U=3, meaning it's for women.

V means type and has 3 number options:
U**V**WXYYY-ZZZZ
1. Garments
2. Shoes
3. Bags
Example 3132001-9999
Example V=1, meaning it's a garment.

W means category and has 6 options:
UV**W**XYYY-ZZZZ
1. Outerwear

2. Mid-layer
3. Base
4. Skirt/dress
5. Swim
6. Accessories

Example 3132001-9999

Example W=3, meaning it's a base layer, the garment closest to the body.

X means subcategory and has 3 options:
UVW**X**YYY-ZZZZ
1. Tops
2. Bottoms
3. Suits

Example 3132001-9999

Example X=2, meaning it's a bottom. There are pants, shorts, and tights in this collection. You can easily add on specific subcategories for these if you prefer.

YYY means style number and you can have 999 styles in each subcategory.
UVWX**YYY**-ZZZZ
That will last you a while. If you're worried it isn't enough, you can always add one more Y. We start by giving our first style in the subcategory the number 001, and then we add on. This will give an indication of how early in your brand's history the style was created.

*Example 3132**001**-9999*

Example YYY=001, meaning it's the first style in the subcategory bottoms.

ZZZZ means color number.
UVWXYYY-**ZZZZ**
Each garment style can come in different colors. Create your own color-code system: for example, white and beige colors in the range 0000—0999, yellow colors starting at 1000, red colors starting at 2000, and so on. You can also adopt existing color codes from your supplier, to keep it simple. Bear in mind, though, that adopting the code system from one supplier can be confusing when you change supplier.

*Example 3132001-**9999***

Example ZZZZ=9999, meaning it's our darkest color: black.

Style-Number-System Overview
Style-Number Format: UVWXYYY-ZZZZ

U	V	W	X	YYY	ZZZZ
Gender	Type	Category	Subcategory	Style	Color

Example Number: 3132001-ZZZZ (Women's Tights)

U=1	V=1	W=3	X=2	YYY=001	ZZZZ
Gender	Type	Category	Subcategory	Style	Color
Woman	Garment	Base	Bottoms	1	ZZZZ

Style-Number Guide

PLACE	MEANING	NUMBERS	DESCRIPTION
U	Gender	1	Unisex
		2	Man
		3	Woman
V	Type	1	Garments
		2	Shoes
		3	Bags
W	Category	1	Outerwear
		2	Midlayer
		3	Base
		4	Skirt / dress
		5	Swim
		6	Accessories
X	Subcategory	1	Tops
		2	Bottoms
		3	Suits
YYY	Style	000-999	Style ID
ZZZZ	Color	0000-9999	Color code

9.4 Define-The-Collection Tasks

1. Determine the styles you're going to make.

2. Decide if it's both men's and women's.

3. Decide the colors/variations per style.

4. Decide the sizes you want the styles in.

5. Determine who your customer is.

6. Determine price/style and a total collection price structure.

10.
The Design

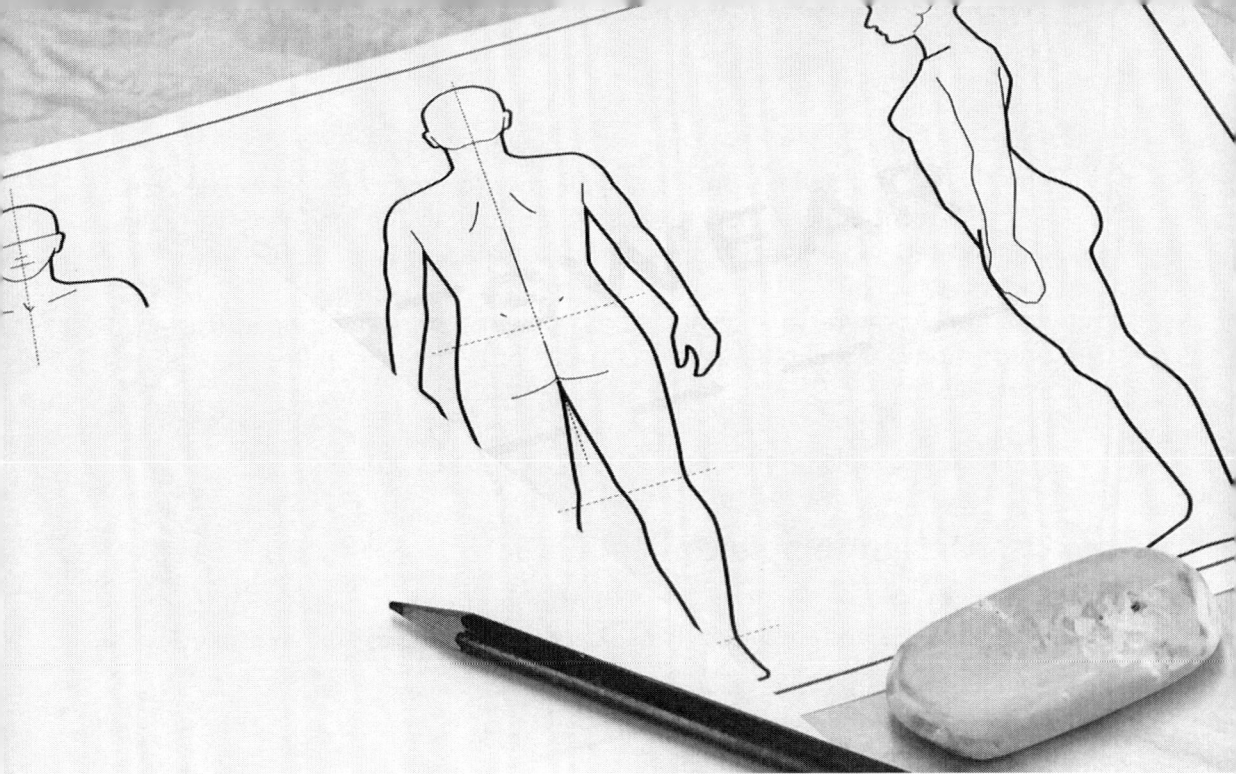

10.1 How To Design Without Knowing How To Draw

Do you need to know how to draw to start a clothing brand?

The short, direct answer is *No*—you can start and run a successful brand without knowing how to draw. But for your sake—and ultimately for the brand—yes, it would help significantly if you could visualize your ideas.

Here are our thoughts on this and a couple of steps you can take to get your design juices flowing:

The purpose of an illustration is to visually communicate your design ideas. This sketch will be the groundwork for your entire product development and the first link in the entire chain. Somehow your product ideas need to come out on a sheet of paper, on a computer, or in a physical form like a prototype. From this draft, you or a designer can make a tech pack with flats; the pattern-maker can make the measurement list; and the factory can make a prototype.

The technical drawings, the flats, will go into your tech pack. The flats are the front and back views of a design. If the garment is really complicated, you might want to add a side view as well.

Flats are drawn to normal body proportion, not 9-head fashion proportions, and should be as "correct" in terms of real-life proportion as possible.

You have a couple of different options for how to proceed:

Use Design templates

A number of websites specialize in offering finished and downloadable Illustrator design templates. These can be changed to suit your needs.

Outsource

If you have the budget for it, you can always hire a designer to do the job for you. You'll still have to explain your thoughts to the designer in order for him/her to do her job and start sketching the ideas.

Some factories also provide this step in the process as a service for companies that don't have a designer. They can actually help you design and make the entire garment in the process. You'll go through the same steps, where you visually and verbally show what you have in mind. They'll also have garments in their showroom that you can pick ideas from to help out in the product-ideation stage.

Learn to draw

If you want to be in full control and absolutely on top of the design process, then there are no shortcuts—learn how to draw. Practice till you can visualize your idea on paper or a screen. For hand-drawn sketches you can use pencils, markers, watercolor, gouache, collage—whatever makes you happy and inspired.

Generally, the easiest and fastest way to land a design is to make several quick hand sketches. To learn how to do this, take time and look at yourself in the mirror, wearing similar apparel to that you intend to design. Look at proportions, shape, balance, seams, details. Also go to your own wardrobe, pick a garment out, put it flat on the floor and start sketching it. Look at proportions and seams. When you've done this on several styles, you'll start to get the hang of it and also understand how garments are sewn together.

Dissect competitor samples. Either take garments from your own wardrobe or bought samples, and deconstruct the products. Cut out what you like from different styles and sew new ones together. This way you'll learn how garments are constructed plus you'll get closer to what you want your own styles to look like and what finishing details they should have. Later bring this to the factory and show them what you want to achieve.

There are tons of online classes for drawing—you just need to decide you want to learn and commit, put in the work, and soon you'll have no trouble doing quick sketches. However, you do not have to be able to draw amazing fashion illustrations to run a successful apparel business.

Use croquis templates

Another way of doing it is to print out tech-pack sketches from the Internet showing similar styles, and redraw them with your own designs on a Light Box. You already have the main frame for the design and proportions—adjust the length and width, and redesign the lines to suit your taste.

You can also use the help of a croquis template: the apparel drawing can be done on top of the croquis, forcing the lines and proportions into shape.

It'll be a huge advantage for you to have drawing skills—not only to articulate your own designs but also for when your team grows. When you have to read an employed or contracted designer's work, you'll know the thinking behind it, you'll know what and how to "see." This is ultimately the most important skill: to be able to SEE. See what it's going to be, see what the design's going to look like in the intended material, with the intended details and trims: to visualize how the garment is going to move, behave, and feel.
If designing is not part of your background, don't underestimate the importance of having a designer involved in your brand. After all, apparel design and the products form the core of your business.

10.2 How To Get Your Design Inspiration Going

Where do you find your inspiration? Here are a few pointers to get you inspired.

Who, What, Why, How?

Ask yourself the question WHY? Why does this product exist? What should it do to the person who uses it? And how should the person wearing it feel?

The human body itself plays a major role here, because the garments you design will be used by a person/body. The garments should facilitate the wearer's experience: for example, the pockets should be in the right place for you to be able to put your hands in, and the sleeves should be cut in a certain way so that you can move properly, etc.
Try to have a "no bullshit" approach in the design phase. Keep it simple and user-friendly.

WTF moments

Everything can inspire you: Life, simple things, a conversation on the bus between two strangers, architecture, the material itself, photography, behavioral patterns, and illustrated picture books. Try to see what's NOT there as much as you see what IS.

Are there opportunities and things that can easily be improved—for example the service in a store, or the making and finishing on a product, or someone's way of saying hello? You know, those moments when you go, "WTF?"

Look and see!

Take a load of photos wherever you go. You don't have to look at them all the time, but you know where to find them if you need to. Pics of shadows, materials, birds, flowers, faces, outfits, packaging, structures, patterns, nature itself, lighting—EVERYTHING that you go, "Oh!" about. The only thing you need to do is LOOK and SEE—it's all out there and it's free. Force yourself to look in fields other than apparel, too, otherwise your designs will end up looking like someone else's... and that you do not want! The products you design need to somehow "speak" YOU. You can draw your ideas first, with old-school pen on paper. The lines need to come freely and never be forced. If it feels forced, work on something else till the lines come to you naturally.

Keep a notebook with you at all times. Write stuff, draw stuff, and tape things in it. It can be very inspiring to flip through old notebooks from time to time.

Keep it personal

Keep the designing personal. You're your own muse in a way. If you need to design trail-running shorts, you know what a trail runner needs from a pair of shorts, since you're a trail runner yourself. If you're not your own customer, then you're in deep trouble. You could argue that you'll look at product development with fresh eyes and see problems from different angles, but you can never put yourself in a trail runner's state of mind and body as they run if you've never run on a trail. You'll never be able to understand the features, the feeling someone needs to have in your garment or by using your product. Let your designs "speak *you*" and be your own customer.

Steal with pride...

Everybody copies in one way or another. "There's nothing new under the sun," as they say. But what *is* new is the way YOU combine things you've seen and registered. Hopefully you'll improve on what you've seen—otherwise there's no point in doing it at all. So, do "borrow" from others, tweak, improve, add the "you" to it—and congratulations, you're an innovator!

If you get tired, learn to rest, not to quit.

Stop thinking and start doing

Get your hand going and start doodling. Just get those lines down on paper. Don't overthink; just let the hand do the drawing. It's always better to have more drawings than you end up using.

Go for a run or walk

Of course you get stuck from time to time. The design just won't "come" to you, and you don't know how to solve a problem or improve on something. The best way to not force things, and to open up your brain's capacity to think, is to go for a run, bike ride, walk, or something similar—whatever you prefer. It works wonders! Perhaps it's the fresh air or the increased blood flow—who knows—but it works!

Make a habit of it

Always look for inspiration around you. Make a habit of sketching and collecting stuff you like. Keep a file of inspirational pics or drawings handy for new collections. This way you'll be off to a flying start when it's time to design.

24/7

A designer's brain is always on. It's always registering and seeing things. The intake doesn't run on a clock or just from nine till five. It's constantly on, looking and mixing things up, connecting different ends and sometimes putting them into new, interesting outcomes. Ask yourself why you like or dislike stuff, and learn from the answer.

There you go! As you can see, it's pretty simple. Just LOOK, SEE, SENSE, and REGISTER. Now go make amazing things happen with that information!

To design is much more than simply to assemble, to order, or even to edit: it's to add value and meaning, to illuminate, to simplify, to clarify, to dignify, to dramatize, to persuade, and perhaps even amuse. To design is to transform prose into poetry.

−Paul Rand

10.3 Designing The Collection

When you have a structure for your collection and an idea of what type of styles you wish to have, it's time to start sketching. Revisit your inspiration, the brand image, and your customer profile. The styles should fit in with your brand vision and identity. For example, if you're an activewear company, you'll focus on activewear; you'll have to give the customer the connection between the brand image and the product. They need to correspond.

Keep the next tips in mind while you go at it:

Focus

It's easy to want to do everything at once, but it's best to narrow your focus to only one or a couple of categories, like just outerwear, or just tops, and grow from there. If you start big, you won't have the budget anyway to do it all.

Balance

Have the overall spirit of the collection in mind, to ensure cohesion, consistent color story, and shared materials.

Edit

Yes, please do! It's so easy to get carried away—you have so many ideas you want the world to see, but too much will just be confusing. If the garments don't have hanger appeal and are not strong enough, they won't sell anyways. If you have trouble editing by yourself, get some people on board who know what they're doing—stylists, for example.

Line language

When designing, make sure that the lines in the design tell the same visual story in all garments. For example, if you use a lot of angular shapes and sharp seams/lines, but have one piece that has all rounded shapes, that piece is going to feel off; it's not going to be cohesive.

Red thread

Think about having a red thread throughout the whole collection or the few styles. And don't limit this thinking only to the designing—think also about styling and merchandising. How is the collection going to be merchandised in the stores and how do you want the pieces to be styled in the lookbook?

Generally, the design part represents about 10 percent of the workload in an apparel business. Make sure you really, really enjoy it and that you have fun doing it.

Paper and pen are ALWAYS a good start in the design phase. Once you've got a clear sketch drawn out of front, back, and details, move on to the computer and translate that in an Illustrator file, called The Tech Pack. The Tech Pack consists of front, back, and side views of the style; instructions on fabrication, trimmings, stitching and lamination; inside sketches, sketches of details, logo and branding positioning; and color versions for the style. This is then sent to the factory so they can make you a prototype.

Whatever you decide to design, or if someone else is designing for you, it's vital that you find your voice and that *the garments speak you, your brand and your vision.*

Own the design

Stay on top of the design process. Learn to make sketches out of your ideas. If you don't know how to, practice until you can. Your product is your business, and if you leave it all to someone else, you'll be lost without that help. Not having design in-house puts you in a fragile, exposed position.

Do epic stuff that's true to your values.

If you want to be original, be ready to be copied.

–Coco Chanel

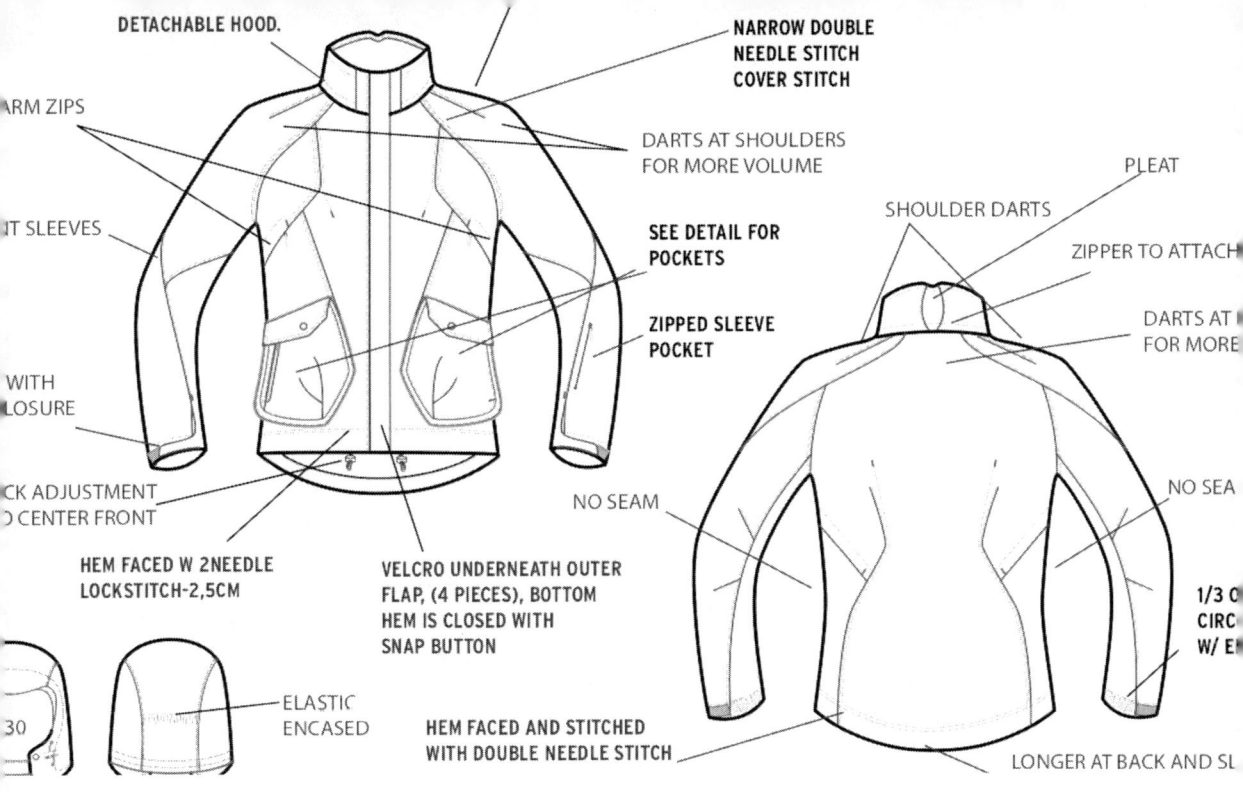

DETACHABLE HOOD.

NARROW DOUBLE
NEEDLE STITCH
COVER STITCH

ARM ZIPS

DARTS AT SHOULDERS
FOR MORE VOLUME

PLEAT

SHOULDER DARTS

ZIPPER TO ATTACH

IT SLEEVES

SEE DETAIL FOR
POCKETS

DARTS AT
FOR MORE

ZIPPED SLEEVE
POCKET

WITH
LOSURE

CK ADJUSTMENT
CENTER FRONT

NO SEAM

NO SEA

HEM FACED W 2NEEDLE
LOCKSTITCH-2,5CM

VELCRO UNDERNEATH OUTER
FLAP, (4 PIECES), BOTTOM
HEM IS CLOSED WITH
SNAP BUTTON

1/3 C
CIRC
W/ E

ELASTIC
ENCASED

30

HEM FACED AND STITCHED
WITH DOUBLE NEEDLE STITCH

LONGER AT BACK AND SL

10.4 What Is A Tech Pack, Why Do You Need It, And Why Is It Important?

The tech pack

A builder would never build a house without a blueprint—and it's exactly the same for a garment. Manufacturers need to know what you have in mind, what the garment looks like front and back including details, what materials you have in mind, what trims you want on your garment, and what type of fit it should have.

The tech pack is the most important document in your product-development process, and needed in all areas of bringing your brand to market. The patterns are made based on the tech pack, the sourcing is done depending on what materials and trims you want, and the price calculation is based on the garment sketches. The sketches can later be used in your line sheet and workbook.

A tech pack is required for all styles in your collection.

When the manufacturers have your tech pack, they can product-develop without having to talk to you and check details with you every time they're wondering about something. All the information will be there, visible, for them to do their job. Often, people on the factory floor don't speak English, so sketches need to be correct and very clear. Think about a tech pack like this: From the moment you hand over the tech pack, it should be clear enough that you don't have to explain or instruct anything further. All the information needed for that specific garment should be clear and visible in the tech pack. Efficiency and productivity will be higher and you'll have fewer misinterpretations along the way.

The more details you put in the tech pack, the better information you give the manufacturer. This limits the amount of errors in your products and in the end will save you money and time.

How to make a great tech pack

Tech packs are for the most part made using Adobe Illustrator. The document is later saved in a smaller PDF size that can't be edited, and sent to the pattern-makers and factories. It's also possible to buy templates to use as a base, so you don't have to start from scratch every time you design a new garment.

If you want to be in full control of your product, learn the program and make your own sketches and tech packs. This will give you the flexibility to make exactly what you intended, without having to depend on anyone else. As with everything, there are good and bad tech packs. The better yours are, the more accurate protos you'll get.

The document should consist of several pages. The number of pages depends on the complexity of your garment. A basic T-shirt tech pack may only have four pages, while a complicated jacket could have twelve or more.

Preferably the tech pack in Illustrator should be divided into different layers: one for the main information, one for sketches, one for colors, and one for text. This will make your life easier when copying and pasting info on different pages.

Tech-pack information

Information needed on ALL pages in the tech pack:
- Company name and logo
- Style number and style name
- Season
- Date
- Page content: e.g., front and back instructions, trims and accessories instruction, hood detail, etc.

First page: Color options
- Color options. The style in X amount of colorways. Write down the color name and code below each colorway. You can also indicate—e.g., using a colored dot—whether the style is new, updated, or carry-over. Mark the same way if a special colorway is new.

Second page: Overview instructions
- A black-and-white front and back sketch. No colors, no shading, no frills—keep it neat and clean and very visible and detailed. All stitching, down to the smallest bar tack, should be included in the sketch. No text on this page—only the front and back sketch. A large sketch size is advisable. Some factories are huge and will print out the sketches on poor-quality printers, making copies of copies to have in different departments. You want to make their jobs easier by making the sketches clear and visible.

Third page: Fabric instructions
- Front and back sketch, with different color shades in the areas of different materials. Here it should be clear where all the different materials go on the garment.

- At the side or bottom of the page, have small squares showing the different shades of color and a text describing the intended materials.

- On the sketch, show what fabric goes where, with the help of arrows and text. Show the manufacturer both in written form and in color/ texture where the different materials should be placed.

- Keep the text away from lines in the sketches. It should be CLEAR and visible.

Fourth page: Instructions for trims and accessories
- Front and back sketch, black-and-white.
- Arrows and text on what trimmings should go where on the garment.

Fifth page: Stitching and lamination instructions
- Front and back sketch, black and white.
- Arrows and text on what type of seam/stitch should go where on the garment.
- For laminated areas you can indicate—e.g., with a different color—on the seam you want taped, or mark an area with a pattern.

- Do detailed sketches of special seam constructions if you want a specific construction on your product. You can also include pictures if you don't know exactly what the construction is.

Sixth page: Detail instructions/hood instructions/inside instructions
- Depending on what details you want to communicate, this is the page to put it on. For an inside instruction, draw the inside of the garment and write where all the details should go and what finishings you want. Here as well, you can have pictures if you're not sure exactly what you want.

- For hood details, it's a good thing to do two different pages: one for the outside of the hood and one for the inside. Write down where everything should be and do detailed sketches for the desired construction.

- If you want a specific pocket construction, draw it out or include a picture.

Separate pages: Body silhouette
- If the factory is making the patterns, you can have a body silhouette "wearing" the intended garment. This way you show the pattern-maker the desired fit.

Separate pages: Measurements instructions
- If you wish to have the measurements in the same document, you can have a separate page for this. Use arrows and text to instruct what measurements go where on the garment.

Last page: Logo instructions
- The black-and-white front or back sketch and your labels, print or branding that you want to be visible, or on the inside of the garment. Write distance from seams to indicate where the branding/logo should be placed on your garment.

A reminder: keep everything neat, clear and VISIBLE. The arrows should point to the exact thing you want highlighted and not below, above, or to the sides.

Keep proportions accurate when designing products. Visually, you want a sleeve to end where a sleeve "usually" ends on a normal garment—e.g., on a pair of pants, the waist width should be proportionally wide to the length of the legs. If you don't really know what the proportions are, take a similar garment to your intended design and place it flat on the floor. Make the proportions similar.

When the tech pack is done, make sure you triple-check it. Get rid of typos and mistakes.

Mistakes in the tech pack end up as production mistakes...

The aim is to arrive at your intended garment as soon as possible, with as few prototypes as possible. The "normal" procedure is to have two prototypes and one salesman sample before the bulk production. After showing the salesman samples to buyers, you'll probably want to see a size-set and preproduction sample to make sure everything is as intended. This is not mandatory, but if you want to have full control and make sure you get what you've ordered, it's a wise move.

When in doubt as to how much info is needed, too much is better than too little. Your tech packs and the information within will be a big part of your brand/branding. If they contain sloppy, ugly sketches, text errors and poor information, this will have a negative effect on your business.

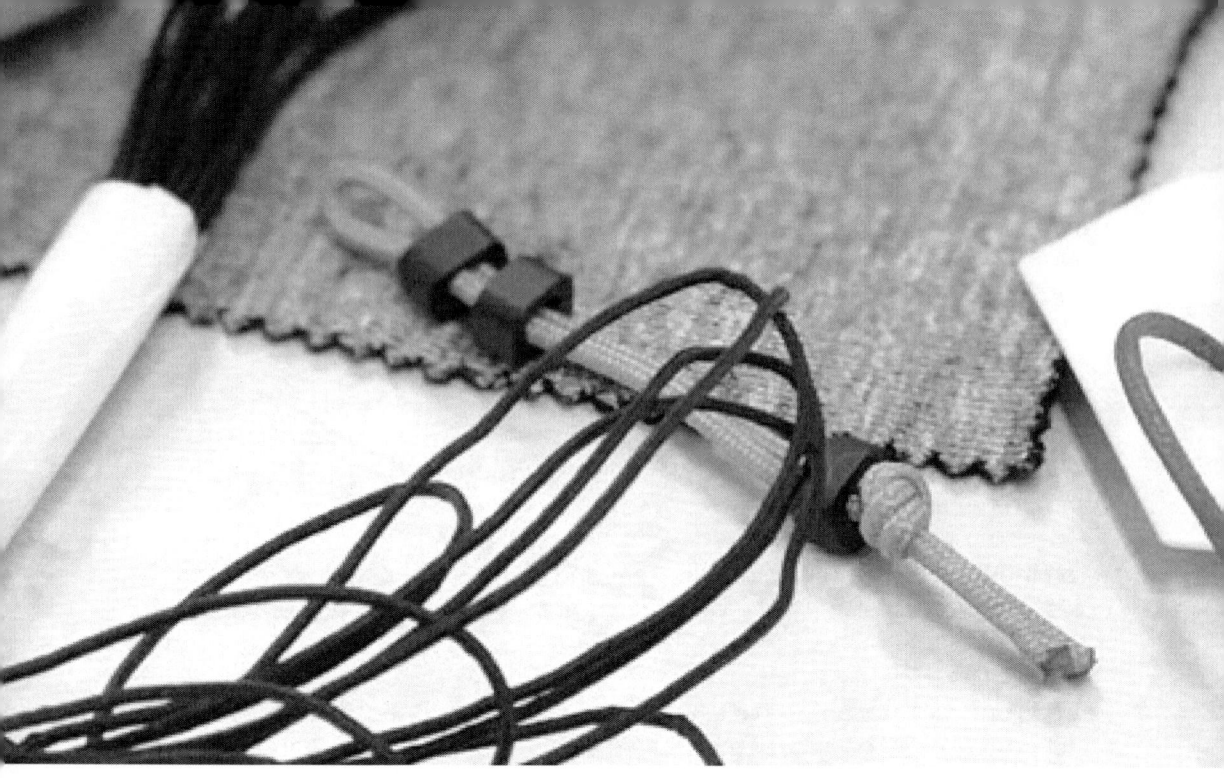

10.5 Bill of Materials and Measurement List

The BOM

A bill of materials, or BOM, is a comprehensive list of the components required to make your product, as well as instructions for gathering and using the necessary materials. You use a BOM for communication between you and your manufacturing partners.

The BOM functions as the recipe and shopping list for creating your final product. It explains what, how, and where to buy required materials, and includes instructions for how to assemble the product from the various components ordered.

All manufactured products start with the creation of a bill of materials (BOM).

The results from work you've put into business activities such as sourcing will end up in the BOM, so it's important that it's well organized, correct, and up-to-date.
When you outsource manufacturing activities, it's especially important to create an accurate and revision-controlled BOM. Anytime the BOM

is handed off to a contract manufacturer, it should be correct and complete—if it's not, expect production delays.

This list is later sent together with the tech pack (the garment specification) and the measurement list to the factory. Only when the factory receives all this information can they start making the first prototype and you can get a rough first price quotation. The factory will be able to give you an accurate price quotation after making the first prototype.

Example of a BOM: template downloadable in the Member Zone.

> Make sure you have a complete BOM for every garment.

Reasons for having a BOM

You get a custom-made shopping list
The BOM mentions each raw material needed, and in which quantity, making procurement of materials much simpler. These can also be scaled up and down according to budgets.

Never run out of materials again
With a clear list of materials, quantities, and inventories, you'll be able to manage what you need to ensure you never run out of materials again.

Better planning
With a comprehensive list of what's needed to complete a project, planners have all the data they need to map out how long the project will take and how many people need to be involved.

Better costing
With better planning comes more accuracy in terms of timeframes. This allows you to cost up jobs and orders more effectively, which means more profit.

All departments work as one
The very process of creating a BOM ensures all departments are working as one. When creating an accurate BOM, you need input from design, procurement, manufacture, and sales to ensure the document is 100 percent accurate.

Measurement list

The measurement list, also called a spec sheet, is a document containing measurements for specific measuring points on a garment. This list is followed closely by the pattern-makers, who use the information listed in the spec sheet to make the patterns for the intended product.

The measurement list should include three pages indicating:
1. Garment measurements for one size. Usually it's the company's fit size, M or S for women's, and M or L for men's.

2. Size grading—measurements for all the intended sizes in that particular style; e.g., S to XXL.

3. "How To Measure" illustration. This will show how you measure and how the factory should measure to get the desired measurements. If you measure differently, you'll get different numbers and a different fit.

Correct and updated

All of the above documents must be accurate before they're sent to the factory.

It's important to date each document—this way, every time you change and update them, you'll be able to keep track of developments and changes.

After each prototype review, the tech pack, BOM, and measurement list should be updated with the changes made on the prototype, if there are any. Again, add the new date every time you modify the document.

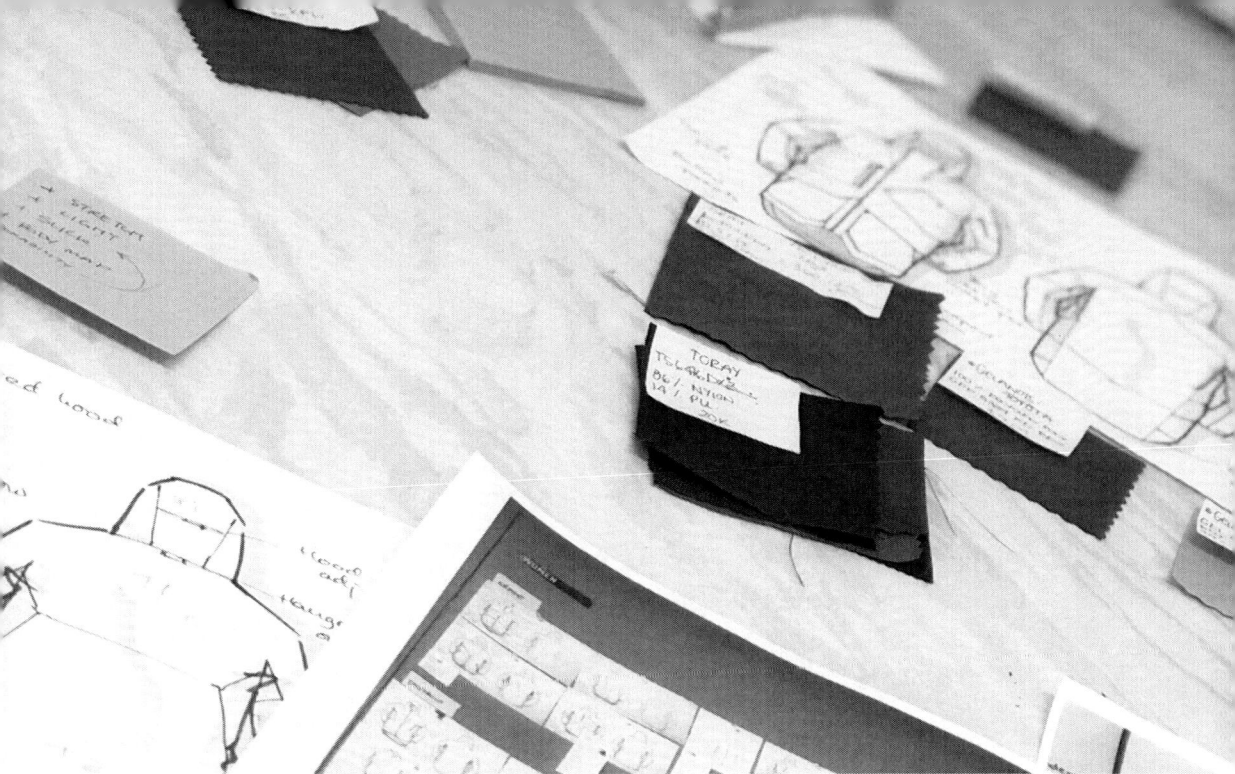

10.6 How To Brief A Designer

If you're not the one designing your collection, you need to find someone who's going to translate your thoughts and ideas into actual products. It's crucial that you provide this person with a clear and detailed explanation so they can take that idea and turn it into a tangible concept, collection, and products. The best way is to give your designer a brief. First, one for the entire project if you need that, or a brief for each and every single product. Your designer will know exactly what to design, what type of materials to source for, and at what price point the product will land. The idea is to have as few unanswered questions as possible when the designer starts.

The brief

1. INTRO AND VALUES
Describe your brand/business in a couple of sentences plus its values.

2. BRAND POSITIONING
Describe your market positioning.

3. VIBE AND FEELINGS

Describe the vibe and feelings your brand evokes.

4. LOOK AND FEEL
Describe the aesthetic you want to have.

5. COMPETITION AND UNIQUENESS
Describe your main competitors and what makes you unique.

6. RANGE/PRODUCT PRICING
Describe the price structure and target product price.

7. CONCEPT/PRODUCT DESCRIPTION
Describe the concept and the products you want to have.

8. PROJECT DELIVERABLES
Describe the project. List the deliverables for the end of the project.

9. BUDGET
Indicate the amount of money you've allocated for the project.

10. TIMELINE
State the milestones and the final deadline for the entire project.

Download the How To Brief A Designer Template, the Project Design Brief Template, and the Product Design Brief Template in the member zone.

10.7 Design Tasks

1. Design all styles in the collection.

2. Decide the materials (fabrics and accessories).

3. Make sure there's a red thread in the collection. Make it cohesive.

4. Determine the type of fit you want for each style.

5. Produce tech packs, BOMs, and measurement lists for all styles.

6. Order branding package.

11.
Sourcing

11.1 Sourcing—The Materials

The materials

Almost at the same time as conceptualizing the collection comes the need to think about materials. They need to tell the same story as the concept and the design—they go hand in hand.

It may be the material that actually triggered your inspiration; sometimes you see some really cool material that you just need to do something with, so the material is the starter of the whole design process. The same goes for trimmings.

It definitely helps if you know something about materials—that way you know what to source for and what the different materials can do for your design. If you don't, get someone on board who knows fabrics and trims because this is such a major part of the design/concept. It's crucial to know what you need for your design and what the fabrics can do. The materials have a huge effect on the garment and what it's intended to do. Just to give you a quick example, heavier woven fabrics can be more durable, whereas stretchy fabrics are usually more comfortable in tighter silhouettes. So it's pretty vital to know exactly what type of fabric you need when designing your styles.

The easiest way to source your fabrics is to go to fabric fairs. Suppliers can also help you out sometimes if you have an idea, and can guide you to the best fabric choice. But be careful—if you go this route, your selection will be quite narrow when you come to discussing minimum quantities, prices, and lead times.

Generally it goes like this: European suppliers have lower minimum quantities and somewhat higher prices. Asian suppliers have better prices and higher minimum quantities. If you're a European brand, it might be easier to go for the European suppliers so you don't have to think about taxes, tolls, and lengthy shipment times. If your production will be in Asia, it's smarter to pick materials from Asia as well. That way you don't have to ship the thing all over the planet.

There are a few things you can do when sourcing materials, if you have trouble reaching MOQs:
* Buy sample yardage—but you'll have to pay a surcharge, so the price goes up and the quantities down.

* Buy stock fabrics. Ask what the supplier has in stock; the minimums are usually low for stock materials.

* Ask for leftover materials. Sometimes fabric suppliers get canceled orders and end up with materials no one will buy. If they've overproduced a material, it ends up as dead stock, and you can get it for a better price. Keep in mind: it doesn't mean it's crappy quality. Just ask for leftover stuff.

* You can also get materials from factories. Some factories have leftover fabrics from previous manufacturing.

* Buy uncolored material and garment dye (when you dye the whole finished garment instead of only the material and then sew it together) instead of buying already died fabric. Check that the composition of the material is okay for garment dying.

Your pricing calculations and price range will steer your search more than anything else. Look for fabrics you can afford—otherwise your garments will be way more expensive than intended.

Before you place a bulk fabric order, make sure you have the prices, delivery, and payment terms confirmed, so you don't get any nasty surprises later on. Remember to include the shipping costs in your price calculations.

Your materials are all sorted. Now you need a factory that can actually *make* what you've designed.

11.2 Material Sourcing—Fabrics And Trims

How to source fabrics and trims

Before going to fairs or contacting suppliers and manufacturers, it's advisable to have your business already registered and planned. Having your logo and brand name in place would be a plus, too.

The fairs are business fairs, and your company needs to be registered in order for you to attend. Let's say you haven't come that far in your brand development and have no registered company or logo. Don't worry—you can register your intended company name, provided you have a business card. Print a few at home or at your local supplier. Whatever you do, make sure you're armed with business cards—you will be exchanging them at every interaction!

Here are three sourcing options with pros and cons, dos and don'ts:

1. At fabric/trim fairs

Before you go to a fair, it's good to have a clear image in your mind of what you like and want. A good tip is to go downtown and look at competitor garments to give you an idea. Have a look on the insides of garments: usually on the left inside you'll find a care label that notes exactly what the material is. Also take a look inside your own wardrobe for materials you like. Take a close look at the care labels and instructions. The preparation phase before going to a fair is very important. Why are you going in the first place? What materials and trims exactly are you looking for? How many, in what weights, and for what specific garments? You should prepare a comprehensive, structured list of every single material/trim needed. Put together a little folder of swatches/trims you've found, either from cutting competitor's garments or from other supplier swatches. Bring them with you and show the reps. This will help guide them in the direction you're looking for. If they don't have what you want, they might suggest other vendors, or have better suggestions for your intended materials.

What information do you need to give the reps so they can help you find what you're looking for?

- Fabric: What type of fabric is it? A woven, a knit, a waterproof material with membrane?

- Fiber and composition: Should it be a durable polyamide, 20 percent cotton/80 percent polyester, 100 percent merino wool?

- Weight: 140gr/m2 for a base layer? A little heavier, at 350gr/m2, if you're looking for an outerwear material, for example.

- Color: Have some color swatches in hand in case you're in a time constraint and need to find stock materials or see a color card.

Before arriving at the fair, give yourself time slots for each material, to make sure you stay focused, on track, and that you don't lose time. The risk might be that you leave the fair having missed some of your material.

It's best not to ask for minimum quantity or price at the first meeting. It's just not the done thing. You can get that information later when you find the fabrics you like.

If you find something you like on the spot, by all means ask the sales rep if they have sample meters/yardage in stock and order a couple of meters/yards to sew up a prototype and test the material. You usually have to pay for the sample meters and postage. In the beginning it's really hard to know what to look for, so the best way to find what you like is to go through many swatches. Eventually you'll get a more honed eye and you'll get inclined towards certain materials. Trust your gut and let your hands and eyes do the job for you. Is the material soft, or hard and noisy? Start to take notice of how materials behave and what makes you go, "Ah!" Put those to the side and order swatches. It's always better to have too many swatches and to pick and choose in the studio, than to have too few and no plan B in case things go south.

If you happen to hear the term "MOQ," that's a Minimum Order Quantity: the minimum amount of meters/yards they require you to buy per fabric.

Before you leave the fair, try to make sure you have a plan A, B, and C for every material you're looking for. At least you'll have a couple of options in case one of them doesn't work out.

As you start to receive swatches, mark them with their arrival date. After a while you'll have many swatches to keep track of. You can also sort them by material type or by supplier—whatever works for you. And, no, a big pile in the corner of your studio doesn't count as sorting! If you find what you like, ask the supplier to send you testing results so you can see how the material performs: durability, colorfastness, pilling, etc. Since you have the swatch, throw it into the washing machine and see how it performs—the results will help you in the selection process.

2. From your studio

Perhaps you can't or don't want to attend fairs to source your fabrics and trims. How can you get the materials you need? Contact suppliers by phone and email, explaining what you want in a detailed manner. They'll send you swatches that correspond to your description.

How do you find the right suppliers? You google. This is a very tricky way of finding materials, however, if you don't know what you're looking for and if you don't already have contacts. First of all, like with planning before going to a fabric fair, you need to know what you're looking for. When you contact a supplier via email, be short, very descriptive and to the point. This will increase your chances of getting the right materials. Once the supplier has your "wish list," they'll find the materials that best match your description and send you the headers. You'll receive the batch and look through them.

Once you've narrowed them down to a couple of options, contact the supplier again and ask for MOQ, lead time and price. With the info received from the supplier, you calculate and pick the material you want. And remember: Prices and MOQs are negotiable. Lead times can be moved a little but only roughly—you should expect it to take the time you're quoted.

3. Through your manufacturer

Most manufacturers can help you source your materials. Here, as above, they'll require a detailed explanation of what you have in mind. Send swatches, pictures, competitors' garments—whatever you need to send to best explain what you're looking for. Depending on how much time you have, letting the manufacturer help you source can be a quick and effective solution. The manufacturer will have the price in mind from the beginning and will restrict your choices. Of course, manufacturers have a limited amount of materials, but as a start it can save you time, money, and a great deal of headache.

General info

So, you've found your intended material—now what? How do you proceed? The next step is for the supplier to dye your material in the exact color you want. Send the supplier a Pantone ref or clip of the color you want. After a couple of weeks, the supplier will send you the lab dips—usually two/three color options per intended color. The best way to review these is both in daylight and indoors to see which options best match the Pantone ref. Then, either okay the best option or, if none are good enough, comment: "Too red—please add more yellow/too dark—please make slightly lighter," etc., until you get exactly the color you want.

If you're under time pressure, there are some ways you can save time. When discussing with suppliers, you can ask them which materials and colors are always in stock. This means you can order your bigger quantities directly without waiting for the supplier to do the lab dips, and then produce the big order.

For parts of the material offer, suppliers usually have a color card. These are the colors most used for that specific material. Again, if you're under time constraints, pick a color from the color card.

Logistically it's a good idea to plan your manufacturing and source materials from the same continent. If your factory is in Europe and the fabrics are coming from somewhere in Asia, you'll have to pay for the fabric shipping, have longer lead times, potential extra costs, and the bureaucracy headache of toll paperwork. Be smart from the beginning and plan for a smoother process.

Tell suppliers and manufacturers what you need. The more specific the information you provide, the quicker you'll get what you need.

11.3 Finding A Factory

Finding the right manufacturer who meets all your criteria in terms of quality, ethics, and communication is a crucial part of running a successful apparel business. Can they make the products you've designed, on time, at the right price, and in the right way?

Involving a factory early on in the process is advantageous. It's not until your specific factory has made a product sample that you can make a correct price calculation. This price calculation is essential for your entire business, to ensure you ultimately make a profit and can thus continue your venture. Secondly, you need the factory to make a correct, well-made salesman sample. You need this to proceed with your marketing and sales activities such as photo shoots and showing to potential buyers.

Determine your needs

Before you even start looking for a manufacturer, you need to determine your needs.

1. Start off by defining your collection. Different styles may require different manufacturers. You need to know what type of garment you're

making, the materials you're using, and whether any specific techniques are required to make your garments.

2. Determine your price point. When you prepared your business plan, you made a decision about the price level for your collection. You can now go back to that and determine whether you'll get the margin you want when manufacturing at that exact factory.

3. Decide how many garments per style you want and can afford to make, because manufacturers have minimum quantities (MOQ). The MOQ is for one style and is the minimum quantity a factory will produce in one batch.

EXAMPLE

Factory MOQ/style is 1000 pieces.
You want to make 10 styles at that factory.
This means you have to produce 10,000 garments, to meet their MOQ.

Finding the factories

Right—you know what styles you want to make, how many, and so on. But how do you go about finding a factory?

1. **One of the best ways is through recommendations.**
As with all recommendations, you'll get a reference from someone you trust that the factory is okay. Ask around if you have contacts in the industry. Let your fabric suppliers recommend factories for your products.

2. **Go to an industry trade show.**
This is a great way to meet many suppliers in one place. You can view reference products and get quick answers as to whether they fit your criteria. Even if you don't attend the trade show, it's a good idea to check out their website. Look up the exhibitor and brand directories.

From there you can google or pick up the phone and talk to them. Don't rely solely on a website for information. Here are a few trade shows we recommend for you:

- Performance Days: Functional Fabric Fair
- ISPO: The World's Largest Exhibition For The Sports Industry
- OutDoor: Outdoor Sports Summer Fair
- Première Vision: Fabric and Manufacturing Fair
- Texworld Paris: Fabric and Trim Fair
- Texworld USA: Fabric and Trim Fair
- Hightex: Int'l Technical Textiles and Nonwoven Trade Fair
- Istanbul Yarn: Int'l Yarn Fair
- Perú Moda: Int'l Tradeshow of Textiles, Apparel, Footwear and Accessories
- International Apparel and Textile Fair: Int'l Apparel and Textile Fair
- London Expo: Int'l Trade Fair for Garments, Textiles and Accessories
- Apparel and Textile Sourcing Miami: Apparel and Textile Trade Show
- Techtextil North America: Int'l Trade Fair for Technical Textiles and Nonwovens
- F&A Show: Fabrics and Accessories Trade Show
- Yarnex India: Int'l Yarn Exhibition
- Milano Unica: Int'l Textile Fair
- Source Africa: The African Apparel, Textile and Footwear Trade Event
- Pitti Immagine Filati: Exhibition on Yarns, Fiber and Knitted Fabrics
- SpinExpo: Trade Fair for Yarns and Fibers
- IntertexMilano: Int'l Textile Exhibition
- Ideabiella: Fabrics for Men's Wear Exhibition

3. Competitors' websites, trade magazines, and online searching are further options—though this can be time-consuming and there's no guarantee you'll find what you need. No matter how you find the manufacturer, you need to talk to them about your project and see what they're capable of and willing to do. Ask them for references and speak directly with the referring brands to hear what it's like working with that specific manufacturer.

4. Visit your library.
Okay, it's a bit old-school, but Libraries can be a valuable source for finding a manufacturer. They can give you access to great directories that otherwise would be too expensive for you.

Location

Your manufacturing location depends on your strategy. Do you want the garments made locally for sustainability and patriotic reasons? Do you want to make them in a low-cost country to reach a certain price point? Whatever you decide, consider that you need to visit the factory, and look at transportation costs, work culture, and potential tolls and administration. Here we list the advantages and disadvantages of producing locally vs overseas.

Local clothing manufacturing

Advantages
- Easier, cheaper, and less time-consuming to visit
- Labor standards
- Easier communication
- Similar time zones
- Market it as locally made goods
- Faster and cheaper shipping
- No or lower import duties or tariffs

Disadvantages
- Higher manufacturing costs
- Smaller choice of potential factories

Overseas manufacturing

Advantages
- Lower manufacturing costs
- Greater number of manufacturers to choose from

Disadvantages
- Labor standards
- Language and communication barrier

- Time zone difference
- Cultural differences in negotiating and schedules
- More costly and time-consuming to visit
- Lengthier and more expensive shipping
- Duties, tariffs, and administration

Reaching out

Once you have a list of factories, it's time to start interviewing them. Read the next chapter, Twelve Questions To Ask A Clothing Manufacturer, for pointers on what to discuss when emailing, speaking over the phone or meeting in person.

What matters most are the relationships you build with them. From the outset, your mentality should be that you're in this together, and that both parties should be equally happy with the collaboration. Keep this in mind if it comes down to negotiating prices later on in the process.

It's wise to meet in person and visit the facilities before starting a collaboration. You'll see how they operate, get a sense of how they do business, and have time to sit down and plan together for the future. If the factory knows your story, your concept, and where you want to take your brand, they'll be more emotionally involved and will perhaps go that extra mile for your products to turn out amazingly.

Factory checklist

Use this checklist when discussing with factories, to see if you're a good match:

- Social certifications
- Factory's overall capacity for new customers
- Minimum orders by fabric, color and style
- Location—country and distance to port
- How long has the company been in business?
- Past and present customers with similar products
- In-house facilities, and where is their outsourcing done?
- Printing, embroidery, washing, dying, etc. Need to make sure they're working with compliant subcontractors
- Average turnaround time for specific styles after all approvals
- Inventory of their equipment and maintenance schedules

- In-house auditors, auditing procedures and records of audits
- Technical staff available for assistance
- Communication: Do they write or speak English? Do they have a complete understanding of your questions or comments? If they don't understand you when you're talking with them at a sourcing trade show, how are you going to communicate with them?
- Work in Progress (WIP) reports—discuss what they will provide
- Response time?
- Sample quality—any issues due to poor communication skills?

Final word of caution

Please make time to check credentials and get references so you have reliable feedback on the people, consultants, or companies you're sourcing from!

Almost all quality improvement comes via simplification of design, manufacturing, layout, processes, and procedures.

–Tom Peters

11.4 Twelve Questions To Ask The Clothing Manufacturer

What to ask when contacting a manufacturer for the first time

Before you start selling your collection, you need to find a manufacturer. The first reason for this is you need ensure your quality standards are met and that the sales samples will look like the products you'll sell. Secondly, you need the cost estimations from your intended manufacturer. Costs vary from factory to factory, and you need to be on top of your price calculations and business model before kicking off.

Finding a good manufacturer is a vital aspect and challenge for an apparel company. As mentioned, there are many ways to find factories: trade shows, online, contacts, branch organizations, etc. But it can be really tough finding a factory that suits your needs in terms of communication, quality, and delivery. One time, we started working with what we thought was a great factory that promised us the moon. Six months later it turned out that they weren't at all capable of making the product we asked for. It was a complete waste of time. Recommendations are of course extremely valuable, and if you've already found a good manufacturer, make sure to nurture that relationship. Don't push them and treat them like crap thinking that you easily can replace them with another factory. You can't. In order to improve your chances of a successful collaboration with a factory, there's a range of questions you can ask. Once you've got your shortlist of manufacturers, it's time to pick up the phone and start calling. Pose these questions to see if there could be a fit between your brand and their manufacturing.

Entrepreneurship is all about the relationships you build.

---

1. Are they taking on new customers?

Factories are sometimes overbooked and put a freeze on taking new customers. If so, don't waste your time here. Hang up and call the next factory on your list.

2. Can they make your products?

Ask them what kind of products they make. If you have a specific need, check that they can meet it. Let's say you're making a jacket with taped seams—then you need to confirm that they have a seam-sealing machine to do that. Let them know the products you want to produce.

3. What brands are they working for?

This can give you an indication of the quality level if you're familiar with the reference brands. Also, ask for references you can contact about their collaboration.

4. Are they working with third-party suppliers?

Sometimes manufacturers outsource parts of their production to third-party suppliers. If they do, check what parts they can't do by themselves. Remember that if they work with a third-party supplier, it can be more difficult to control that part of the process. It's one more link in the chain that can lead to delays and misunderstandings.

5. Can they provide price estimates?

Ask for a quotation. Remember, for an accurate price estimate you need them to make a prototype. It's only then they'll know what your product will cost. Do they work with CMT, FOB, or some other way?

6. What services can they provide?

Can they do patterns, grading, prototypes, fabric sourcing, maybe even design? It can be a quick and easy solution to hand over more than the actual production work to the factory. But at the same time it'll give you less control. It can be like the proverbial black box: you put something in, don't know what happens inside, and then something comes out that's not exactly how you pictured it.

7. What are the minimum quantities?

What's the minimum amount of products they're willing to make? Is this minimum per style, color, or size? It makes a big difference. If they're willing to take on lower quantities, how much is the surcharge?

8. What is their capacity?

Are they scalable? Though your first batch of garments will generally be pretty small, you're going to want to grow down the line. Is the manufacturer ready to help you with that?

9. Do they have terms and conditions you can take a look at?

Here you can see their payment terms, for example. There are quite a few things you want to include in an agreement with a supplier.

10. How much do they charge for samples?

If you're new, factories typically charge two to three times the production price for a prototype.

11. When do they have time?

How quickly can they help you with prototypes and when can they fit in your bulk production?

12. Do they have any certifications?

You have certain standards for your brand when it comes to sustainability and work ethics. Make sure the manufacturer meets those expectations. Are they certified? Can they guarantee a good working environment?

If you can get the answers to all these questions, you'll be able to make your shortlist of manufacturers even shorter. Trust your gut feeling. What are they like to interact with? If they're hard to reach, it's a warning sign that they'll continuously be hard to reach. Don't forget to let them know about your business, brand, and goals. They need to be on board with your values and vision. You'll both be investing time and money in each other's businesses. Hopefully you'll find a good match and you'll be ready to get started.

11.5 Abbreviations

After sourcing and ordering material swatches from suppliers, you'll receive sample headers. The swatch hanger will contain detailed information about the material. The information includes fiber and composition. Usually it only states the abbreviations, and if you don't know your textile abbreviations you'll have a hard time understanding what you've just received.

Here's a list of the most common textile abbreviations:

CA	Acetate
CO	Cotton
CTA	Triacetate
CU	Cupro
CV	Viscose
EA	Elastane
EL	Elastodiene
HF	Hemp
HR	Cattle hair
HS	Horse hair
HZ	Goat hair
JU	Jute

LI   Linen
PA   Polyamide
PAN   Polyacrylic
PE   Polyethylene PES Polyester
PP   Polypropylene RA Ramie
SE   Silk
WA   Angora
WG   Vicugna
WK   Camel
WM   Mohair
WO   Wool
WP   Alpaca
WS   Cashmere WV Virgin Wool

3-Step Formula For Success

1. Surround yourself with the right people.
If you're going to accomplish great things, you need a team of great people.
2. Have a learn-it-all mindset.
3. Be ready to play the long game.

-Jeff Bezos

11.6 Sourcing Tasks

1. Contact factories. Decide upon a match.

2. Contact material suppliers. Ask for samples.

3. Decide on material.

4. Order material for prototypes.

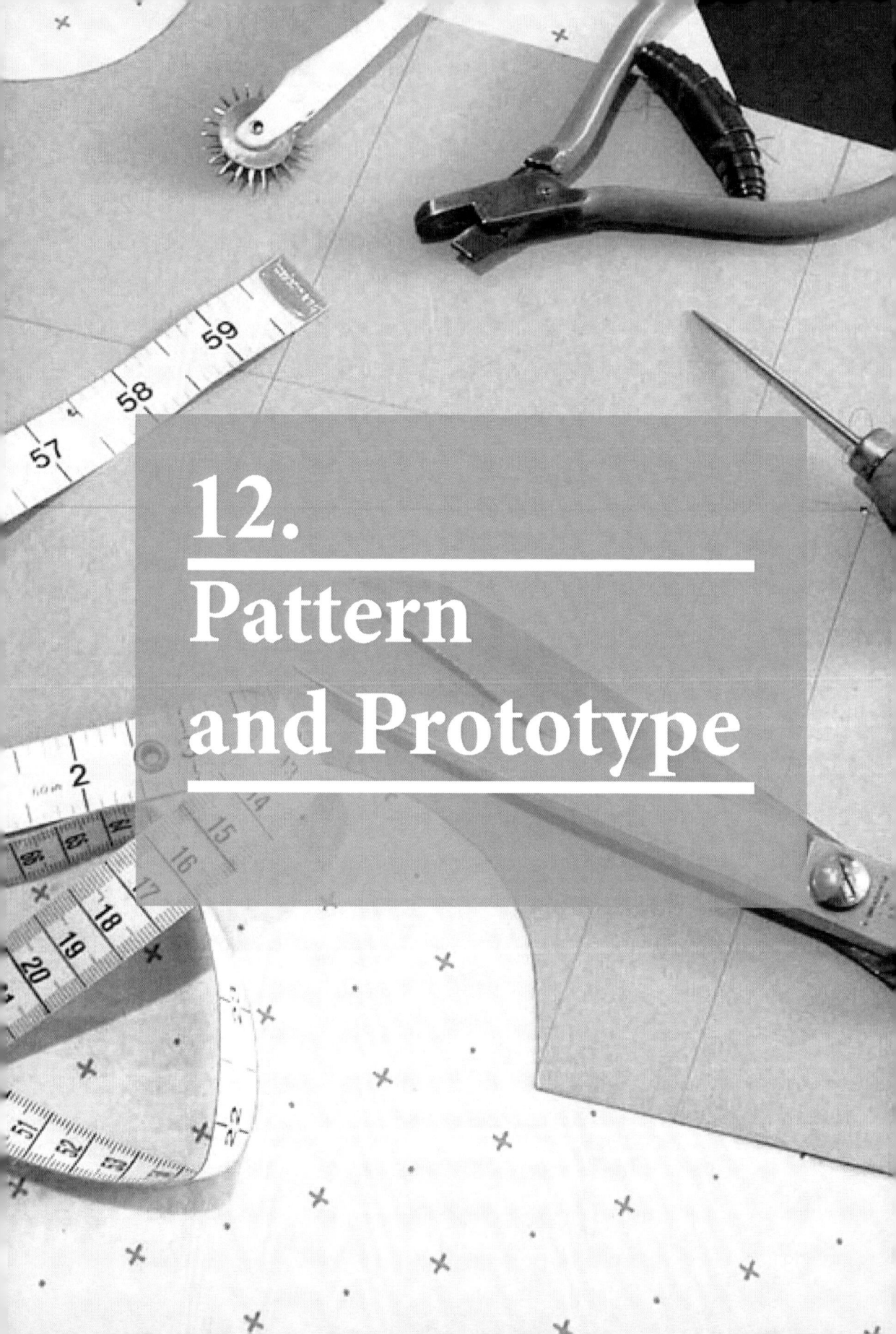

12.
Pattern and Prototype

12.1 Patterning The Collection

Apparel is made to be worn. People only want to wear comfortable garments with a good cut. It doesn't matter how great your design is if the pattern is horribly cut. It's one thing to have design lines drawn on a sheet of paper, but another to actually be able to pattern the style and later on sew the thing together. That's why it's ideal if you or the person designing the styles has some sort of pattern-making knowledge. That way, you'll know how to put a garment together, and you'll know it'll be possible for the factory to produce your styles.

A great method is to start by draping your ideas using muslin material on a draping form, working in 3D from the beginning. Cut pieces of muslin, apply them to the form and put the style together that way. Another method is for the pattern-making to start flat, on large pieces of paper, where the "form" is translated in flat pattern pieces, which are later applied on fabric, cut out and then sewn together into a 3D shape.

To be honest, it's really hard to find awesome pattern-makers. We've only met a handful. This is such a crucial part of your garments and collection. If there's one area that warrants you spending a lot of money in, it's here.

Imagine this: You walk into a store, look around, see something you like; you pick the hanger up, look at the item, touch the fabric; you start to really, *really* like it, and then you go to the fitting room. Your excitement soon dies when you put the garment on—it fits horribly. Will you buy that garment? Hell, no! Or imagine a similar garment—you go to the fitting room, put it on and it fits like a glove. You feel comfortable, you can move really well in it and you feel great. When you walk out of the fitting room, you're already thinking about how many colorways to buy since the garment was so fantastic. Two very similar situations—two very different outcomes.

Designing apparel is the easy part. Understanding product development and working with people is the hard part.

The fit and patterning of a garment is mostly about comfort and freedom of movement. Of course you want, for example, to be able to stretch your arms when you drive and not feel restricted by your jacket.

Pattern-makers work in three different ways:
1. Manually, on paper.
2. Draping in muslin on a draping form.
3. Creating patterns directly on the computer. The two leading pattern-making programs are Lectra and Gerber. Most manufacturers have these programs.

The best way to find a great pattern-maker is through personal referrals. Find out who she/he has worked for before, and on what types of garments. You preferably want someone who specializes in your field. Keep in mind that the best are almost always taken or very busy so be street-smart and figure out a way to have them work on your stuff.

Working with a pattern-maker

If you don't have pattern-making skills you need to find someone to help you out. Either look for an external pattern-maker or work with the manufacturer's in-house one. Going the external route can be advantageous if you want things to move along quickly, be able to have physical meetings easily, and want a full product-development package ready before contacting several manufacturers. Working with the factory's in-house pattern-maker can be advantageous if you want one point of contact and a lower price.

Draw the design. Have a finished, clear vision of what you want. Have full front, back and sometimes side view sketches and some detail sketches. Bring the intended fabric and some fit references (such as samples or pictures where the fit's correct) to the meeting. Go through exactly what the overall idea of the product is, so he/she knows the end consumer, then explain details. Try to cover as much information as possible. The clearer you are, the better she/he will understand the product and details, and the more accurate the first pattern will be.

Make sure you agree what the work should include; e.g., the first raw draft, or a full detailed pattern, or a full detailed pattern with size grading. Everything should be clear—no room for misunderstandings.

A well-fitted garment will have a huge market advantage as there are so many ill-fitting ones out there!

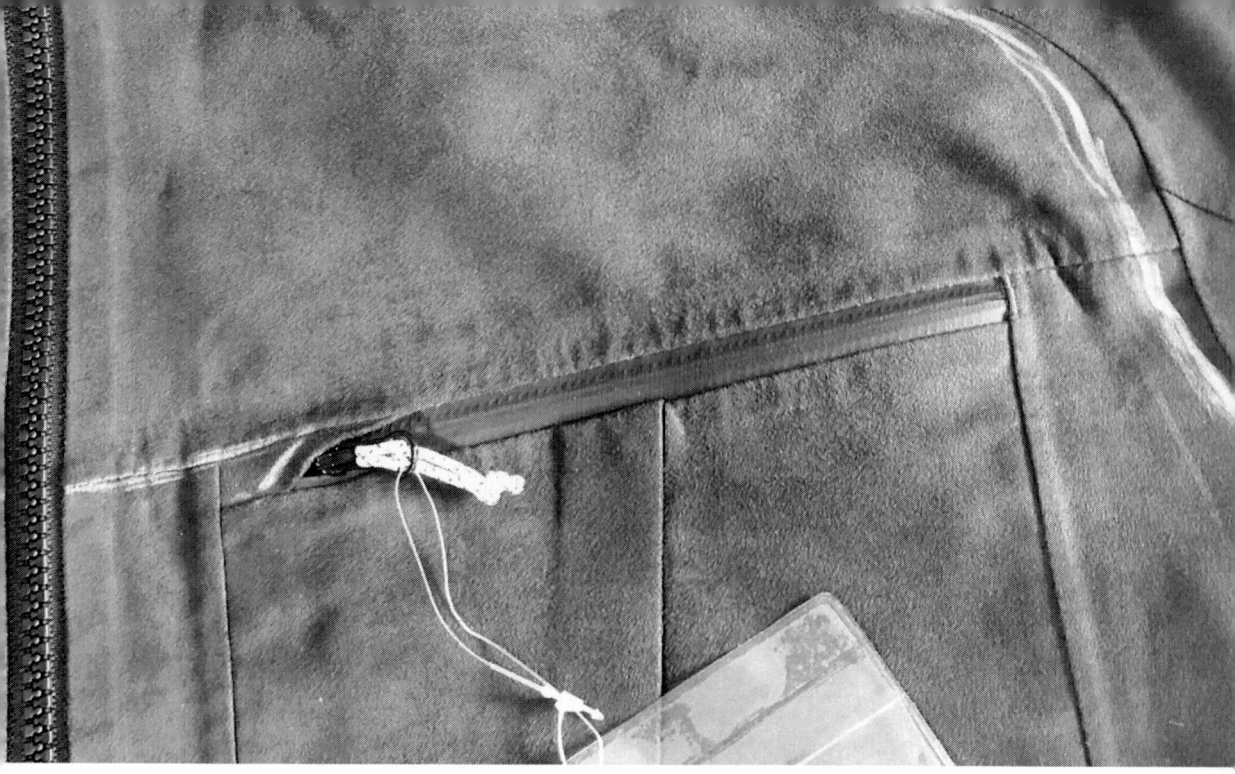

12.2 Prototyping

Proto 1, 2 (and sometimes 3) and salesman sample

Finally it's time to make the first samples. Now you're going to see your ideas materialize into an actual product. Normally you'll have your intended factory make the prototypes. See to it that the factory has your chosen fabrics and trims, then send over your tech packs, BOMs, measurement lists, and patterns. If you're in a rush and your materials haven't reached the manufacturer yet, you can ask them if they have similar materials in stock, to make the first sample. It's preferable, but not essential, that you have the first prototype made in the intended fabric. It'll help a great deal with the silhouette and fit if they make the first proto in a fabric with the same characteristics as you're planning to use.

This is not the time to sit back, wait, and hope for the best. There's a pretty big chance that you've got a clearer picture of your product in your mind than you were able to communicate to the factory. Especially if you haven't worked together before, there's definitely a risk of misinterpretations. The more time you spend together, in person, discussing the styles, the better result you'll see. If you only communicate electronically, the proto will probably miss the mark. If the factory is far away and you can only go once throughout the whole production cycle, the best time in our opinion is to visit the factory with the comments for proto 1. Ideally you should visit before you start a relationship, during the sample-making, and right before the bulk production to make sure everything's on track and exactly how you want it. If there are still question marks, you can fix those before the bulk production.

The first prototype arrives with a load of questions: is the pocket shape tilted enough, is the hood brim wide enough, is the sleeve well articulated, is the length too long, etc.? Remember to step back, take it all in, look at the front, look at the back and look at the sides. Just *look*. What is your first spontaneous feeling?

There will always be comments on proto 1

We've never seen a perfect proto 1. The order for how to comment a proto is usually as follows:

- The pattern-maker measures the proto and records the discrepancies. If the garment material is somewhat stretchy, never try the garment on before measuring it—you might stretch it, which will give you faulty measurements.

- A fit model is brought in and the style is fitted on her/him. Make sure the fit model's body measurements correlate to your ideal customer and size. Comments are written down.

- All adjustments should ideally be made on the proto, for as much information as possible to stay with it—think of it as your bible.

- After the fit session, the designer sits quietly with the proto and examines it in detail, inside and out. All the aspects that haven't been looked at during the fit session need attention now. The more comments the better at this stage.

The pattern-maker makes changes on the patterns. The fit and proto comments are then communicated to the factory. Now the factory has all the information needed to start with proto 2. If proto 1 was really good, and you feel there's no need for a second proto, you can go right ahead and make the salesman sample directly. Of course this should be as accurate and as similar to the bulk production style as possible.

It would be ideal if you or someone else could use or test the first proto. Make sure you get to keep the first proto—sometimes you have to send it back to the factory with all the comments. This depends on your agreement with the factory. Usually the factory keeps a sample.

While testing the sample, you'll notice things you didn't think of during the fit session: pocket bags that are too small, sleeves that are too tight, details that don't actually work when you start using them. The more testing the better, also when it comes to the material.

Communication

The most important thing in the sampling stage is the communication. Let the factory know your overall company idea. Let them know your values. Tell them about who your customer is and where the products are intended to be used. All this extra information helps the factory immensely, especially when it comes to understanding certain decisions you'll make.

Factory visits are an important step in the production process. The people you meet and the connections you make are so much fun. It sure helps a bit if you bring some good chocolate to the meetings—always appreciated!

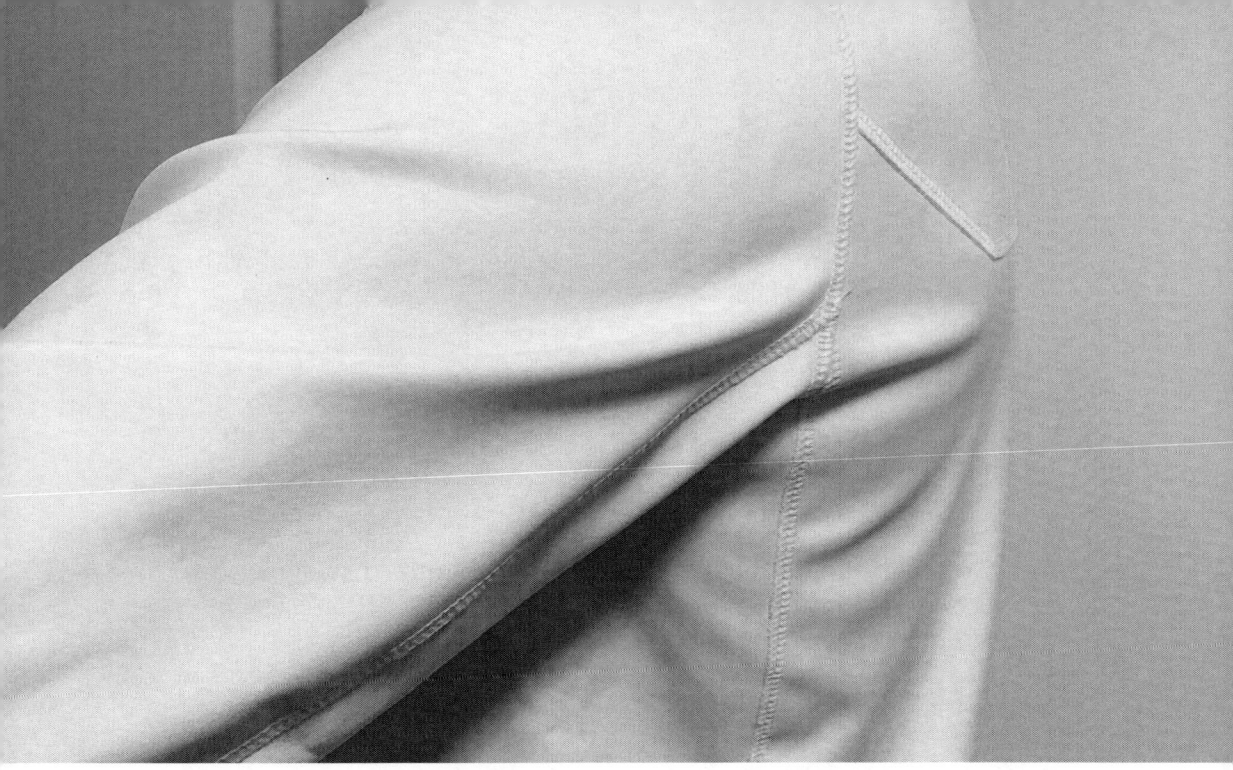

12.3 How To Successfully Fit A Garment

By this stage, there's been an enormous amount of work and thought processes to get all the information to the factory. Now the product needs to look good, feel good, and behave as intended.

When opening the package with your first proto, you'll have mixed emotions flooding your body. You'll feel really excited and at the same time extremely nervous and anxious about the result. We've never seen a PERFECT first proto—just to set your expectations straight. There are always changes on the first proto, both in fit, details and workmanship. No matter how extraordinary your design, what counts ultimately is the fit and comfort of your product. Comfort is key in all apparel, and varies according to type. Full-performance or urban apparel needs functionality in the fit. The wearer should feel extremely comfortable and never hindered in their body movements. The products should look great on, and should function and move with the body in line with use.

Before you start

As soon as the garments arrive at your studio, unpack them, let them lie flat on a table for a little while and then measure them. I know you'll be super eager to try them on but this can wait. It's important to measure the garment before you've tried it on otherwise you'll stretch the material. Measuring the proto is important because you'll see the discrepancies from the original measurement list. Armed with your discrepancy info, you'll know what's right and what's off when fitting the garment.

All garments should be fitted on a live model. They can feel how the garments sit on the body and how they move. If something's uncomfortable you'll know it and have a chance to improve.

Your brand has an ideal customer in mind—which means specific measurements that you'll stay consistent with throughout all the products in your range. Your customers should feel familiar with your measurements. They should know that when they buy different garments from your brand they have the same size and type of fit, no matter the product.

As for the fit model, this person should have the same measurements as your expected customer. Decide on the sample size. Either it's L for men's and M for women's, or M for men's and S for women's.

Be consistent and stick with the same model throughout the whole product-development process. You'll have a better result fitting and commenting on the garments.

Tips

Have a little fit-session box with all your necessary tools and extra garments—e.g., some base layers and long johns in case you have to fit outerwear; an extra mid-layer for fitting a winter jacket. You don't want to be running round the studio looking for stuff. Be prepared and efficient. The model doesn't want to wait unnecessarily.

Supplies needed

• Tech pack printout/style

- Commenting sheet/style
- Measurement list/style
- Fit model with the right measurements (your brand ideal measurements)
- Mirror—full-length
- Pins—straight
- Tape measure
- Chalk, marker pen or narrow marking tape
- Scissors
- Camera

Good lighting in the studio helps you see everything clearly. Start with looking at the measurement-discrepancy list. What's off and what's correct? With this information, you'll know how to look at the garment, what to change and keep.

Then start with the overall feeling of the garment. What catches your eye? Do an overview, then go deeper into detail. Start from the top and move downwards.

The garment usually tells you what needs to be adjusted. There should be no pulling or tugging, no creases, no bagginess or droopiness. If it's a yoga top you're fitting, then let the model do yoga movements and see if the garment moves with the body and not on the body.

Have the model move, run, jump, sit and put her arms over her head. Do the movements that are required for the intended use, be it yoga, skiing, biking, etc. Preferably the model is used to wearing your type of garments and will feel if something is off.

What to look at

Ease: What's the general fit on the body? The model should be able to move comfortably in the garment no matter the material.

Set: This refers to creases and wrinkles in the garment due to poor fit. The garment can be too snug or too lose.

Balance: When looking at the garment three-dimensionally, it should "hang" proportionally on the body. There should not be any pulling to the back or pressing over the chest. The left and right sides should be symmetrical.

Line: The design lines on your garment should follow the body lines. If the intended design has normal side and underarm seams then these should be visually right on the vertical sideline. Check that the lines you've intended in your design are placed exactly where you want them to be on the garment. Draw new lines if you're not satisfied.

Note

If the garment is tightly fitted, bear in mind the seam placements. You want the seams moved away from places where the wearer can get chafing. For tops, the problem areas are the underarm, right on the shoulder seam, right on the elbow, and right over the chest and nipples. For bottoms, the problem areas are right over the knee and the inner leg/crotch seam. If possible also avoid seams over the seat.

If you have tops, mid-layers, jackets, and bottoms in your collection, make sure to fit them in correlation to each other—meaning that if you have a mid-layer that should go over a top and under a jacket, make sure you fit all of them, layer on layer. Can your model move comfortably in all layers?

Let's say you're fitting a trekking jacket. Your customer will probably wear a backpack sometime. Make sure the model tries the garment on with the gear. Does the hip belt sit below the hand-pocket opening? Do the shoulder straps land right on the shoulder seams? Do you have ventilation zips on your jacket—can the model open and close these with the backpack on?

What's the intended fit? Look at the sketch and compare to the garment on the model. If the mid-layer was intended to have a really dropped back hem, does the garment on the model have that?

Remember the details

Garments with pockets can be tested to see if the pockets are big enough, make sure a phone fits in the phone pocket, the ventilation zippers are in reach, and that thigh pockets are big enough to fit stuff in. Make sure to test all the features on the garment—that they're easily maneuvered and in reach. If pockets are too small, that'll be irritating, and if the pockets have the wrong construction, for example, your things will fall out when you sit down... No one wants to lose their phone nowadays!

On garments with Velcro tabs, hood adjustments and cord stoppers, double-check that everything's easy to use, preferably adjustable one-handed.

Several protos need to be fitted: 1st proto, 2nd proto, salesman sample, size sample and preproduction sample. The closer to bulk production you are, the fewer things you'll have to change and comment. The preproduction should be spot on, identical to the bulk.

On the first proto you'll also have to make sure labels, trims and embroideries are exactly where you intended them to be. If not, measure and indicate the changed position in the tech pack and comments notes.

Testing, testing, and more testing

As early as possible in the process it's good to start testing your products, both in terms of physical performance and washing. Put the garment in the wash and see how it behaves. Also, take the sample out for a ride to see what needs to be changed. The sooner your garment's tested in real life, the better. It goes without saying that the test person should be the same size as your fit model, otherwise you'll not get a correct fitting/testing evaluation. When a product is tested in real life, all the small changes will make a huge difference to the final garment and its performance.

Even normal everyday use is better than no use/testing at all. If you yourself are sample size, it's a good idea to test everything yourself because you'll know when something is off. A seam that's chafing, a strap you can't reach, a leg entry that's too wide, something that's just plain ugly... You'll see it all.

Fit sessions are time-consuming and should never be rushed. This is the time to really look at the garments, because if you want to make any changes, the time is NOW. Make clear, highly detailed notes and explain everything like it's meant for a three-year-old.

In the next post we'll guide you through the steps of commenting a garment.

It's all down to you!
The effort you put in, how much you want it
and how much you're prepared to sacrifice for it.
Excuses are lame and will take you nowhere.
Take responsibility and put in the work.

Take 100% responsibility!

12.4 How To Successfully Comment A Garment

In our previous chapter we explained step by step how to go about fitting a garment, what to think about in the process, and the tools needed. In the fit session you looked at the fit, movement and volume of the garment. Now you need to zoom in on all the details, making and workmanship. We're talking about commenting your garment.

It's all about communication

The prototype comments will be your way of improving the garment, making sure every single detail is as you intended it, and that your customer gets the quality garment he/she pays for.

The way to comment a garment is by looking very closely at it and comparing it with the sketch and your instructions. Look carefully at all the details and making. What's incorrect? What do you want to change? Comments are made in text or visually by making adjustments on the proto.

You can draw, cut, pin and tape on the garment—do whatever it takes to visually state the changes you wish to make. This information is later sent to the factory to be implemented in the next sample.

Quality control

Think of the proto commenting as a little quality control. Have they attached the pocket bags as you indicated in your tech pack? Are the seams straight, and are they as narrow as you want them to be? Is the zipper sewn in flat or is it wobbly? Are the eyelets punched in correctly or are they damaged because of too much pressure in the eyelet machine? Are there thread ends all over the garment and is the lamination sloppily done? EVERYTHING should be commented and YES, it's okay to comment, "Please improve the workmanship!" if you feel it's bad.

Not sure what's off with your garment? Buy a competitor garment in the same price range as yours and compare. How are the details done and finished? Are there any loose thread ends hanging all over the garment? Is the zipper puckering? You can also use the competitor sample to show the factory what you're looking for in workmanship. Generally, the workmanship reflects the price of a garment. You usually get what you pay for.

It's entirely up to you

Can't the factory do the comments for you? Nope—this is your most important task in the product-development phase. This is where you take your time and sit with the product, look through every single cm/inch on the garment: the making, the trims, the treatments, stitching—EVERYTHING incorporated in the product. Nothing should be neglected.

The comments and improvements on your protos are entirely your responsibility—not the factory's. Of course the factory wants the best for your products as well; the more you sell, the more you order and buy from them. But YOU have to check everything, double-check again, and communicate in such a way that nothing gets lost or misunderstood.

We can't stress this enough: You can't afford to be lazy about this! Input = Output

---

First season after launching our own brand, we developed a couple of jackets. One of them was pretty complicated. We'd been through the full proto process successfully and had been to the factory for proto comments, handover and review with the team. Everything seemed under control before going into bulk production. Still, when we received the bulk shipment, all the jackets in that style were missing the lower-part adjustment. It wasn't crucial for the style, but it was a default. We sold all the products but had to give the retailer a discount. No jackets were returned because of that default, thankfully, but to this day we still feel the anxiety when we think about it. There's no such thing as over-explaining in the product-development world.

If a picture is worth 1000 words, a prototype is worth 1000 meetings.

–Tom & David Kelley

12.5 Pattern-and-Prototype Tasks

1. Create patterns.

2. Create prototypes.

3. Fit and adjust for each style. Communicate comments to sample-makers.

4. Adjust and create samples until satisfied. Finish with SMS (salesman sample).

5. Create graded patterns.

13.
Pricing

13.1 Garment Price

When you reach this stage in your apparel brand startup project, it's time for a reality check. By now you'll have gathered a lot more information and actual cost figures. You know which garments your collection is based on, the price for fabrics, trims, and production including prototypes. Armed with this information, which you didn't have when first starting out, you can now redo your budget, making it more accurate. Back when you prepared your business plan, you thought about the price level you wanted to position your clothing brand at. Now let's see if it's all realistic.

Your price is the sum of your costs and profit:

$$Cost + Profit = Price$$

Garment cost

Your budget includes a host of expense entries related to overheads, administration, samples, production, sales, and marketing. Ultimately it's the profit from the garment sales that should cover all those costs. Just looking at the pure production cost, you have everything from pattern-making to fabrics and trims. To help you keep track of all costs associated with producing each style, use a costing sheet. On it, note down the costs of all components in the garment. Fill out a costing sheet for each item right from the start—it'll be a vital tool when it comes to running and adapting your business financially, to ensure you stay in full control of production costs.

Profit

You must make a profit—otherwise you've got an expensive hobby rather than a business. The markup depends on your negotiation skills and the type of apparel you're making. But a typical industry example looks like this: the wholesale price is twice the production cost, and the retail price is twice the wholesale price.

Garment price

When talking garment price, you have to differentiate between the following two prices:

Wholesale Price

The price your retailer is buying your garment for. Since it's a business-to-business transaction, it's listed without VAT.

Retail Price

The final price that the end customer buys the product for. This is including VAT. How do you calculate the retail price? Read the next chapter, Pricing Strategies, to look at different options for determining your price. We take a look at three different strategies, their advantages and disadvantages. Again, you can use the costing sheet to calculate the garment retail price based on production costs.

Pricing terms

When you talk to manufacturers, they'll give you the production cost using different terms. Let's take a look at the most common terms, to ensure you understand what the price covers:

CMT: Cut, make, and trim

Cut—the supplier cuts the fabric and then bundle by style, size, and color.

Make—the different sewing steps.

Trim—the finished products are trimmed and packed for shipment.
CMT doesn't include fabrics, accessories or transport.

FOB: Free on board/Freight on board

FOB includes all charges for making the garment and transportation to the shipping port. It doesn't include the shipping, duty, or other costs from that point on. FOB includes making, fabrics, accessories, and in some cases product development.

> It's easier to explain price once
> than to apologize for quality forever.
>
> *-Zig Ziglar*

COGS: Cost of goods sold

Includes all expenses related to producing the garment. This includes construction, materials, grading, and shipping.

Do the numbers add up for you? Does the retail price match the quality of your garment? Do the garments reflect their price? Go back and see if there are any unnecessary costs that you can adjust in order to make ends meet. Check that the price matches the product quality and that you make a profit to reinvest in your project. You're doing something you love so make sure your business is sustainable.

Work with your manufacturer to have full transparency on the pricing. This way you can check where costs lie and you can price-engineer to get the profit/margin you want. Preferably only work with manufacturers that have full transparency in their costing.

> The bitterness of poor quality remains long after
> the sweetness of low price is forgotten.
>
> *–Benjamin Franklin*

13.2 Pricing Strategies

How To Price Your Product

One of the most common questions we receive is: How should I price my products?

The short answer is: It's totally up to you—it's *your* clothing business. However, there are a few common strategies you can use to figure it out. Here we'll go over three different strategies for pricing your apparel.

Pricing strategy 1

This strategy is based on your target cost. The target cost is the price you pay for producing the garment. Then you add your desired margin to that cost to calculate the retail price. The margin should typically cover all your costs, both fixed and variable. If your margin doesn't cover your costs, you'll soon be out of business. As a rule of thumb you should aim for a margin of at least 50 percent.

Target cost

To facilitate your product development, you should figure out your target cost before you start contacting manufacturers and suppliers. When you know your target cost, you know what fabrics and trims you can afford, as well as how much you can spend on the actual manufacturing cost. Also, knowing your target price before contacting suppliers and manufacturers will show them that you're professional, which will benefit you in the long run. And you want to build a long-lasting relationship that's based on transparency and honesty.

Margin

The margin is what keeps you in business. The margin should be sufficient for you and your business partners to be able to both reinvest in your business and live off it. It should also cover all your production costs and overheads.

Advantages of pricing strategy 1
• You don't need to do much market research.
• It guarantees your desired margin.

Disadvantages of strategy 1
• It requires you to know your margin and target price.
• It doesn't take the market and competitors into account.
• It could give you a too-high market price, leading to no sales or an undervalued price.

Price your garment to match its quality and don't forget to make a profit.

Pricing strategy 2

The second pricing strategy is about positioning. One of the first things we recommend you do when starting up your apparel brand is perform a thorough market scan. You read about it in the Market Scan chapter. Get to know what's out there, who your competitors are, who's doing well and who isn't, the prices, and what would make your brand different. Looking at prices of similar products enables you to set a baseline for you to then adjust. You'll position yourself in relation to all the other products on the market.

Advantages of pricing strategy 2
- It's quite simple to find out your competitors' prices.
- There's a big chance these prices are validated with the market.

Disadvantages of pricing strategy 2
- It doesn't guarantee you the margin you want.
- You compare yourself to brands that have a different, possibly unknown, business setup. They may have different production volumes, margins, and strategies.

Price = Cost + Profit
Price—determined by your strategy and market
Cost—controlled by you
Profit—make sure you always make one

Pricing strategy 3

Create a premium label. You're setting your price based on premium factors such as quality, exclusivity, customer service, and brand image. You're setting a fairly high price to reach a niche group of people, trying to achieve a certain level of prestige.

Advantages of pricing strategy 3
- It can give you high margins and greater profitability.
- Your brand can be perceived as higher quality.

Disadvantages of pricing strategy 3
- You limit your customer base.
- It requires a lot of marketing and brand positioning.
- Sets higher demands on your brand in terms of quality and service.

Whether you use one of the strategies above or a completely different one, it's important to go back to your numbers on a regular basis. At the very least, you should go over your numbers when you're preparing your budget, then when you receive your samples, and once again when the bulk production is done.

Calculating price

How do you calculate the price for your products? Let's take a look at two examples. The markup depends on your negotiation skills and the type of apparel you're making. But a typical industry example looks like this:

$$Wholesale\ Price = COGS \cdot 2.2$$

$$Retail\ Price = Wholesale\ Price \cdot 2.2$$

EXAMPLE

You know the cost of producing your garment is €/$100.
You want to determine your wholesale and retail prices.

COGS = €/$100

Wholesale Price = 100 x 2.2 = €/$220

Retail Price = 220 x 2.2 = €/$484

You can use these formulas to figure out your target cost. Using the same markup, your calculation looks like this (2.2 x 2.2 = 4.84):

$$Target\ cost = \frac{Retail\ Price}{4.84}$$

Calculate using the margin

You should always aim for at least 50 percent margin, if you want to be
in business for the long run. Let's take a look at how you can calculate
your prices based on your goal margin.

$$Wholsale\ Price = \frac{COGS}{1 - \frac{Margin}{100}}$$

$$Target\ cost = Wholesale\ Price \cdot (1 - \frac{Margin}{100})$$

Your wholesale price should be €/$40.
You want a 55% margin, and you want to find out how much your garment will cost.

Target cost = 40 x (1-55/100) = €/$18

Product Name		Date	
Product Code			
Product Description		APPAREL ENTREPRENEURSHIP	
Range			

Sketch

13.3 Garment-Costing Example

How much does it cost to make a garment?

Putting salaries, facilities and other overheads aside for the moment, we're now going to look at the product-development costs. Below is a typical example of the costs involved in making a hoodie.

The cost of developing a hoodie

Hoodie-Costing Example

Apparel Design	
Design	€/$35
Pattern-maker	€/$200
Costing sheet	€/$45
Print	€/$200
Labels and hangtags design	€/$35
Subtotal apparel design	**€/$515**
Product Development	
FOB	€/$25
Prototype 1	€/$50 (2x FOB)
Prototype 2	€/$50 (2x FOB)
Prototype 3	€/$50 (2x FOB)
Salesman Sample	€/$50 (2x FOB)
Shipping prototypes	€/$100
Subtotal product development	**€/$300**
Preproduction	
Updating patterns	€/$100
Grading	€/$100
Sample size set	€/$200 (4 sizes: S, M, L, XL)
Subtotal preproduction	**€/$400**
Total development cost	**€/$1 215**

The costs involved

Design
To save time and money, you can use a pre-made hoodie design and its tech pack. Spend a bit of time modifying the tech pack and put your own print design on it.

Pattern-maker
The garment fit—and thus the pattern—is a crucial part of your product development. You need to work with a skilled pattern-maker to get it right. The patterns for this hoodie example cost €/$200.

Costing sheet
To help you keep track of all costs associated with producing each style, use a costing sheet. On it, note down the costs of all of the garment's components, and finally, calculate the garment's retail price. This is a vital tool in the financial operation of your business.

Print
In our example, we've got an idea for a print but we need help with the execution to make it stunning. We launch a project with 99designs for €/$200.

Label and hangtags
Decide which types of labels you want for your garment. In this example, we make a neck label, a flag label on the side of the garment, and a hangtag for information when the garment is hanging in a store.

FOB
Our manufacturer has given us an FOB price (free/freight on board) which includes all charges for making the garment and the transportation to the shipping port. It includes fabrics and accessories. It does NOT include the shipping, duty, or other costs from that point on.

Prototypes
If you're a new partner to your supplier, your prototypes typically cost two or three times the FOB price. The first prototype is never perfect. You'll likely need two to three prototypes before you're pleased—then you'll make a salesman sample that you use for photos and sales.

Preproduction
The initial patterns need updating after the prototype process. Use your pattern-maker or ask the manufacturer's in-house pattern-maker to do

it. The prototypes are made in the same size. Before bulk production, you need to grade the pattern for your desired sizes.

Size set
This is a set of samples in all your sizes that you'll later produce in larger quantities. Order a size set to make sure that the grading is exactly according to your specifications. The size-set samples will assure you that you're producing what you actually want and will order.

Production

Decide on the production quantity for each style in your collection in line with your sales strategy and business model. You also need to take the manufacturer's MOQ into consideration when deciding how many pieces you want to manufacture. If you've received an FOB price, as in this example, simply multiply that by the number of pieces you're producing, to get the production cost.

EXAMPLE

FOB = €/$25

Producing 100 pieces:
100 x 25 = €/$2,500

Producing 500 pieces:
500 x 25 = €/$12,500

In general, as with all production, larger production batches mean a lower price per piece.
Talk to several manufacturers and ask for price quotes. This way you get a benchmark as to reasonable costs for producing your particular garment.

Development and production cost

Let's take a look at the development and production cost per style. In our example, the development cost is €/$1,215. The bulk production costs are taken from the previous example.

EXAMPLE

Cost per style of making 100 pieces:
(1,215 + 2,500)/100 = €/$37.15

Cost per style of making 500 pieces:
(1,215 + 12,500)/500 = €/$27.43

It's no surprise that the price per piece drops when you produce larger quantities. If you keep using the same hoodie style in your next collection, you don't have to redo your product development, and thus save those costs.

13.4 Pricing Tasks

1. Calculate the garment price. Does the margin match your business strategy?

2. Review all of the entries in your budget. What can you adjust?

14.
Production

14.1 Bulk Production

At the end of your product-development cycle, it's finally time to get sewing and make all the garments in larger quantities.

Hopefully you had a great sell-in and have taken orders and actual production quantities for each and every style in your collection. Or, if you had insufficient order quantities on certain styles, you could either drop that style or pay a surcharge to manufacture the exact amount—it's your choice.

Set a time schedule together with your manufacturer. Decide when you need the garments in the warehouse and count backwards. If your business model is direct to consumer, there's no need for SMS, etc., so you can count that out.

Decide what you want

Your first step is to decide how many styles you want to produce, and in how many variations. You now have exact orders from your buyers after your selling period, so use this information to place the manufacturing orders. You know which styles, colors, and sizes your buyers want.

Determine the exact quantity for each variation before you start talking production with the factory.

Book your production early

You need to discuss the time schedule with the factory early on in your product-development phase. You know when you have the delivery drops for that particular season—just count backwards to determine your production deadline. Factories usually plan their production a year ahead. Based on what and how much you need to produce, they'll work out how it fits into their schedule. Reserving your production slot gives you a clear timeframe within which to develop your styles.

Order materials

Since it can take a couple of months to produce your fabrics, you need to take care of this well in advance before the clothing production starts. Don't forget to include transportation times in your schedule.

Preproduction samples

Before moving on to bulk production, you need to have approved a full-size set of each style and a preproduction sample.

Service-level agreement

We recommend that you write an agreement with your supplier that clearly states what both you and your partner should deliver, and what your expectations are. A written agreement will clarify whether you've understood each other during the discussions. In the event things are subsequently not up to par, you've already agreed what should happen. Have all the dates and critical information confirmed in writing by the manufacturer. The information you should agree on includes quantities, shipping, payment, insurance, quality, and delivery dates.

You can also add a non-disclosure agreement stating that the partner cannot discuss your product with anyone outside your project.

Quality control

For every sample during product development, it's important that you put in the work: measure, comment, adjust, and communicate as clearly as possible with the factory. It's your responsibility to double-check that they've understood you and the changes you wish to make. This is vital to ensure your garments come out as intended. Right before, or right at the beginning of your bulk production, it's time for you to check that your garments are made according to your agreement. Preferably travel to the factory and perform the quality control there—that way, if you need to change something, you'll still have time for corrections before it's shipped. The more time you can spend at the factory, the better. Try to visit at least once during the product-development and production phases.

Ask the manufacturer about their quality-control setup. If you feel this won't be enough, you can always involve a third-party quality-control company.

Packaging and shipping

All styles are finished up, steamed, pressed, and folded, then placed in a plastic bag. Every style and color is later packed in a box and shipped to your warehouse or distributors. Check with your manufacturer that the boxes are optimized before shipping. They should be clearly marked with the destination address. You should also receive full documentation for shipping, tolls, etc., from your manufacturer.

To sum up the production phase there are quite a few things to coordinate and you need to start well in advance. Don't think it's just a case of picking up the phone, ordering a production, and receiving your garments in next to no time. Put your project-management hat on and be thorough in all the details along the way. Make sure things are agreed, written down, and confirmed. With signed orders from your customers, you have a promise to keep and a brand reputation on the line.

14.2 Manufacturing Checklist

You want to be in full control of where you are in the production process. Keep track of delays, update your partners on current status, mitigate risks, and stay on top of your game. Use this production checklist to monitor progress and manage your project.

Tech pack, BOM and measurement list package

The tech pack should preferably be in PDF format so everyone can read it; the BOM and measurement in Excel format. Make sure it contains all the necessary information for a smooth production.
Source material

Research and look for fabric, trims, and accessories based on your concept and need. Order fabric swatches and accessory samples from different suppliers so you can see and feel the materials before deciding.

Order fabric and accessories for prototypes

Once you've found your materials, don't forget to actually order enough to make all the prototypes you want. Typically you'll need around three prototypes per style. If there's a time constraint, you can always make the first prototype in a similar fabric that the manufacturer has in stock.

Create pattern

With the tech pack as input, let a pattern-maker create the pattern for your garment. You want the patterns in digital format, which is standard today.

Create prototypes 1, 2 and possibly 3

The manufacturer starts with proto 1. Continue to arrange the making of proto 2, and if needed proto 3.

Fitting and adjustments prototypes 1, 2 and possibly 3

To make proto 2 and 3, you need to give feedback from previous prototypes after fitting and adjustment.

Create SMS—salesman sample

The last sample, which looks like the garments you'll produce. Everything is as it should be, from labels and accessories, to fit and fabric.

Sell collection and finalize orders

Show and sell your collection with your SMSs.

Order fabric and material for bulk production

The sales orders and manufacturer minimums will tell you how much material you need to order. Stay on top of delivery times and don't forget to order in time.

Finalize production pattern

Does your pattern need final adjustments? If so, create the final production pattern.

Grade pattern for sizes

Grade the pattern for all your intended sizes.

Finalize production prototypes

To include final adjustment and to verify the bulk production, make final prototypes—preferably in all sizes.

Cut, sew, and trim

Let the manufacturer do their magic and make your garments.

Quality control

Check production to verify that it meets your service-quality agreement.

Pack and ship

The bulk production needs to be packed and sent to the designated destination.

> **Handing over your work to a supplier and hoping they will figure out exactly what it is you want won't happen. You need to know what you want, how your products should "work" and be able to communicate it.**
>
> Suppliers are only as good as you are.
>
> *–Paul Arden*

14.3 Quality Control

What is quality?

Quality is the degree of excellence in products or services. It's important to remember that quality is relative, and what one person believes is good quality may be seen as poor quality by someone else. The aim is for the customer to be satisfied—that's you and your end consumer. Quality is important in any aspect of your business. Customers expect value for money. It's easy to say you'll have a high-quality brand—but what does that actually mean? You need to think through and describe what quality is to you and your apparel brand. Set standards.

The quality standards of a product are often related to its price point. Every part of product development should be the best possible for the fee you pay.

Even though you'll set standards, quality is something that may change from time to time. There'll be new suppliers, new manufacturers, new workers, etc.

Below we list some of the areas in which things can go wrong. There's no such thing as a smooth production run. You need to know where problems could arise in order to be able to prevent them.

Once a production run is finished and shipped, it's too late to do something about it. If retailers receive faulty goods, it could ruin your reputation and brand—that retailer might not want to do business with you in the future.

> **The process is everything. It's the business.**
> **Designing is only one percentage of building a brand;**
> **the rest is, well, all the rest that needs to get done.**
> **There's ups and downs, the constant hustle; you love it,**
> **you hate it—this is the entrepreneurial game.**
> **If you don't love the process,**
> **then building a brand is not for you.**
>
> If you don't love the process, you've already lost.
>
> *–Gary Vaynerchuk*

What is quality control?

Quality control means ensuring, at a minimum cost, that the quality requirements of a product are being met at every stage of manufacturing, from raw materials to boxed stock.

Determine your requirements

In the apparel industry, product quality is based on performance, reliability, durability, visual and perceived quality of the garment. During the product-development and manufacturing processes, there will always be a certain portion of defective goods. It can be economical for you to allow for a small percentage of defective goods, instead of screening the entire load. This is referred to as Acceptable Quality Level, or AQL.

You need to determine your quality requirements and communicate them to the manufacturer. The manufacturer will then examine them, refer to past performance, discuss with their quality-control and production departments, then send their feedback to you. You can then revise your quality requirements and reach a mutual agreement with the manufacturer about the AQL.

Maintaining an adequate standard of quality also takes effort.

Risk assessment

A risk assessment should be carried out as part of the quality-control process. This assessment identifies potential failure points in the manufacturing and internal and external supply chains. The risk assessment takes into account materials, design, manufacturing processes, suppliers, customer use, performance tests, durability tests, washing tests, and use tests.

How to control quality

Quality control needs to be practiced right from the initial stage of sourcing materials, through to the final, finished garment. Quality involves fabric, accessories, construction, colorfastness, design, and the finished garment.

To secure your quality standards, you implement a Quality Management System (QMS) that suits your business. The QMS determines a strategy, responsibilities, an action plan and process to realize your quality goals and ensure continuous improvements.

Typically, a number of products are picked at random and their quality is checked against a number of predetermined parameters. Below we list a range of standard parameters and defects that are examined before, during, and after production.

No matter how many pieces you produce, be it 200 or 5000, you should decide with the manufacturer how to go about the quality control— either in-depth, checking every single product, or by spot-checking.

Use a Quality Control Specification Sheet. It should include the following:

Quality control before production—materials

The following parameters and defects are checked prior to cutting:
- Shade matching
- Fabric construction
- GSM (grams per square meter)
- Diameter
- Dyeing levelness
- Ecological parameters if required
- Softness
- Shrinkage
- Matching of rib, collars and cuffs
- Fabric holes
- Vertical and horizontal stripes
- Knitting defects such as missing loops, sinker lines, etc.
- Bowing
- Skewing
- Yarn defects such as thick and thin places
- Dirt and stains

Quality control during production—product-making

These parameters and defects are checked during the making of the garment:
- Cutting patterns
- Cut components measurements
- Cutting shapes
- Fabric defects
- Other specific parameters as required by customers—e.g., rib, collars and cuffs matching
- Stitching defects
- Sewing threads matching
- Stains
- Measurements
- Labels
- Trims and accessories

Final quality control

These parameters and defects are checked during the making of the garment:

Packing and Assortment
- Wrong model
- Wrong quantity
- Missing labels and tags
- Wrong size and color assortment
- Wrong folding

Fabric defects
- Wrong shade
- Uneven dyeing
- Holes
- Knitting stripes
- Thick and thin places
- Stains
- Oil stains
- Sinker line
- Poor softness
- Higher shrinkage
- Crease marks

Workmanship defects
- Open seam
- Puckering
- Needle holes and marks
- Unbalanced sleeve edge
- Unbalanced placket
- Insecure shoulder stitch
- Incorrect side shape
- Bottom hem bowing
- Uneven neck shape
- Cross labels
- Broken and missing stitch
- Non-secured buttons

- Untrimmed threads and fabrics
- Poor ironing
- Double stitch

General defects
- Shade variation within garment parts
- Shade variation between garments
- Defective printing
- Defective embroidery
- Defective buttons

Measurement Deviations
- Garment length
- Body width
- Shoulder length
- Arm hole
- Arm opening
- Sleeve length
- Placket length
- Placket width
- Neck width
- Neck opening
- Hemming width
- Rib or collar width

Sustainable parameters

In addition to the above parameters, the following may be relevant to you if you have a sustainable approach:
- pH range
- Formaldehyde levels
- Extractable heavy metals
- Chlorinated phenols (PCP, TeCP)
- Forbidden amines of MAK III A1and A2 categories
- Pesticides
- Chlorinated organic carriers
- Biocide finishes

- Flame-retardant finishes
- Colorfastness to water
- Colorfastness to acidic and alkaline perspiration
- Colorfastness to wet and dry rubbing
- Colorfastness to saliva
- Emission of volatile chemicals
- Other specific parameters as required by customers

It's your responsibility to check the manufacturer's work while the goods are still in the factory, and specifically before the entire bulk production is completed. Ideally, visit the factory before they start sewing the full production run, to make sure everything is as intended—that way, if there are any problems, they can be corrected at once. Include your quality requirements in your terms of agreement.

The above is only applicable to products—but you should have quality standards for *all* aspects of your business; e.g., customer service, shipping, returns, etc.

The quality remains long after the price is forgotten.

– Sir Henry Royce

14.4 Production Tasks

1. Confirm delivery deadlines with suppliers.

2. Order all materials.

3. Approve size-set samples and preproduction samples.

4. Order manufacturing. Cut, sew and trim.

15.
Sustainability

15.1 How To Run A Sustainable Apparel Brand

The apparel industry is the third most polluting industry in the world, after the meat and oil industries. With major global issues caused by the apparel industry, it's more important than ever to start taking responsibility and implement sustainability practices in apparel businesses.

Today, the average apparel consumer buys 60 percent more clothing items per year than 15 years ago. Unfortunately, consumers also keep the products for half as long as they did 15 years ago. It's common knowledge that we consume enormous amounts of products, get rid of them and buy new.

An estimated 92 million tons of textile waste is created every year from the clothing industry, and it's estimated to increase by about 60 percent between 2015 and 2030, with an additional 57 million tons of waste generated annually. The anticipated total clothing waste in 2030 is 148 million tons, which is equivalent to an annual waste of 175 kg per capita across the planet.

These alarming numbers have made the entire industry question the way we do business. You and your brand can contribute to driving change within the apparel industry: by raising awareness through information and education, every consumer can be a catalyst for change!

How can we run apparel businesses that make little social and environmental impact?

Through the Apparel Entrepreneurship community, the most common questions we get regarding sustainability implementation are: "Where do I start?" and "What do I need to do?"

This chapter is about how to run a sustainable brand. You've surely heard about environmentally friendly brands, eco-friendly brands, ethically made, responsibly made, consciously made, and sustainable brands. A load of different names—but what do they actually mean?

Being a sustainable apparel brand means having as little impact on the planet as possible. It takes care of the people involved in and around the business and has a sound and profitable business setup.

A sustainable brand means that the generations to come need a healthy planet to live on. It means that the customer buying your products is safe, never harmed by your products due to dangerous chemicals. It means that employees manufacturing your products work in a safe environment and are paid fair wages.

We can't go back and undo the harm, but we can make things better now and in the future. For sure, the best way to develop products that won't end up in landfill is by designing long-lasting products that your customers love. Products that will be taken care of, products that will be sold in second-hand stores or handed over to relatives and friends. Products and systems designed for a closed loop. Take ownership of what's happening with your products, throughout the entire lifespan of the product: when it's made, when it's in the consumer's hands, and when it's reached its finish line.

Why run a sustainable apparel brand?

What are the advantages of running a sustainable apparel brand? It's complicated and hard as it *is* to run a clothing brand—so why bother with the sustainability side? Why make it even more difficult?

Besides the obvious reason of wanting a healthy planet for the coming generations, there are huge advantages.

Competitive advantage

Established brands that are not sustainable have a hard time becoming sustainable. Conscious customers care what brands they're buying and when a brand transitions into sustainability, there's no authenticity. Conscious customers will choose sustainable brands over non-sustainable. The younger generations buy brands that they can belong to, that they share the same values with.

Financial opportunity

Environmentally friendly brands have an advantage by already having a customer base that's ready to pay more for the garments and invest in the company and its products. You can—and should—charge appropriately to cover all your costs.

Lower the environmental footprint

By making better choices at each step of the process, you can lower the overall environmental footprint. Because you care, because it's the right thing to do and because you know the consequences if you don't.

Streamlined supply chain for increased efficiency

When you run a very conscious business and can track where everything comes from, have consolidated suppliers and manufacturers, and a clever logistical setup, you'll run a more efficient business. Sustainable design improves the environmental outcomes and can reduce your total costs in the long term.

Improved brand value and reputation

It means you stand for something and it means you care about the environment and the people living on this planet.

Awareness

Brands have a responsibility to bring awareness to the public. Customers can't make better decisions if they don't know the truth. When you're transparent and have traceable products, your customers will get to know where the products come from, how they're made, and the impact they have.

Circular economy

A circular economy is a regenerative system in which resource input and waste, emission, and energy leakage are minimized by slowing, closing, and narrowing energy and material loops. This can be achieved through long-lasting design, maintenance, repair, reuse, remanufacturing, refurbishing, recycling, and upcycling. This is in contrast to a linear economy which is a "take, make, and dispose" model of production.

Areas for improvement

We don't want to scare you into sustainability, even though sustainability is without a doubt the way to go. Rather, we want to show you what can be done better.

In order for you to better understand how the apparel industry harms the environment, we've put together a little list with points that can be improved upon:

- Pesticides and high water consumption in cotton production
- Chemical treatments and finishings, bleaching and dyeing of materials and finished garments
- Fossil fuel used in synthetic fiber
- Waste in material factories and clothing factories
- Carbon emissions in transportation
- Packaging waste—plastic and paper
- Energy consumption during production
- Bad working conditions, long working hours, forced labor, child labor
- Clothing that ends up in landfill or is burned. Fact: Only 14 percent of clothes are recycled

Greenwashing

Sustainability has been a trending topic for a while. Some companies have taken this seriously and changed things for the better, and some just *say* they have, to generate positive PR and sell more products. By marketing sustainability, companies tap into the conscious consumers. But to falsely market sustainability is called greenwashing. Greenwashing causes long-term damage to a label's reputation. If the brand eventually does do something good and changes things for the better, unfortunately no one's going to believe them.

In order to avoid greenwashing as a brand, you have to:
- Be authentic, honest and transparent.
- Do what you say you'll do and have evidence for what you promise.
- Practice what you preach. If taking care of Mother Nature is your calling, then living a non-sustainable life is very hypocritical. You represent your brand. Sustainability should be your lifestyle.

Mindset

To start a sustainable apparel brand, you need the right mindset. Once you've chosen to launch your brand there's no going back. Either you go full speed at it, or you don't. Again, the conscious customer who's going to be attracted by your brand's values wants honesty, authenticity, and transparency. To start this type of brand means serious commitment. If you think about it, there's no such thing as a sustainable brand. As soon as you start producing something, those products will have a negative environmental impact. First of all, make the decision that you want to reduce the harm, then decide on the degree you can commit to. Start from there and improve it bit by bit, over time.

Alternative business models

Innovation and implementation of leasing models—does your brand need to *sell* all it products? Could you experiment with leasing certain product types? What about alteration models, where customers can come in with one garment and leave with a new, altered piece?

Thought experiments

What if nothing in your collection was disposable? What would that product look like and be made of? What would the company setup need to look like to facilitate this business model?

Business success will depend on your being innovative, flexible, and knowing your core values. Brands need to invest in technology and sustainable-design methods. To stay relevant, companies have to become transparent, implement innovation strategies, and explore new business models, whilst giving customers the best-value products. Consumers are getting picky and well-educated. Small brands can go a long way with very little money—they just need to be brave, check the numbers, and take calculated risks.

In order to make the most of the possibilities, you need focus, planning, and strategizing. Sustainability is the new playing field and offers huge opportunities—we're talking a €/$500 billion fashion-industry opportunity.

15.2 Sustainable Marketing and Sales

Brand values. Attract the right customer.

Customers buy into your values and story. People want to be part of a bigger community, with like-minded peers. Sure, customers will like your products, but they'll love *you* for your values. Dig deep and be very concise with those core values; be honest with what you're here to achieve and why you want to do it. What is that personal story that made you care so much? What has affected you so deeply that you wanted to start an apparel brand based on those values?

Create emotional attachment through your values and your brand's responsible approaches. And remember to include your customers at every step of the way on your entrepreneurial journey and towards decreasing your carbon footprint.

Customers want to belong, especially when there's a great cause. Let your customers be part of your world, to help raise environmental awareness together.

• Be authentic with what you're here to achieve.

• Take accountability for your impact.

• Make it public: tell the world what, why, and how you're doing it.

- Include your customers via social media, contests, and events.

> Everyone can do simple things to make a difference, and every little bit really does count.
>
> *–Stella McCartney*

Have a clear, concise declaration about your business strategy

We're sure you've seen Patagonia's mission statement 100 times. And if you haven't, here it is:

Build the best product, cause no unnecessary harm, use business to inspire and implement solutions to the environmental crisis.

It's so simple and so clear. Everybody, from the people who work there to the end consumers, knows in a couple of sentences what the brand is about and what they're here to do. By knowing your mission and vision, you'll know exactly where you're going, and all your decisions will be easier along the way. You'll know where you stand and what you need to achieve.

Have a clear mission and vision! This is your framework and purpose!

Whether you decide to raise awareness for issues surrounding child labor, the ocean, or endangered animals, choose it and stick to it. If it's too broad, you'll confuse your customers and your employees. Keep it clear; it'll be easier for you to focus and prioritize—and eventually gain traction for your goal. When creating your vision and mission, it should include the 3 P's of Sustainability: People, Planet, and Profit.

Market scan

It's important to have complete knowledge of the market you'll position your brand in. What are brands saying about their goals, what products are they pushing, and what materials are they using? Sustainability can be "attacked" from many angles—what are their USPs? What will your USP be to differentiate your brand from the rest? What vocabulary is used around sustainability, and what are the stories that are being told?

Also, take a look at what your competitors are doing that's great—and what they're doing that sucks.

What materials are they using and how much do they charge? Understand what's happening in the market, to better position yourself and to ensure you don't have the same USP as someone else. Look at business models, price ranges, materials, and product structure. Are those brands transparently revealing their suppliers and manufacturers? This information is important when you position and structure your collection and design your styles.

What are your USPs?

Today, being unique and different is more important than being better. New, innovative business strategies will give your brand a competitive advantage. This applies to startups and existing brands. There are always new possibilities, and if your company is quick to action, you can change things up and try out new stuff constantly. Answer these questions to figure out your USPs:

• What's so special about your business idea and product?
• What sustainability problems are you trying to solve?
• What problem does your actual product or brand solve?
• Why should customers buy your brand instead of something else?
• What impact do you want to make? What is the message that you want your customers to know you for?
• What steps are you taking to reduce harm to the environment?

It's a crowded space and you need to get noticed—and noticed for the right reasons.

Marketing—the brand

As we explained earlier, sustainability is widely used in PR and marketing to gain customer trust. This needs to be done in a clever way, by telling your story. Storytelling connects your customers to your brand. People do business with *people* and they want to know and feel that there are real humans behind the brand. Honesty, transparency, seeing behind the scenes, the heart and soul, the ups and downs. That's what makes people care deeply about brands.

Communicate clearly and loudly your story, your WHY and your VALUES in everything you do.

It doesn't matter how many great things you're doing if no one knows about it. And it's not enough to say things once. With the constant flood of information, people forget quickly and need to be reminded of the great things you're doing as a brand. Talk about the big picture, the impact you want to have. Getting nerdy and super-detailed about your products and fabrics will let your customers know that you know what you're doing. They should get to see and learn about every step of the product's journey.
What do you want the world to know about your brand? Bring customers in on your sustainability journey. The honesty will make them love you more.

Marketing—the product

The above was about how you market a sustainable brand—but how do you market a sustainable product?

You do it through awareness, education, inspiration, and motivation. Help customers make better choices. By informing them on all levels about the big picture, the vision, the concept and idea behind your collection, the materials used, and the manufacturers that made your products, you make sure your customers are so informed and familiar with your brand and products that it'll be hard for them to not buy your stuff. By this point, you and your brand should be top of mind when it comes to the type of products you're offering, be it activewear, jeans, or whatever your specialty is.

Label it
Tell the world on the hangtag, on the website, and in the store by labeling the product. Make it visual, so people see—and remember—that

you're a sustainable brand, use eco-friendly materials and components, and made the better choice for them.

Use certifications
Ask suppliers and manufacturers to provide you with the certifications used. Become a member of different organizations and talk about it in all your media.

Offer a service
Repair, resell, rent, and recycle. Give customers the possibility of opting for longer garment life or afterlife care for their products. Could you offer a once-a-year garment service, like in the car industry?

Activism
Talk loudly about it, get involved in debates, make a stand, and get involved with charity and organizations. Your customers need to know that you care for real and that you stand proudly for what you believe in.

Use emotions. Create emotional attachment to your products through ethical and environmentally friendly product choices.

Sales

Direct-to-consumer businesses have to focus on finding customers with the same values and this also applies to B2B models.

Work with agents, distributors, and stores that already sell sustainable brands. They know why sustainability is important and you won't have to spend time educating them. Their conscious customer base will be your target customer.

- Be your own sustainability messenger! When you put *yourself* forward, your enthusiasm, authenticity, and dedication will be very noticeable and contagious.
- Work with agents, distributors, and retailers with a sustainability focus —you won't have to educate them; they already know the importance of being a responsible brand.
- Pitch your values—heartfelt content will speak more than facts about your materials. Connect on a deeper level with your buyers.
- Tell them what you're trying to achieve with your brand—stories sell.

- Tell them the benefits of your product.
- Simplify and make it easy for people—share facts and information for better and easier choices.

> Who are businesses really responsible to?
> Their customers? Shareholders? Employees?
> We would argue that it's none of the above.
> Fundamentally, businesses are responsible
> to their resource base.
> Without a healthy environment
> there are no shareholders, no employees,
> no customers and no business.
>
> *–Yvon Chouinard*

15.3 Sustainable Product Development

Collection

We've discussed the brand idea, USPs, vision, and mission—all the reasons why you're in business. Now we're going to narrow it down into constructing a sustainable collection and its actual designs.

Niche
The narrower, the better. When you start with a small collection or even one product, you can focus on nailing those eco-friendly materials. You can focus on finding that specific sustainable and ethical manufacturer you need for your products. Unless you have unlimited funding, starting small and niched will give you a huge advantage in terms of making things great from the start.

Collection structure—styles and price
Every piece in your collection should have its "raison d'être" and its own placement, not cannibalizing on another style in the collection. There should be very clear and distinct product differentiation in order to make it clear to your customers what the product is intended to do and why they should buy it.

Cohesion

The collection should look like a collection and not a bunch of products put together. Think about merchandising; think about store windows; think about outfits for your website, etc. To keep even more cohesion and to work cleverly with materials, you can consolidate your materials to keep the collection tight. More consolidated materials mean less shipping across the planet. Try also to source as close to home as possible.

Timeless-color strategy

There are on-trend colors and there are timeless colors. The ones you pick will pretty much dictate how long your customers will use your products. Help your customers want to keep your product much longer in their wardrobe.

Edit

Keep what's necessary: the greatest environmental damage is caused by the overabundance of stuff. If you feel that some styles in the collection aren't really great and don't have a clear positioning in the range, ditch them. Keep only the strong pieces that have a clear positioning.

Think a step ahead

By knowing what you have in the collection now, you can plan what to add in the coming season. Are there certain new and innovative sustainable materials that you want to implement?

Design

If we're looking at the fast-fashion model, there are 15 or more seasons/drops per year. This model is of course neither sustainable nor easy to follow as a startup. Traditional product-development cycles are 6-12 months—it would be impossible for a small brand to produce so many products.

So how many pieces should you start with, when launching your collection?

At the beginning, we would recommend starting small. It could be one segment and even one product—only T-shirts, for example, or only tights. When you own your positioning in the marketplace, it's easier to expand from there.

If you have the budget and team to have several products, start with a small range. When you have a small range—for example, a couple of bottoms and a couple of tops—customers can buy outfits or mix and match the products themselves. You give them options to buy more than one product. Keep the collection together through material, usage, and details.

The 30/30/30/10 rule

When thinking and planning for upcoming collections and product drops, you can apply the 30/30/30/10 rule. There's no need to renew all your products, every collection.

The rule goes like this:

- 30 percent new: totally new styles; can be in new materials.

- 30 percent carryover: styles that are exactly the same as last season, no changes except for very small tweaks that will be unnoticeable by customers (an additional bar tack, for example). Materials can be the same, and some new colors.

- 30 percent updated: the updated styles can be changed, new materials used, new treatments, but the changed style should resemble the old version. Customers or buyers should be able to see the update.

- 10 percent showstoppers: these new styles should be pushed in terms of innovation, technology, material usage, and styling. This is where you can experiment. These styles will not be your most-sold items—they're meant more as marketing pieces. They'll lift the entire collection up.

Sustainability starts with design

Around 80 percent of a product's environmental impact is decided in the design stage. This is where all the critical decisions are made concerning materials, manufacturing, product lifespan, afterlife, and recyclability. The average lifespan of a product is 2.2 years. A good product should be designed to function, be cared for and kept way longer than 2.2 years. The best thing for the environment in all aspects is a great-functioning product that lasts a long time. After choosing environmentally friendly materials and ethical production, look at how to reduce your impact through design. Could you use design techniques to reduce waste? Could you design clothes with multiple uses and functions? Could you prolong the product's lifespan through design? Could you foster good consumer use, such as wash, care, repair, reuse and recycle through your design?

These design options can be very creative and fun, and will for sure pique customers' curiosity through your stories.

There are certain components to consider when designing a product with low environmental impact:
- Timeless design
- Well-functioning design
- Zero-waste pattern-cutting
- Minimal seam construction
- Outstanding fit
- Multifunctional or transformational design
- Minimal waste
- Ethical production
- Design to reduce water, energy, and chemicals
- Design for disassembly—products that can easily be taken apart at the end of the product's life
- Design for longevity—use durable materials
- High quality in design and all components
- Repair/secondhand services
- Recyclability
- Design for closed-loop manufacturing—no waste; everything is recycled and reused

THINK ABOUT ALL THE COMPONENTS AND THE ENTIRE PRODUCT LIFESPAN. About 95 percent of the textiles landfilled each year could be reused or recycled.

Garment standards

Before each product is introduced to the market, you can implement standards that it should meet, to make sure every product has passed your sustainability test. The standards should include design, materials, manufacturing, usage, and afterlife.

Example of standards:
- Clear purpose for the product
- Timeless design
- Durable materials and construction, reinforced seam areas where needed
- Versatile product
- High-quality materials and manufacturing
- Designed for easy care—cold washing, no need for special treatments
- Designed with the afterlife in mind, what can and should the customer do with the garment when they're done with it?
- Have an afterlife plan

Sourcing suppliers and supplier selection

The biggest part of a product is the materials used to make it. Before contacting any suppliers to source your fabrics, it's a good idea to learn the fabric basics. What are the different types of materials, what are their properties, and what is their environmental impact? If you're new to sourcing and finding suppliers, start by visiting fabric fairs to see, feel, and understand the different offers on the market.

How do you know who to work with? How do you know which suppliers are better than others? By talking to them and by researching them, you can see how transparent they are. Try and work with suppliers who are certified and have made sustainability a priority in their business. It can be hard to find great suppliers—so when you find them, you want to work on building a great relationship and grow with them. It's a good idea to not have too many suppliers. Consolidate your materials for a more streamlined supply chain.

KEY—Ask your manufacturers and suppliers a lot of questions and don't be satisfied with vague answers!

Sourcing materials
When choosing materials, think about how the garments will be used. Select durable materials that don't need any special cleaning.

Material suggestions:
- Recycled materials like recycled polyester, recycled nylon, recycled wool.
- Biodegradable materials like silk, bamboo, hemp, castor oil materials.
- Organic cotton, hemp, Tencel, linen, modal.
- "Pure" 100 percent materials. If you intend to recycle the entire garment, pure 100 percent fibers are easier to recycle than blends.
- Mixed materials. As an example, a 50-percent-cotton/50-percent-polyester T-shirt will last twice as long as a 100-percent-cotton tee with normal usage.
- Dead stock and leftover materials. These are completely fine materials that end up as surplus in factories or that certain designers/brands no longer want to use.
- Certified materials—this can guarantee a cleaner process.
- Stock materials. These types of materials are already produced, in certain colors, and are waiting to be used.
- Use solution-dyed materials or plant-based natural dyes instead of dyes and inks that contain toxic heavy metals like cadmium and beryllium. Also, work with suppliers who recycle their waste.
- Non-fragile materials that need extra care. Preferably the materials you pick should be washed effectively in cold water, with no special care and harsh detergents.
- Repeat patterns/prints—select materials that have a repeat pattern with no beginning or end, so that the entire roll of fabric can be used.

To check your materials for toxic chemicals, you can use the Safer Textiles tool on their website: http://safertextiles.eu

Quality

Quality and long-lasting products are important components for a sustainable brand. It starts in the design phase where the product's lifespan can be improved by, for example, moving seams away from friction points, avoiding fragile details, including reinforced construction at, for example, pocket edges, zipper endings, cuff hems, and hems. Quality touches all components, including materials and trims. Implementing quality control into your processes becomes even more important for sustainability reasons. Include rigorous tests on material, washing, and usability to make sure your products live up to your quality standards.

Animal welfare

Your material choices also affect certain animals. We won't go into detail about this, but the use of leather and fur means that animals need to be killed. We're glad that the industry is going in the right direction, with London Fashion Week banning fur and big designers also banning leather, angora, cashmere and mohair from their collections.

Staying away from exotic skins, fur, leather, silk, mohair, cashmere and angora is of course the obvious choice if you care about the planet and the animals living on it. There are still some better options when it comes to wool and down if you're concerned with animal welfare.

When using wool, you should make sure you can trace it back to the farm it comes from, and that you can guarantee the wool is non-mulesed.

You can go one step further and also check that the farm follows The Five Freedoms of animal welfare for its animals:
1. Freedom from thirst and hunger
2. Access to adequate shelter
3. Freedom to behave naturally
4. Freedom from stress, pain and fear
5. Prevention or treatment for injury, disease or parasite infection

To guarantee that your material or yarn comes from fairly treated animals and authentic, ethical and sustainable farms, certifications are extremely important—preferably from third parties like New Merino and ZQ and not from wool companies themselves. Read more about wool certifications in the certifications and organizations list at the end of this chapter.

If you want to use real down in your collection for those warmer products, opt for recycled down or traceable down where the down comes from responsible sources that respect animal welfare and can be traced. The ducks from responsible farms are never live-plucked or force-fed and are treated humanely.

Read more about down certifications in the certifications and organizations list at the end of this chapter.

Ethical manufacturing

When you've found great trusted and sustainable suppliers, they can guide you to trusted ethical manufacturers. Suppliers and manufacturers work together and of course they can help you find the right partner. Here, as with suppliers, choose manufacturers that have ethical standards and sustainability as a priority. Your aim should be to only work with manufacturers that operate ethically and comply with their respective national employment laws and regulations.

Here is what you should consider:
- Code of conduct—factory to operate with a thorough code of conduct contract.
- Green factory—the manufacturing plant should be energy-efficient, low in water and chemical usage.
- Ethics—Freely chosen employment, minimum age of employment, no discrimination, terms of employment: rates of pay, working hours, safe and healthy working environment.
- Certifications—Bluesign, Fairtrade, GOTS, Oeko-Tex.
- Recycled waste—factory to recycle its wastewater and leftover materials.
- Audits and unannounced visits. Third-party audits and personal visits.

The above are areas manufacturers work on to operate in an ethical and sustainable way—but you as a brand can also make better choices to minimize the damage during the manufacturing process:
- Local manufacturing—support local manufacturing plus the goods won't have to be shipped across the planet to your warehouse.
- Vertical supply chain—by working with vertical suppliers you'll have both the materials and the manufacturing in the same place. This usually speeds up the production process, cuts lead times and is a bit cheaper. Also, the goods don't have to be shipped from place to place, lowering the carbon footprint.
- Minimize packaging—products are usually packed in plastic, paper, or carton. Decide what you don't need and communicate with the factory.

- Minimize waste—Around 15 percent of materials end up on the factory floor. How can you minimize this—and if you can't minimize, what else can you do with the scraps?
- Reuse, recycle waste—can you produce something else from your waste scraps?
- Produce according to the demand—it's better to pay a certain surcharge to produce a lower quantity than produce the MOQ and have those products sit in your warehouse and later end up on sale.

Logistics

As soon as the factory has manufactured your bulk production, they'll want to ship it to your warehouse—or your house if you're a startup with no studio yet. What smart decisions can you make at this stage in the process, to have your goods sent to you fast but with as little environmental impact as possible? Once they've arrived, how will you ship the goods to your customers? All shipping is bad—that's why local manufacturing is a plus. It's definitely a balancing act to have your goods transported from one place to another in the most eco-friendly way.

Source materials and production within the same continent, to reduce shipping. When sourcing all materials close to home, you'll not have to ship them across the planet.

Ocean and rail shipping instead of truck and air: Shipping by ship will take longer and needs some proper planning. If you're tight on delivery deadlines, then shipping by air is the only option. This will of course be much more expensive. Shipping by train is green but this also needs some planning. Truck shipping is very flexible but here you have to think of the truck being full both ways, otherwise it's not a good option.

Optimized full boxes: There are several options when shipping your products: hanging or folded. Folded garments will take less space and you can optimize your boxes better than if you ship hanging products. Hanging goods need bigger boxes and you can pack fewer products into one box.

Plan the transport, full transport both ways if possible: Look at all the legs of transport your product has to go through to reach its end destination, the customer. How can you optimize each and every stage of the transport?

Energy-optimized warehouse: If you have your products in a warehouse, choose a modern facility that's optimized for low energy consumption.

Efficient storage and picking in the warehouse: Have structure and set guidelines in place to ensure optimal picking of your products.
Shipping partners that compensate for fuel emissions: Talk to different companies and compare.

Packaging and presentation

In the garment industry, every product is individually packed, with more or less packaging, be that plastic bags, paper, or both. The protection is needed to ensure the garments reach their destination safely, without being damaged, misshapen or creased. But you as a brand have a choice to make when deciding upon the packaging for each garment. And think one step further: do you need any packaging at all for certain products? If you're an online direct-to-consumer supplier, do you need the polybags for each product?

Point of sale
What POS presentation materials are your retailers using for your products? All the presentation materials can be made environmentally friendly—you just have to look for better options.

7 ways to make your packaging and presentation materials more environmentally friendly:
1. Recycled and recyclable materials in hangtags/labels: Ask your supplier what alternatives there are. When it comes to hangtags and labels, pick recycled materials over virgin.
2. Recycled fiberboard hangers: Opt out of the traditional plastic hangers. Go for steel or fiberboard.
3. Reusable shopping bags: This can be a great way for your brand to be extra visible, too—on fabric totes, for example. Or have no shopping bags at all. You decide. But the traditional plastic bag should never be an option.
4. Recycled presentation interior material: A creative and exclusive approach can be to find unique furniture and interior material.

5. Reduced packaging: Try to eliminate as much extra unnecessary stuff as possible.
6. Recycled packaging: If you absolutely have to use packaging, go for the recycled and recyclable options and indicate clearly to your customers how to recycle it.
7. Packaging to be multifunctional: By being extra creative you can come up with ways to use and reuse packaging.

Product care and afterlife

You've done everything you can so far to ensure you have a low environmental impact. Now the product is in your customers' hands. This is where information and education are extremely important. And no one but you can provide this.

What we know is that the most sustainable products are those that last a very, very long time. Through great consumer education, this can be achieved.

Showing your customers the sustainability roadmap for a product's entire lifespan will enable them to understand the full process and see what effects their actions can have.

Here's what you can do to make your consumers more aware, informed, and educated:
• Have instructional care labels and hangtags.
• Offer a repair, resell, and recycle service—brands should promote prolonged life for their garments by offering repair services, taking back products for resale or recycling—a closed-loop system.
• Educational website.
• Provide simple and clear care and laundry instructions.
• Provide styling guidance—give consumers tips to encourage longer use of your products.
• Have clear fit advice—provide extra-clear size and fit instructions on your website and packaging to ensure that your customers get the right fit and can actually use their newly bought garment.

15.4 Certifications

Your Textile Certification Guide

Apparel Entrepreneurship's guide to textile certifications, standards, and organizations for sustainability. There are many certifications and standards out there helping us consider the environment and ethical work environments. Read up on the certifications in this guide and determine which are important to you and your brand. Also, ask your customers to keep their eyes open for these certifications as a way to guide them toward better product choices.

Better Cotton Initiative (BCI)

This was created in response to the current impacts of cotton production worldwide. BCI promotes measurable improvements in the key environmental and social impacts of cotton cultivation worldwide to make it more economically, environmentally and socially sustainable.

Source: http://bettercotton.org

Bluesign

Indicates all the input streams, from raw materials to chemical components, and resources used are assessed in terms of their ecological impact. It's essentially a label that helps identify fabric and apparel producers that have analyzed their manufacturing chain and are constantly investing in research and development in an active effort to reduce their ecological footprint.

Source: http://www.bluesign.com

Cradle to Cradle

Indicates a product that's either completely recyclable or biodegradable, and made with the lowest-impact manufacturing processes that are not harmful to people or the environment in any way. The certification program applies to materials, sub-assemblies and finished products and is a chance for companies to demonstrate eco-intelligent design.

Source: http://www.c2ccertified.org

Fairtrade

The symbol indicates that the product has met certain social, environmental, and economic criteria that support the sustainable development of small-scale producers and agricultural workers in the poorest countries in the world. The Fairtrade organization essentially gives consumers the opportunity to help reduce poverty and instigate change by purchasing Fairtrade cotton and several certified food items.

Source: http://www.fairtrade.net

Global Organic Textile Standard (GOTS)

Indicates that the product is definitely organic through every stage of production from ginning to the labeling of the final product. This includes all aspects of manufacturing from use of biodegradable and toxin-free dyes, to low-impact waste treatment and water-supply systems in factories, fair-labor practices and final products that are free of allergenic, carcinogenic or toxic chemical residues. This officially and internationally recognized standard is currently one of the most trusted organic textile certifications.

Source: http://global-standard.org/the-standard.html

Global Recycle Standard

Indicates that the product contains recycled content of some sort. This is often in the form of recycled polyester or rPET, which is often found in sportswear and cotton/rPET fabric blends.

Source: http://textileexchange.org

GoodWeave

A non-profit organization based in Washington, DC that seeks to end exploitative child labor in the carpet industry, offering educational opportunities to children and support to communities affected by exploitative practices. They do this by certifying carpets and rugs free from exploitive production. In order to earn the GoodWeave label, rug exporters and importers must be licensed under the GoodWeave certification program and sign a legally binding contract to adhere to the no-child-labor standard. Importers agree to source only from GoodWeave-certified exporters in India, Nepal and any other country in which GoodWeave rugs are available. In the United States and other rug-importing countries, only licensed importers are legally permitted to sell carpets carrying the GoodWeave label.

Source: https://goodweave.org

MADE-BY

The sign is a label that indicates a fashion company's environmental responsibility and fair labor practices throughout the entire supply chain. The MADE-BY organization works with brands that use organic cotton and work with sewing factories with enforced social codes of conduct.

Source: http://www.made-by.org

This product has been given the OE 100 Standard, which guarantees that it is made of 100% organic materials that have not undergone chemical treatment or manufactured in ways to endanger the environment and local communities.

OE-100

Indicates that a product is made from 100-percent-organic fiber that has been tracked and verified throughout the entire production chain. Textile Exchange awards the certification.

Source: http://textileexchange.org

Oeko-Tex

The standard indicates that the textile product is free of certain groups of harmful substances, ensuring that all certified products are harmless to health. The certification standards fall into three levels: 100, 1000 and 1000-plus as the highest. The certification indicates that everything from fabric, threads, interlinings, hook-and-loop closures, hooks, etc., have met the criteria.

Source: https://www.oeko-tex.com

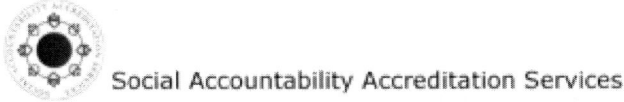

Social Accountability Accreditation Services (SAAS)

Supports social responsibility by ensuring the implementation of credible social standards designed to protect people and their communities. SAAS evaluates and accredits auditing organizations to assure they're qualified to hold their clients accountable for such social standards. SAAS is the only global accreditation body whose mission is to support the implementation of social and labor standards.

Source: http://www.saasaccreditation.org

SCS Certification

Measures the amount of recycled content that has been diverted from the waste stream in a certain product. The SCS organization also grants certification to companies that meet certain criteria for in-house recycling schemes.

Source: http://www.scsglobalservices.com/

USDA Certified Organic

Is often recognized for food labeling, but accounts for all agricultural crops. These include cotton, wool, and other natural fibers that come from animals that have not been given antibiotics or growth hormones and receive organic feed, and plants that have not been grown with pesticides, synthetic fertilizers or ionizing radiation. All products that are labeled as USDA certified organic have to meet the standards, whether the raw material was grown in the US or elsewhere.

Source: http://www.ams.usda.gov/AMSv1.0/NOP

Zque

Indicates responsibly manufactured and environmentally safe wool. Wool with this accreditation has been produced in an environmentally, socially, and economically sustainable manner, to high animal welfare standards, and is traceable back to its source. Most Zque wool is merino wool raised and produced in New Zealand.

Source: http://www.zqmerino.com/home/zq-merino/

ASIA

World Fair Trade Organization (WFTO)

WFTO members are social entrepreneurs and artisans, farmers and campaigners, innovators and fair trade pioneers. They are spread across more than 70 countries.

Fair Trade enterprises are 100 percent committed to fair trade in everything they do. Their social mission is in their DNA. They work to a different business model that puts the needs of people and planet first. They are social enterprises, cooperatives, family businesses and other social businesses that truly prioritize the goals of fair trade.

Fair trade enterprises are a unique breed. They were born as alternative business models in the struggle against inequality and injustice.

Source: https://wfto.com/standard-and-guarantee-system/our-product-label

Fair Wear Foundation

Fair Wear Foundation is a non-profit organization that works with brands, factories, trade unions, NGOs and sometimes governments to verify and improve workplace conditions for garment workers in 11 production countries in Asia, Europe and Africa. FWF keeps track of the improvements made by the companies it works with. Through sharing expertise, social dialogue, and strengthening industrial relations, FWF increases the effectiveness of the efforts made by companies. FWF's more than 80 member companies represent over 120 brands, and are based in Europe; member products are sold in over 20,000 retail outlets in more than 80 countries around the world.

Source: https://www.fairwear.org

Two Organic Standard Certifications

The Organic Content Standard Certification verifies that a product has met organic standards throughout its journey from raw material to finished product. When a product is certified to OCS standards, OCS works with producers to ensure a final product contains the accurate amount of a given organically grown material.

Source: https://www.soilassociation.org/certification/fashion-textiles/types-of-certification/ocs-textiles-certification/

Ethical Trading Initiative (ETI)

The ETI has a very simple mission: to protect workers' rights in global supply chains.

The Ethical Trading Initiative adheres to nine base code provisions: Employment is freely chosen; Freedom of association and the right to collective bargaining are respected; Working conditions are safe and hygienic; Child labor shall not be used; Living wages are paid; Working hours are not excessive; No discrimination is practiced; Regular employment is provided; and No harsh or inhumane treatment is allowed.

Source: https://www.ethicaltrade.org

B Corporation

B Corporation is a new type of corporation which uses the power of business to solve social and environmental problems. Certified B Corporation businesses are unlike traditional responsible businesses because they meet comprehensive and transparent social and environmental performance standards, institutionalize stakeholder interests, and build collective voice through the power of a unifying brand.

Source: https://bcorporation.net

Sourcemap

Sourcemap.com supports sustainable decision-making through their platform for supply-chain transparency, where producers share detailed information about their processes with their buyers and their buyers' buyers, all the way to the end consumer. A Sourcemap Ecolabel points to information on a product's components and their origins, as well as optional environmental and social footprints.

Source: http://www.sourcemap.com

Cotton made in Africa

Cotton made in Africa is an initiative of the Aid by Trade Foundation (AbTF) that helps African smallholder cotton farmers in Africa to improve their living conditions.

Source: http://www.cottonmadeinafrica.org/en/

Responsible Down Standard

The Responsible Down Standard is an independent, voluntary global standard, which means that companies can choose to certify their products to the RDS, even if there's no legislation requiring them to do so. The RDS was developed and revised over three years, with the input of animal welfare groups, industry experts, brands, and retailers. The standard recognizes and rewards the best practices in animal welfare.

Responsible Wool Standard

The Responsible Wool Standard is an independent, voluntary standard. On farms, the certification ensures that sheep are treated with respect to their Five Freedoms and also ensures best practices in the management and protection of the land. Through the processing stages, certification ensures that wool from certified farms is properly identified and tracked.

People for the Ethical Treatment of Animals (PETA)

People for the Ethical Treatment of Animals (PETA) is the largest animal rights organization in the world. PETA focuses its attention on the four areas in which the largest numbers of animals suffer the most intensely for the longest periods of time: the food industry, the clothing trade, laboratories, and the entertainment industry. PETA works through public education, cruelty investigations, research, animal rescue, legislation, special events, celebrity involvement, and protest campaigns.

Fashion Revolution

Fashion Revolution is a global movement that wants to unite people and organizations to work together towards radically changing the way our clothes are sourced, produced, and consumed so that our clothing is made in a safe, clean, and fair way.

Who made your clothes? If you want to ensure that the garments were produced ethically, look for clothing brands that participate in the Fashion Revolution. This will mean that their manufacturing processes ensure fair wages to all employees, and production stages are fully traceable and transparent. Fashion Revolution doesn't yet provide an actual certification.

Source: https://www.fashionrevolution.org

Sustainable Apparel Coalition

The Sustainable Apparel Coalition is the apparel, footwear, and textile industry's leading alliance for sustainable production. The Sustainable Apparel Coalition's vision is of an apparel, footwear, and textiles industry that produces no unnecessary environmental harm and has a positive impact on the people and communities associated with its activities.

Source: https://apparelcoalition.org

Higg Index

Developed by the Sustainable Apparel Coalition, the Higg Index is a suite of tools that enables brands, retailers, and facilities of all sizes at every stage in their sustainability journey to accurately measure and score a company or product's sustainability performance. The Higg Index delivers a holistic overview that empowers businesses to make meaningful improvements that protect the well-being of factory workers, local communities, and the environment.

Source: https://apparelcoalition.org/the-higg-index/

Ecolabel Index

Ecolabel index 107 Ecolabels for the apparel industry's local and global certifications.

Source: http://www.ecolabelindex.com/ecolabels/?st=category,textiles

Outdoor Industry Association

The Outdoor Industry Association is a membership-driven trade organization for the outdoor industry. In collaboration with our members, we're a force for the industry in recreation and trade policy, sustainable business innovation, and increasing outdoor participation.

Source: https://outdoorindustry.org

Textile Exchange

Textile Exchange is a global non-profit that works closely with our members to drive industry transformation in preferred fibers, integrity and standards, and responsible supply networks.

Source: http://textileexchange.org

NSF Global Traceable Down Standard (Global TDS)

The NSF Global Traceable Down Standard establishes a framework for a down supply chain, animal welfare, and traceable-content claims assurance program. The standard includes criteria for animal welfare and prohibits the practices of force-feeding and live plucking. It also defines traceability requirements, from parent farm to factory, to ensure that compliant down is the only down material used in finished, certified goods.

Source: http://www.nsf.org/newsroom/global-traceable-down-standard

NewMerino

NewMerino is an independent and single-focused organization with the goal to make it easy for retail brands to establish a transparent supply chain of verified merino, with full traceability to responsibly managed farms operating to internationally recognized animal welfare and land-management standards.

Source: https://newmerino.com.au

> Buy less, choose well, make it last.
> Quality rather than quantity:
> That is true sustainability.
> If people only bought beautiful things rather than rubbish,
> we wouldn't have climate change!
>
> – Vivienne Westwood

15.5 Sustainability Tasks

1. Decide on a sustainability strategy—what will you focus on?

2. Incorporate sustainability in your brand values.

3. Decide on USP for your brand.

4. Decide on sustainability design rules for collection and styles.

5. Make garment-standards list.

6. Decide on supplier standards.

7. Decide on manufacturer standards.

8. Decide on material criteria.

9. Make a garment life-span plan.

10. Decide on recyclability standards.

11. Make a responsible logistics setup/plan.

12. Create a packaging and presentation plan.

13. Make product-care standards.

16.
Sales

16.1 Sell It!

Sell it to your target customer

Once you have your salesman samples and your story ready, it's time to sell. Either you sell it yourself or you get a salesperson on board to do it for you. Selling goes hand in hand with marketing, and it should be integrated in everything you do. Let's take a look at the most common ways of selling your product.

Wholesale

This is the traditional way of selling your garments, where you get help from a retailer with an already-established customer base. They'll take a big chunk of your margins, but they can probably reach a larger audience quicker than you can. Hopefully you've checked out some stores where you really want to have your brand, and where your target customer is a shopper. A good way to meet potential retailers is to exhibit at targeted fairs. You get to merchandise your garments in your own space, which helps to tell your story. The trick is to be proactive. Contact retailers well in advance of the fair and invite them to your booth. Make sure to book as many appointments with them as possible. By the way, when preparing for exhibiting at a fair, remember to bring a full-length mirror. People want to see themselves when trying on your samples.

When you're not showing at fairs, you should pack your product samples in garment bags and invite yourself to the retailers. Hustle your brand into the busy buyers' schedules and give them a private presentation.

Schedule buyers' meetings if you have your own showroom.

Agents and distributors

It can be time-consuming and hard work to sell your products to retailers. Especially if you're small or trying to expand into new markets. One option is to enlist the help of agents or distributors. Agents know the market and help you find retailers. They help you sell the products and take a commission for that. They're not involved in delivery or after-service. Distributors, on the other hand, buy the products directly from you and distribute them into the market. They also take care of after-sales service.

Consignment

Consignment is a bit tricky. The only time we would recommend selling your products on commission is if you have products in stock and need to move them out of the warehouse. The store is not really responsible for your products, the shop doesn't buy the products, and what doesn't get sold is shipped back to you. In a way, you just rent the shop floor and pay a commission. The advantage is that you get to test the market and your product.

Online—Direct to consumer

We're all aware that selling online is increasingly popular. It's understandable that companies are finding new ways to reach end consumers. Selling direct to consumer has some advantages: you have a bigger margin, which you can reinvest in your business; you can afford to use better materials and higher-quality production; you get the advantage of having direct contact with customers. No one knows your brand better than you, and no one can answer questions about your brand and products better than you. You get instant feedback and can feel the pulse of your business quickly.

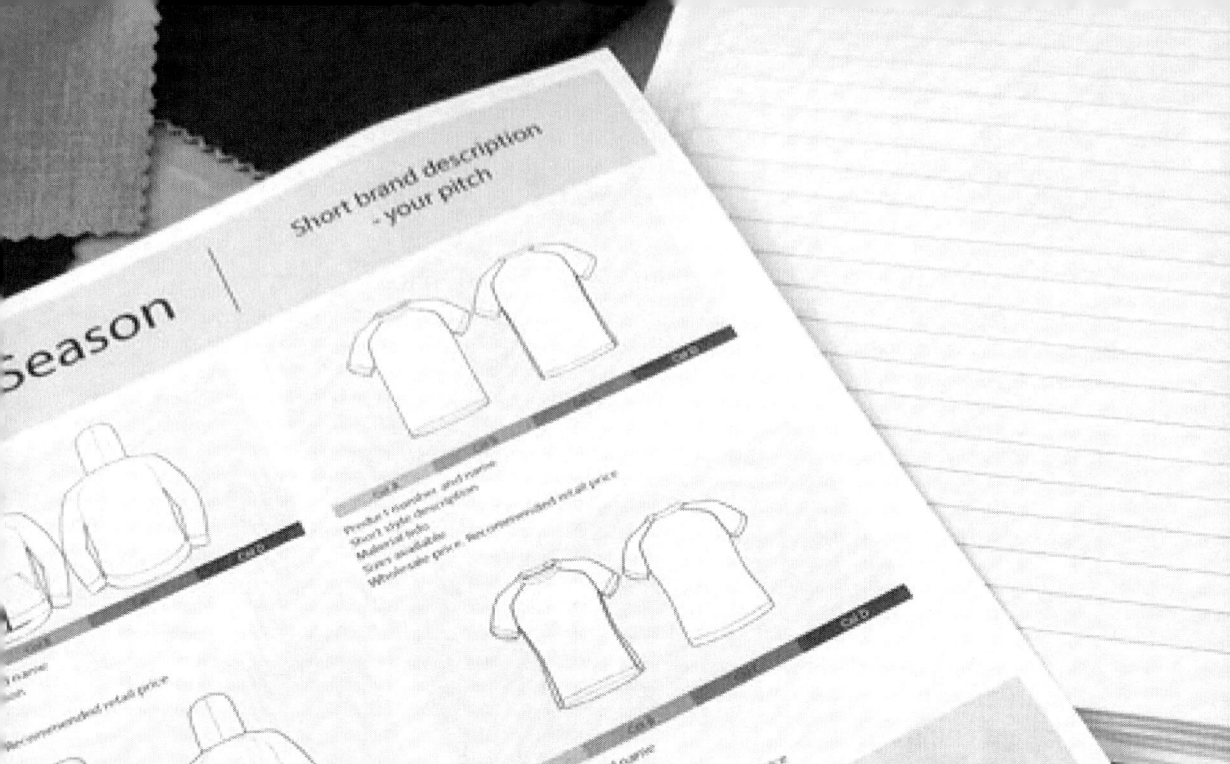

16.2 What Is A Line Sheet And Why Do You Need One?

If your business model includes retail, you'll eventually have to present your collection to buyers, for wholesale and retail purposes. Buyers will need all the relevant product information in order to place an order. Together with the line sheet, you'll provide your pitch, an order form, and your lookbook. The lookbook should show your spirit, the vibe of your products and brand. The line sheet should make the buying job as smooth as possible. The order form should always be present so that you're ready to do business.

What is a line sheet?

The actual line sheet is a document with your entire line information, delivery dates, and contact info. This document should be easy to read, understandable, and contain all the product information. It should make buying—and subsequently selling—easy. If your collection is somewhat larger, then consider grouping your products into product groups. Generally, the most expensive product category goes first. There should also be a logical price structure—and here, too, place the most expensive product first.

Here's the list of things that should be incorporated in the line sheet:
- Your company logo, on every page of the document
- Your brand's story (short version)
- Season (Autumn/Winter, Spring/Summer), on every page of the document
- Style name and number
- Style description
- Style drawing or clear photograph, preferably front and back, plus the most important details
- Sizes available
- Material information, preferably with material swatches
- Color information, written and visual, preferably with Pantone number
- Delivery dates and order cutoff dates, on every page of the document
- Order minimums (if you have any, per style), on every page of the document
- Wholesale price and recommended retail price
- Sales agent's contact information, on every page of the document
- Mark NEW for new styles
- Mark BEST SELLER for your best-selling styles
- Payment Terms: e.g., full up front, 50 percent up front and 50 percent after delivery, or 30 days after delivery

Keep every page as clean as you can; some buyers want to take notes about every product, and they need some space to do that. Plus, a cluttered line sheet is just going to be confusing and hard to work with.

Bear in mind that some buyers won't be able to meet with you in person to see the collection. This means they'll have to depend on the information in your line sheet to make a decision as to whether to buy your line or not. The more details and clear content you present, the better. BUT it should be visually appealing and in sync with your brand's graphical profile! Buyers usually have many line sheets and order forms, and you want yours to stand out.

Sensitive information

This information is extremely sensitive and important for you and your buyers, so don't hand the line sheet out to anyone who's not serious about buying your line. Your business "secrets" and pricing strategies are in the line sheet and can easily be copied. When handing over the line sheet, you should also include an order form. You don't just want them to see what you have to offer—you want them to BUY your collection. Have organized, pre-filled order forms to make the ordering process as smooth as possible. Nailing this will greatly improve your chances of getting orders in.

Be consistent!

Getting an audience is hard.
Sustaining an audience is hard.
It demands a consistency of
thought, of purpose, and of
action over a long period
of time.

-Bruce Springsteen

16.3 What You Need In Your Sales Kit

Selling or pitching your brand and products can be highly rewarding. There will be instant recognition if the "audience" likes what you're selling and if they get the concept.

To succeed with your sales presentation or pitch, either to your sales reps or a buyer, there are some things that need to be covered.

First, set the intention of the meeting. Decide what you want to achieve and then prepare—mentally and physically.

Intention

What is it EXACTLY that you're trying to achieve in this meeting? Are you trying to blow their minds with your unique concept and your particular way of designing your products, for example?

What outcome do you want to have achieved when you walk out the door? Do you want to have made a 100 percent connection with the buyer? Do you want to have the buyer place an order for a minimum of X dollars/euros?

> 90 percent of selling is conviction, and 10 percent is persuasion.
>
> *–Shiv Khera*

Mental preparation

- Know the store properly: what they offer, who their customer is, etc.
- Know the buyer's name and something personal to make it easier for you to get a good rapport.
- Know facts about the industry that you can share with the buyer—it'll give you an advantage and position you as an expert.
- Know the brand's story. Know what makes your brand unique.
- Tell a story about the production phase, or the inspiration behind your products, or why you picked that particular material.
- Know your target customer.
- Know the market you're trying to position yourself in. Who are the competitors and what advantage do you have over them?
- Know the products extremely well—including how they differentiate from the rest of the products in the market. Know all aspects in the product development, including design, materials, and manufacturing.

Physical preparation

- Bring your samples. Preferably steamed, clean, and with all the hangtags and right labels.
- Bring the collection line sheet containing product sketches or pictures, colorways, product info, material info, and fit of the garment.
- Bring a lookbook, if you have one.
- Prices: wholesale and recommended retail prices.
- Delivery dates.
- MOQ information.
- Business cards.
- Pen and Paper.

• Order form—physical or digital (iPad).

Selling can be daunting for some and extremely fun for others. However you find it, it should above all be educational. The more information you acquire from buyers or sales reps about your collection, the more you can improve for the next meeting and in the near future with coming collections.

> We miss 100 percent of the sales we don't ask for.
>
> *–Zig Ziglar*

16.4 Fourteen Ways To Secure More Orders

As an apparel entrepreneur you work incredibly hard on your collection. When it's finally done and you have your great-looking salesman samples in your hand, you should be extremely proud of your accomplishment. Congratulations—you've reached the halfway point. Wait—what? Yup, by "halfway point," we mean you still have the selling to do, getting the end consumer to want to buy your products. No orders = No income. And without sales, there is no business!

Secure more wholesale/retail orders

Here are some points to work on and to make sure you've ticked off before contacting buyers for a sales presentation.

1. Make sure you have a rock-solid concept that stands out. Prepare a clear presentation of your brand, to make buyers understand why your brand is different from others on the market.

2. Know your target customer. When you know who your end consumer is, where he/she shops and what other brands he/she is wearing, it's easier to define a list of stores to represent your brand.

3. Do extensive research on all the retailers you want to present your apparel brand to. The point of this is to make the buyer understand that you know their product offer and customer base and know your products will benefit the selection and ensure sales for the store.

4. Prepare before going to the sales presentation meeting. Have all the garments nicely in line, cleaned up and pressed. Have all the line sheets printed out, have neat lookbooks with you, have order forms and price lists printed. Have color and material swatches with you if needed. Wear some of your own apparel if suitable and be prepared. Know what to ask, what to say, and in what order. Leave information with the buyer so they can process what you've shown and take a decision. Make it easy for them.

5. Know your stuff! It doesn't matter if you have all the products and lookbooks, etc., if you don't know about your products. All of this should be so imprinted in your head that if someone woke you up in the middle of the night, you'd still make a kick-ass pitch!

   • What is the story of your brand?
   • Why is it so great?
   • What is the story with your products?
   • What materials are you using?
   • Why is the color story so fantastic?
   • How is the customer supposed to use your product?
   • Why is your fit so amazing compared to the competition's?
   • What about your quality makes the product so great?

6. Visit the buyers early in the buying period. This will increase your chances of clinching an order. If you present late, there's a risk the store already placed all their orders, and they don't have any money left to buy from you.

7. Ask questions and listen! If you're the one doing all the talking, it can be a bit overwhelming and your presentation will come across as "pitchy." Ask tons of questions about the store, customers, what they're missing, and what their customers are asking for. Be genuinely interested and take notes—this info will help you out later on. Plus, the buyer will feel acknowledged, seen, and heard.

8. Build trust by showing interest in the store way before you're ready to show your line. Show appreciation for the buyers, the store's offer, and the customer base. Be a fan—when the buyer knows you, trusts you, knows you like the store, you'll be in a completely different position when you're ready to do your sales presentation. The trust is there and the buyer will be only too pleased to look at your presentation.

9. Sell to the right store. Make sure you do your research and are aiming at the right store. For example, if your brand is high-end, don't try and sell it to an entry-price store. Don't waste your time and effort. Where is your target customer shopping? That's where you want to place your products.

10. Build a buzz around your brand and its product. Have proof of the hype and proudly mention this to the buyers. People want what other people want. Name-drop other great stores that are carrying your brand.

11. Talk and present to the decision-maker. There's no point in showing your brand to someone who can't take any decisions. You'll waste your time. Meet the buyer who's potentially going to place the order.

12. Be professional. Call, send information, visit them, do your great presentation, build the trust and all that stuff—but make sure you never go over the line to enter the PUSHY area. No one likes to feel forced. No one likes obnoxious salespeople. A salesperson/buyer relationship is like all relationships: it should be 50/50. Both of you should want it as much as the other.

13. Follow up. Buyers are busy people. The fact they didn't get back to you doesn't necessarily mean it's a NO. Respectfully follow up and see if they lack information, if there's more you can do to help in the decision process, etc. Half of the sales come from the follow-up.

14. Ask for the order. This is business. Give deadlines and time brackets for when the order should be placed, follow up, and ask for the order. Sometimes if you don't ask, you'll never know.

Even though you've done everything in your power, there's still a chance that buyers won't place an order. The most important is to walk out of the meeting with as many questions asked/answered as possible, so you know what to improve before the next time or before meeting another buyer

See this period as a learning opportunity, to learn as much as possible about customers, end consumers, and your brand. What's popular, what's not, what do they want more of?

Selling is hard work, but especially fun and rewarding when it's your own products. Review the 14 pointers in the list above before entering the sales phase, and you'll increase your chances for more placed orders.

16.5 Merchandising

When product-range planning, make sure the entire collection is well balanced, giving the customer a wide variety of products to pick from. If you sell retail, you'll not have the final say as to which products are chosen to be sold in a store. You'll have little control over the merchandising and how your products are exhibited in the stores. To better equip the buyers—and yourself if you want to run your own store with great merchandising—it's good to have a plan for how your collection should be put together. You want the collection to keep its core cohesiveness and to have balance in texture, color and styling, so making a merchandising plan could help both your brand and the retail buyers.

One great tip is to appeal to the five senses: sight, touch, sound, smell, and taste. If you succeed in doing this, it'll give your customers a much more memorable experience.

Sight

First of all, it should be visually appealing for the customer, drawing them in with color, proportions, textures, pictures—basically everything that can entice a person's visual interest. Which pictures will speak to them? Which outfits can be put together on a mannequin to create an interesting look? Which color stories can most bring out your collection's story? Which products should be highlighted with extra lighting? What you're doing here is making the customer curious, wanting to get closer and touch the garment, try it on, and finally buy it.

Touch

After you've enticed the customer with interesting visuals, they'll want to try on your products. Qualitative materials with a nice hand will give you a higher chance of a try-on. If the materials are nasty, no one will want to try on the garment, even less buy it.

Sound

A totally quiet store creeps people out. A crazy-loud store stresses people out and has them leave. To improve customers' in-store experience, think about what sounds you can feature, for a more inclusive feeling. What tunes or sound would suit your collection and enhance the mood in the store?

Smell

Smell is directly connected to memory and emotions, and stores try to trigger some of the emotions with different scents. How should your store smell? What emotions do you want to trigger in your customers?

Taste

Obviously taste is more applicable if you sell groceries—but who says you can't take advantage of taste in your store? Many retailers have coffee shops in their stores these days. Nothing beats the aroma of fresh coffee. You can sell other eatables that relate to and complement your apparel brand.

The rule of three

When it comes to merchandising, you can also apply the rule of three or grouping. Which three products or outfits can be placed together to make a great setting? When putting three mannequins together, for example, try to have them in three different outfits but keep them in the same vibe and setting. People like to have several choices—that's why grouping or the rule of three is so effective. It puts the product in perspective, and directs the eyes to look at several things.

Control the merchandising

As a brand, you want to control the way your products are displayed in stores. You don't just want them hung at the far back of the store. A good idea is to give the store visual directions for how to merchandise and display your products. You'll be perceived as professional and competent—which in turn will increase the likelihood that your products get exhibited nicely. Make a sample display in your studio, take a picture of it and hand it over to the retailers.

Color plays a vital role in merchandising. The eye is drawn to color and a pop of color can lift an entire natural-tone collection. Sometimes it's good to just add one pop of color in your range just for the sake of merchandising. It's going to make the whole visual interesting and dimensional.

Provide the store with point-of-sale material such as signs, pictures, backdrops, etc. This can be an added cost for you as a brand but it can be extremely informative in the store, especially if the store is fairly big and you can't train the sellers yourself on your collection.

Another little trick is the pyramid. This refers to placing a product as a center piece and having other products placed below it. It can be done, for example, on a table or a shelf. For pyramids it helps if your garments can be folded neatly and nicely.

With all this information to think about, it's easy to comprehend how important it is to have a great product-range plan that takes merchandising into consideration from the start. It's equally as important to think about the merchandising during the design phase, when you choose materials, and when you price your items. All pieces should have their own place in the range, and should complement each other.

16.6 Running An Online Store

Why you should sell online

We all know that selling online is becoming increasingly popular. An estimated 1.66 billion users made an online purchase in 2017. Data shows that worldwide e-commerce sales will reach €/$4.5 trillion in 2021. Most brands have their own online store today, complementing their brick-and-mortar stores. The traditional way to sell clothes is to work with retailers, distributors or agents. Retailers have their specific location and established customer base, and they sell the products for you as well as handle returns. But they also take a big slice of the pie, usually around half of the product price.

Selling online has several advantages:
- Customers can shop 24/7, when and from wherever they want. There's no need to go to a physical store. More and more purchases are made from mobile devices.
- Customers can read up about the brand concept, the clothes, and check reviews.
- You can interact more easily with your customers without an intermediary between you.

- You can increase your margins or make higher-quality garments for a lower end-customer price. You don't have to pay the retailers.
- You can market-test products more efficiently, thus optimizing your collection.

What's the catch?

If selling online is so great, why isn't everyone doing it, ditching the retailers? Well, because the fact you have an awesome e-commerce site doesn't automatically mean you'll sell. Since you don't have the retailers to do it, YOU have to sell your products.

You'll need to put in a lot of effort to ensure customers find your e-commerce site and buy your awesome products. Most e-commerce businesses pour money into online advertising such as Facebook Ads and Google AdWords. These calculate the advertising costs for each order placed on their site. The fact that you only sell online doesn't mean it won't cost you anything. There are millions of sites out there, and you need to put in the work to let your customers know you exist.

Also, you'll have to handle all the orders yourself, or hire someone to do it for you. How many products do you have to sell to make a profit? Well, you have to pack and send all those orders. The customer service and handling of returns will also fall to you.

How will customers find you?

There are three ways your customers can find you:

1. Brand recognition
The first is through brand recognition. Customers already know about your brand and find you directly online, by searching for your brand. They ask for, look for, or are told about your e-commerce store. This obviously requires significant marketing work from your side.

2. SEO
The second way is through search engine optimization. People search online for topics related to your business and find you that way. If you're really good at SEO, the customer will see your page at the top of search results without you paying for it.

3. Paid advertising

The third way to get noticed is through paid advertising. Use Facebook Ads or Google AdWords, for example, and create an ad to be shown along related search results. The ad links to your site and you pay every time someone clicks on your ad. It's not hard to understand why Google is doing so great.

Running an e-commerce site is a great way to get closer to your customers and increase your margins. But don't underestimate the effort needed to run it and drive traffic to it. The fact you have an online store doesn't mean customers will find it. There are no "rules," and testing different things to see what works best is vital. The most important thing for your website is to keep the customer there as long as possible, to entertain and draw them in to your fantastic world.

> Just having satisfied customers isn't enough anymore.
> If you really want a booming business,
> you have to create raving fans.
>
> *–Ken Blanchard*

Thirty-three steps to build a great online store

Thinking through these 33 points will dramatically increase your chances of securing returning, happy, buying customers.

1. Make a good first impression
Human attention span is very short. You only have about seven seconds to present your offer and answer visitors' typical questions: "What is the site about? Is it interesting to me? What am I supposed to do?" Make your website clear, avoid clutter, and present your information in such a way that your visitor stays longer than seven seconds.

2. Great photos
Have great photos, both product images of your clothes and lifestyle photos that reinforce your brand story. People typically remember more of what they see than what they read, so images are very important.

Photos should be high quality, to make a good impression. Remember that you need permission to publish all your photos. Agree with your photographer as to what you can do with the images.

3. Ease of navigation
It should be easy for visitors to find what they're looking for. Help them to navigate your site, and be clear about what you want them to do. If you don't know how to build up your navigation, take a look at a large selection of modern webshops and see how they've done it. If you then set up your navigation in a similar way, your users will most likely find their way round intuitively since it works like most other online stores.

4. Ease of search function to find what they're looking for
Make your offer easy to find. If you're selling jackets, make it easy for the user to find your jackets and the information about them. Preferably with as few clicks as possible.

5. Show frequent customers what's new
Point out garments that are new and recently added to the online store. Your frequent visitors will appreciate this function. They can directly check what's new without browsing your entire site. In general, update the site regularly to make it more interesting. You want to show that things are happening and moving forward with your apparel brand.

6. Stand out
Make your e-commerce site interesting for your customers. Show them why you're different and what's so good about your apparel brand. Customers won't have any reason to choose your online store if it looks like all the others. Bring forward your unique selling points and integrate them in your content.

7. A great "About" page
Around 70 percent of visitors take a look at the "About" page. People don't just buy products—they buy you, your story, and your brand. Make a great "About Us" page and convey honestly who you are and what your clothing brand is all about.

8. Product recommendations
Display product recommendations based on the products the user views. Take a look at your data and see which garments and accessories are commonly bought together. Based on this information, you can

easily recommend complementary garments your customers may be interested in. A great way to up-sell.

9. Show your top sellers
It's a psychological phenomenon that people typically want what other people want. For this reason, it's a good idea to display your top-selling garments. This adds a layer of trust, telling the user the clothes must be great if other people are buying them. Like the feature for suggesting product recommendations, this one usually comes with the e-commerce system.

10. Ease of checkout
The checkout process should be as quick and efficient as possible. Users don't want to go through additional, unnecessary checkout steps. You need to find the perfect balance here, making the checkout as smooth as possible, while ensuring that the user agrees to everything and doesn't buy something by mistake.

11. Shipping alternatives
Offer different shipping methods, to meet all customer demands. Can you offer same-day delivery or pick-up points for your garments? If you're a small business and don't have any large account discount with a courier, you can use this to your advantage: you're not bound to only offer one courier, but can offer many options.

12. Ask for feedback
One advantage of selling online direct to customer is that you can communicate directly to them without an intermediary player. Take the opportunity to ask your customers for feedback—this will enable you to improve your online store, offer, and apparel brand.

13. Customer service
See to it that you have great support in place to answer customers' questions about your clothes, products, delivery, returns, etc. You can have an FAQ section, live chat, phone and email support. This part is extremely important if you want to be in business for the long run and build that all-important trust with your customers. Superfans will be loyal and spread the word about your brand.

14. Secure payment options
Integrate secure and trustworthy payment options. Which payment system would you feel comfortable using? Can your payment system

accept all the major and popular cards for your target markets? Your website will need an SSL certificate to make payments secure.

15. Localization

People prefer to use sites that are customized to their region. Can the user get your website in their own language? Can they shop in their currency? Localizing your website makes the user experience better and clearer. Can you offer a local phone number for support? There are solutions—Skype, for example—that give you the option of having local phone numbers even though you don't have a physical presence there. Remember that even two different English-speaking regions can need localization; in one place they may call it a zip code, and in another a postcode. Make your customers feel at home.

16. Detailed photos

A picture says more than 1000 words. Present photos showing the details and treatments for your garments. Show more than just the front and back. Show close-ups of your pockets, hems, inside, etc. Make sure colors are displayed accurately on the screen.

17. Speed

Your site needs to load quickly. No one wants to wait for a slow site. You'll lose your customers' interest if the page is too slow. Upgrade your Web host package and make adjustments so it loads quickly.

18. Sizing charts

One disadvantage of an online store compared to its physical counterpart is that customers can't try the clothes on. To mitigate this, you should present easy-to-read sizing charts showing all relevant measurements depending on size, and how to measure them yourself. To further help your customer, clearly state how tall the model in the picture is, and the garment size he/she is wearing.

19. Mobile-device-friendly

You'll be left behind if you have an online store that isn't mobile-friendly today. A large part of all online sales are made on mobile devices, so make sure your site works well on a mobile device—both smartphones and tablets.

20. Description

Provide descriptive information for all your garments. Tell the customer about the materials, design, and special features. Educate the user about your choices. Tell them why the garment is fantastic and about the treatments that enable it to be so. Don't just state "DWR treatment"—tell them also why they need it. Don't assume they understand the design; people can't read your mind. Tell them why your material choice is favorable. You might opt to have a whole section in your online store only talking about your materials.

21. Return policy
Build trust by having a great return policy. Present it clearly on the site so customers know how it works. Think about offering free return shipping of your garments. The advantages with this are that customers will love it and it can boost your conversion rates. Many customers are used to free return shipping and will expect it. If you don't offer it, they'll see this as a negative. The disadvantage of offering free return shipping is that it'll cost you, since you have to pay the courier for it. It can also promote a shopping behavior where the customer orders products they don't really need and don't intend to keep. Do the calculations and test what works for you.

22. Packaging
When it comes to packaging, there are a few things you need to consider. First of all, is your packaging secure, and will your products reach the customer undamaged? You also need to look at it from a sustainability perspective. Consider the environmental impact all your wrapping, bags, and cartons will have. Your packaging should of course look good and represent your brand values and profile. How would it look if someone made an unboxing video with your product? Would you be proud of it? Add something extra in the package to give an unexpected positive first impression that they'll talk about. How does your package look if someone puts it on Instagram?

23. Terms and Conditions
Your terms and conditions should be easy to find on your site and should clearly tell the customer what rights they have. Don't hide in complicated legal language. Look at other brands for inspiration if you don't know where to start.

24. Care instructions
You need to have a section on your site telling the customer how to best take care of their clothes. You know the materials you've chosen and the construction of the garments. Describe how the customer can wash, iron, and handle the clothes to ensure they last as long as possible while having minimal environmental impact.

25. Branding

Your online store needs to represent your apparel brand in the best possible way. The look should make the customer associate with your brand values. It's not only the look you should think about, but also your story. Your website is the place where you can reinforce the story behind your brand and what it's all about.

26. Privacy policy

Today, with laws like GDPR, you need to be on top of how you're handling personal information. Explain how and why you're using personal information and how you do this with cookies. Put your privacy policy where the user can easily find it, and give them the option to agree with your terms as soon as they enter your site.

27. User-friendly

Create the online store with the user in mind. Create a logical structure, and avoid cluttering the site with unnecessary information. Neat and clean helps the user to navigate. Try to create actions that require as few clicks as possible.

28. SEO strategy

Before you even start with your online store, you need to read up on search engine optimization (SEO) or consult with an expert. To have the best effect and to be found on search engines, you need to have an SEO strategy and implement it from the start. Don't leave it all to chance. SEO takes time, so don't waste your time by not implementing it.

29. Have a great blog

A blog is a fantastic way to communicate with your target audience and show them you're an expert in your area of apparel. Create a schedule, and regularly post new content relevant to your clothing brand. Make it interesting and show them who you really are. Honesty goes a long way. This is your chance to educate your customer—e.g., tell them what choices are important from a sustainability aspect. And you'll of course offer clothes making it easier to make those choices. :)

30. Test, track and iterate

Strive to continuously improve your online-store user experience. Test different solutions. Track and analyze user behavior. See what the best options are and adjust accordingly.

31. Email
Ask for permission to email your visitors, and then regularly update them about new arrivals and other relevant information. Email marketing is a great way for you to interact with your audience while promoting your brand and increasing your sales.

32. Technical platform
Choose an e-commerce platform that suits your needs. Start by listing all your requirements for your online store, and look around for one that corresponds to those. Your needs will differ based on whether you're a one-person clothing brand packaging your garments yourself, or a larger brand split in different locations with external stock handling. Online stores may appear quite similar when visiting online, but there are tremendous differences under the surface. If you want a quick and easy solution that enables you to focus on other things than running a website, we recommend you take a look at Shopify.

33. Have an awesome product
This is your foundation. Make an awesome product that speaks for itself. Your garments need to be outstanding if you want all of the above points to matter at all. Put your products first. Focus on getting your collection right, meeting your high standards. Once the sale is made, this is what will keep your brand alive and moving forward.

FACTS:

Using videos on landing pages can increase conversions by 86%.

–DSIM, 2017

It's seven times more expensive to get a new customer than retain an existing one.

–Invesp, 2017

67% of millennials prefer to shop online rather than in the store.

–BigCommerce, 2017

16.7 Sales Tasks

1. Be clear in what you offer.

2. Make a buyers contact list.

3. Organize your sales kit.

4. Present your collection to buyers.

5. Ask for and receive orders.

6. Make a merchandising plan.

7. Create an online strategy.

17.
Order

ORDER FORM

CUSTOMER		Date:	
[Company]			
[Contact Person]			
[Address]		APPAREL	
[Org.no]		ENTREPRENEURSHIP	
[VAT no]			
[Phone]			
[Email]			

SHIPPING ADDRESS (IF DIFFERENT)

[Shipping Address]

PRODUCT	PRICE	QUANTITY			TOTAL QTY	TOTAL PRIC
Women's Styles		S	M	L		
001 Wstyle 1					0	
002 Wstyle 2					0	
003 Wstyle 3					0	
004 Wstyle 4					0	
005 Wstyle 5					0	
006 Wstyle 6					0	
Men's Styles		M	L	XL		

17.1 Receive Sales Orders and Place Production Orders

You've given your all in the sales phase. You've met with buyers, perhaps exhibited at fairs, and connected with all the right people you'd planned to connect with, to show and sell your collection. Good job—it's a really exhausting, very intense period. It's very common to have to show your collection a couple of times before buyers place an order. It can be a good idea to have different packages for them, which you pick out in advance, to best represent your collection. Pick your strongest pieces, to ensure you show the range and diversity of your brand.

The typical sell/order period

Fall/Winter collection
Show collection and sales: January, February, and March. Close sales in March and start to place orders for production materials.

Spring/Summer collection
Show collection and sales: August, September, and October. Close sales at the end of October. Orders for production materials are placed in November.

Typical Sales & Order Periods

Spring / Summer

January	February	March	April	May	June
Show	Show	Close	Place		
Collection	Collection	Sales	Production		
			&		
			Material Orders		

July	August	September	October	November	December
	Show	Show	Close	Place	
	Collection	Collection	Sales	Production	
				&	
				Material Orders	

Fall / Winter

Bulk production

Before kicking off the full bulk production, have the factory send you a preproduction sample so you can check that the latest changes have been made.

It can be tricky to juggle the orders received with the minimum quantity orders for materials and factory capacity. You'll probably have to drop some of the styles that received low orders. It's a risk to produce styles that buyers don't believe in. If the orders are less than your manufacturer's MOQ, you'll almost always pay a surcharge. Try to buy in quantities as close to your orders as you can, otherwise you'll be sitting on stock that you can't get rid of—and that means money locked up that you could have used elsewhere. You'll have to make your own estimations to cover the webshop sales. You don't want to have your stuff on sale. At one point you'll probably have to, but for the sake of your brand, the less sales you have, the better—it'll cheapen your brand.

Communication

A critical point throughout this period is communication. Never assume anything! Get as much information as possible, preferably by email, and have it confirmed—by you or the other party. Make sure you communicate if there are any delays. If any problems occur, lay them on the table as soon as possible. And do status checks with your suppliers/manufacturers from time to time if you haven't heard anything in a while.

Terms of agreement

It's advisable to have a written agreement, called Terms of Agreement or TOA in place with your suppliers/manufacturers describing their undertaking. In addition to outlining what is to be produced and when, it should also have a quality section. This section lists your agreed level of production quality and how to handle defects and deviations from the agreement. In most cases you'll never need to look at the agreement again—but if you do, you'll be glad you agreed on how to handle every situation when you were still happy with each other.

As with everything in business, it's all about the relationships you build. All good relationships are built with time, respect, honesty, and kindness. Share ideas and advice with each other, set targets together so that you know and trust that you're in it for the long run. You want to grow *together*.

Without having a goal it's difficult to score.

–Paul Arden

17.2 Order Tasks

1. Perform customer background check.

2. Get signed orders.

18.
Shipping

CHINA SHIPPING LINE

CHINA SHIPP

18.1 Time To Ship

The bulk production's ready, your stuff looks amazing, the world is anxiously waiting for your collection—it's time to ship. First, you need to transport the garments from the manufacturer to your office or warehouse and then to your customers. Take a look at your agreement with the supplier to see what's included in the deal and what you have to sort out yourself. If your price is FOB, then there's no shipping included, but if your price is COGS then the shipping cost is already included. When arranging your transport, talk to different logistics companies and see who suits you best. Set up a business account and negotiate your price. As always, you get a better price when you have larger volumes, so if you're small it'll be more costly.

Shipping from the factory

If your production is based in Asia and there are delays in production, then you'll have to fly the garments over, to compensate for the lost time. Shipping in containers by ship is the usual route; it's cheaper but obviously takes longer. Air transport is more expensive, but faster.

To avoid tolls and expensive shipping of materials across the planet, it's clever to produce your garments in the continent where you'll sell them.

If you sell in the EU, the ideal solution is to have your materials and garments produced in the EU. This is also very important from the sustainability standpoint. Another sustainability factor you need to consider is the type of packing you'll opt for. Will you go for polybags or biodegradable? Recycled paper boxes or ordinary ones? How will you ship the garments—hanging or folded? Garments delivered hanging will of course look very nice; optimized boxes containing folded and packed garments are better for the environment.

Shipping to customers

Once you've received your awaited garments, you have to distribute them to your customers. You'll need to repackage the garments to fit the orders from your retailers. If you're small and only work with local retailers, you can drive out your orders yourself. If you intend to sell it all online, then there's a bit more to think about: first, you need the picking section, where someone repacks every outbound order. Don't forget that this is a big part of your brand image. How should you pack it? What first impression do you want to give to your end customer? You also need to consider who your logistics partners are. Large market players are usually tied to one logistics partner in order to obtain volume discounts. The advantage of being small is that you probably don't have any volume discount and can use different partners. This means you can offer your customers the additional service of a choice of transport options. Are you going to offer free shipping? If you do, remember that you still have to pay for it, so make sure it's included in your price calculations.

Returns

There will be returns when working with apparel. How can you make this easy for your customers? Talk to your retailers about how to handle this. If you're running an e-commerce business, you can include preprinted return forms.

To summarize: It's important to think about all aspects of shipping and how you can make it easy and hassle-free. Make sure not to underestimate these costs, and be sure to review them to secure the best arrangements possible.

18.2 Shipping Tasks

1. Research and find logistics partners.

2. Arrange shipping from the factory to your warehouse.

3. Arrange shipping to your customers and end consumers.

19.
Marketing

19.1 What's Your Story?

Marketing

Marketing should be embedded throughout the whole company, in every person who works there, and in everything you do. Answering emails and phone calls is marketing; sending packages is marketing; talking to a customer in-store is marketing; the pictures on the website are marketing—EVERYTHING a company does is marketing.

What should be "labeled" as marketing is the communication. And the communication should be honest and straightforward, no bullshit and no excuses. Just tell it as it is! The customer will believe in what you say and in what you'll eventually sell to them. In today's Internet world, information is easy to find. You'd better have a clean business. Let them hear your true voice, from the heart—your ins and outs, your ups and downs, your successes, your failures, and your struggles. You're only human—and so are your customers. They'll want the real thing, not the strained, artificial version. You don't have to come up with stories to tell —everything you do is a story in its own right; no one's ever done exactly what you've done. Your outlook and the values you live by are your own—bring these into your brand and share them with your customers. Sharing your honesty in this way will win you more true long-term customers than anything else.

Facebook, Instagram, YouTube, Pinterest, LinkedIn, Snapchat, Medium, Reddit, etc. are all free to use and there's no restrictions. The only restriction here is you. Let your creativity flow, and start sharing the story of your brand with the world. Let them know about what's great with the product, the process, the materials, and the birth of your idea. Anything you want to share will be interesting to *someone*. Take pictures of your drawings, materials, mood board; interview people; interview yourself; make small movies about your product, or about the product's raison d'être. Storytelling is a powerful marketing tool; an authentic, heartfelt story will ensure your customers forge a strong connection with your brand.

You already know who your intended customer is. Talk directly to them. Post things on the sites where your customers hang out. Keep them in the loop and let them become part of your brand.

Since the Internet is flooded with information, of course you want what you publish to get noticed by your audience—so make sure your ideas stand out somehow and are original.

Focus on making the best product possible.
If your product is crap, it won't matter how great your marketing is.

Your PRODUCT is your marketing.

Let the world know

When starting out your business, you asked yourself the difficult question: "What's different about my brand?" Your story should be about why you and your products are unique. Let the world know why your products are so great and what makes them different from those of the competition. Make the story easy to understand and stick to it. Communicate it as soon as you get the chance. You never know who your next customers or messengers will be. They'll help spread the word.

19.2 Customer Profiles

Avatar, customer persona, profiling, target group, intended customer avatar—they all refer to the same thing: *your target customer*. By identifying your target customer for your apparel brand, it'll be easier to design, strategize your segments, and develop an effective marketing plan.

A customer profile is a detailed description of your ideal customer. You can have one or several profiles, but you should never have more than three. If you have too many, you'll lose focus. Bear in mind that a customer profile represents a *group* of people, a generalization and not an actual description of each and every one of your customers.

How can you sell to your customers if you don't know them?

The goal is to know exactly who your customer is, what they do, where they live, how they shop, etc. The better you know your customers, the more effectively you'll be able to reach them and give them what they want.

This information will help you in your range planning, in the product design and development phases, and in your marketing and sales pitches. The thing is, with the right customer profile, you won't need to pitch that hard; you'll know exactly what your customers want and give it to them.

Everybody in the company should know exactly who these "personas" are, to ensure you're speaking the same "language" in all departments of your apparel business.

Customer profiling in three segments

Let's split the profiling into three segments:

Demographical, Psychological and Beneficial info.

Here are some criteria to question, determine, and check:

Demographical info:
• Gender
• Age
• Marital Status
• Education
• Job
• Income
• Religion
• Country
• Living environment

Psychological info:
• Lifestyle
• Interests
• Values
• Style
• Vacation and free time
• Shopping behavior and motive
• Online and offline shopping preferences
• Goals and aspirations

Beneficial info:
- Which social networks do they prefer?
- Where do they consume their news?
- What challenges do they face?
- What are their pain points?
- How do they decide to spend their money?
- What would make your customers recommend your brand to their friends?
- Best ways to reach your customer

Conclusion

To sum this up: If you want a successful apparel business, you need to have clear customer profiling. There's no right or wrong way of doing it and your customer profiling will be completely unique, based on your mission, values, and business goals. These documents should be alive and change along the way, together with your business. You'll have to adapt to the market and tweak and make iterations as you go. Have these profiles printed out and visible somewhere on a board. Go back to them often, whenever you introduce a new product or segment, create a marketing campaign, or a sales presentation. This will make certain decisions easier along your entrepreneurial journey.

> When the customer comes first, the customer will last.
>
> *–Robert Half*

19.3 Stand Out—Differentiate Your Brand From The Competition

Some of our brand-building customers worry a great deal about this topic. Some brands should worry *more* about this topic and do something about it. The market is crowded out there and it's vital that you differentiate your brand and stand out. Too many companies waste their energy checking out their competition. This can be a good thing in moderation—mostly to see what you should NOT do. When a company does their thing and you end up copying their selection, product, marketing strategy or whatever, you'll ALWAYS end up as number two.

Here are some points to think about and implement, to avoid getting trapped in the "copy and paste" mentality in business:

1. First of all, you have to decide to be different, in order for the rest of the points to make sense. Decide from the get-go that you and your brand should be different from the competition.

2. Show YOU to the world. Let people know who YOU are, and what YOU look like. People like people and therefore connect better to brands that have a face and a person behind them.

3. Tell your and your brand's story: how it came to be, how it all started. Let your customers in—talk about the process and the product development. People remember stories better than facts.

4. Get inspiration from unusual places. In addition to the popular blogs, websites, and magazines that designers follow, try to look in unusual places for inspiration, places that only you find interesting and applicable to your brand. Then mix all that inspiration together and pour it into your brand.

5. Follow your intuition. Only you will know when decisions feel right or wrong. Your brain or other people's recommendations and suggestions might be logical, but only you know in your soul what is right for you and your brand. Take note of hunches you get from your intuition and follow them. Let this guide you in the directions and decisions you take.

6. What do you stand for? What is important to you and what do you believe in? Figure it out and share it with your customers.

7. Keep your ear to the ground. See, listen, feel the vibes and LEARN from what's happening around you, in your industry, in other industries, in your city, in the whole world. What is relevant to you and your brand? How does this affect you and your customers? Take it all in and apply what you feel is relevant to your business.

8. *Do*. Take action and actually do stuff that moves you and your business forward. Test things out. Some stuff will work, some will not—but the more you test, iterate, and actually *do*, the more it'll succeed.

Give a damn about your relationships.

Don't give a damn about what random people say and think.

---

9. Take some calculated risks. Do something in your designs, your communication, or your visual that stands out! You're looking for a wow effect. Keep it interesting and get your customers' attention. Give people something to talk about, be it your product, your marketing, your latest post on Instagram. Whatever it may be, give them reasons to think and talk about you. This should obviously be consistent with your brand's vision, mission, story, and branding.

10. Be consistent. You're the only one who can do YOU. Since there's only one you in the whole universe, by default you'll be different from the rest—provided you stick to you, your gut feeling, and your quirkiness.

11. Deliver. Many companies fail in little things that have a big impact on their customers' perception of them. If you make sure you deliver and actually do what you promise, you'll already have an advantage over your competitors.

12. Never compare yourself or your brand to others. Stop looking at your competitors' sites and offers. It's good to know what they're doing—so you can go in another direction. But if you pay too close attention, you'll unwittingly end up copying them.

13. *Give a damn* about your relationships. By genuinely caring about people (your coworkers, your suppliers and manufacturers, your customers), you'll touch their hearts—and this can have positive, long-lasting effects on your business.

14. *Don't give a damn* about what random people say and think. Nobody knows your potential, drive, ambitions, and dreams. People don't know what you're capable of. If you let yourself be dictated by other people's opinions, you'll never reach your goal!

15. Love it. You have to be *really* passionate about what you're doing. There will be times when you feel a bit low and when things don't go your way. This is when your passion for the brand will keep you persevering and pushing till you get over those obstacles.

16. Come to terms with the fact that most people don't actually give a damn. They have themselves to think about, they have their own lives and businesses—and that's okay. What you do is for *you*. It's your game. Your life. Your business.

19.4 Marketing Tasks

1. Get your story together.

2. Create customer profiles.

3. Communicate your story and values in everything you do.

4. Start your marketing activities as early as you can.

20.

Customer Service

20.1 Customer Care

> Customer service should not be a department. It should be the entire company.
>
> *- Tony Hsieh*

I'm here to help you!

As with marketing, customer care should be present at all times. You're making a great product to meet a specific customer need—and part of this entails paying attention to your customers before, during, and after they purchase from you.

No matter what type of business setup you have—retailers, distributors, or your own e-commerce store—the foundation is *respect*. You make a product for another person, and you want them to be as happy as possible with the whole experience. Think about it from your own perspective: How would *you* like to be treated if you had an issue with a product? If you had questions, how would you like to be received and spoken to? A robot? Someone in a foreign country who barely speaks your language? Or someone who's really there to help you solve your problem in a genuine and sympathetic manner?

If you've made a great product, you may have a long warranty period. Customers will feel reassured about the good quality and confident that if anything happens to their purchase they'll be able to get proper help. When it comes to returns, make sure you have a smooth, uncomplicated return policy. It should be very clear and customer-friendly. Don't tuck it away in minuscule text on the website.

Happy, satisfied customers will be your biggest advocates. They will spread the word and tell everybody about your product if they really love it. Make a product that will blow people's minds.

Your customers are the best influencers.

Turn complaints around

If your customers have any complaints, it should be your goal to turn the situation around and make them into happy customers. There's nothing worse than customer service staffed by people who don't listen and don't seem to want to help. You'll never ever want to buy anything from that company again.

In the early days of our first apparel brand, we had a customer call us up. He explained that the fabric had gotten really beaten up in the area where we had Velcro. Of course, this was not good. We gave him two options: to return the garment and get his money back, or to receive instructions about how to fix the problem and how to minimize it in the future. Unfortunately that specific garment was sold out, so he couldn't get a new one. He therefore chose the second option. We also made sure he got ten percent of the purchase price back, and, as an extra gesture, sent him a brand T-shirt, reiterating our apologies and thanks for his understanding. He wrote back after he received the T-shirt telling us that it was the best customer-care experience he'd ever had. That made our day—and we kept him as a customer!

If your starting point is to make a really good product, you won't have many returns. But problems *will* occur—they always do. It's up to you how you want to deal with them, but always be honest and tell it as it is. For example, if you hit a major production problem, admit it and say your top priority is to fix it right now. Let people know what your plan is. Don't be that company that promises to get back and never does.

The feedback you receive from your customers is vital for your business to thrive, improve, and grow—so remember to treat it that way.

> The customer's perception is your reality.
>
> *–Kate Zabriskie*

20.2 Customer-Service Tasks

1. Implement a customer-service plan and strategy.

2. Listen to your customers!

3. Register and use feedback to improve your business.

21.
After
The Launch

21.1 What To Do After Launching Your First Collection

Reflect

Congratulations—you've launched your first collection. Before starting all over again, it's vital to pause and reflect. Ask yourself all these questions, and give yourself time to think and to answer them as honestly as you can.

- How did it actually go? Go through all the steps and think about the process.
- What went badly, what went smoothly, and what can you improve?
- What is worth changing now?
- What should your priority be?
- Through the design and concept phase, did you have enough time for sketching and sourcing?
- How's your relationship with suppliers and factories?
- Do you have good communication?
- Did they deliver what was agreed and on time?
- Is the quality what you paid for?

- Are they transparent and easy to talk to regarding prices?
- Were the fairs you attended worth it?
- Are your distributors and agents good?
- How does your brand look in the stores?
- Are they going for it full speed or did they tuck your brand away in the corner?

Rushing through the crucially important starting phase is never a good idea. Make sure you give yourself time for inspiration. This is where it all starts—without a great concept and inspiration point, your collection would be pretty mediocre.

Your strategy

Reflecting and looking back is important. Examine the information at hand, evaluate it, and implement it in a new strategy for the future. Yes —*the strategy*.
- Do you have one?
- What are your plans for the coming years?
- How much do you want to grow your brand?
- What's the way to go, to grow your collection?
- How many more stores do you want to sell your brand to?
- If you only sell through your own e-com site, what's your plan for increasing traffic, selling more products, and getting your brand out there?
- Are you happy with your existing customers?

What has the feedback been on your collection and the brand—the bad and the good? Take that into consideration when planning the layout for your new collection.

So many questions—and we're sure you could come up with even more. The best person to answer these is you. Remember, there's no right or wrong answers. Don't get stuck on what could have been or why things weren't done. Focus on how you can do it better moving forward.

Listen to feedback

With the feedback you've received and the stats you've collected from the previous collection, you've got a good restarting point. You pretty much know what will be a success and what won't be so great. Listening to your retailers and customers is very important for your future collections; their feedback will steer you in the right direction. On the other hand, if you listen too much to those retailers who always look in the rearview mirror, you'll never innovate and move forward. You know what you want—it's your brand. Keep this in mind at all times before saying yes to retailers' wishes.

Expand the collection

Do you want to expand your collection? What types of styles should you add? Should you add a new segment? Since you're a new player on the market, you want to set your tone and get customers and retailers used to your brand and style. When that's done, you can expand. Adding on segments when you're new might not be a good idea—but, hey, it's your brand and you do whatever you feel is best for you. If you have backers and a load of money, you can introduce anything to the market—with a big bang.

**No matter how much you try to get things right, some things, big or small, will fail. It's a part of being an entrepreneur.
See this as a lesson, and learn from it.**

Here are two crucial questions to help you analyze and
dig deep into what went well and what you can improve.
There are ALWAYS things to improve.
Having this mentality will help you reach your goals—
then exceed them.

Questions for improvement:
What went right?
What can we do better?

New collection

A good idea is to never start from scratch with a collection. You'll have styles that are selling well—and you'll want to continue with these. "Bad" styles you can drop, but if you really believe in a style, have it carry over to the next season to let customers get to know it. Some styles do actually need a season or two to warm up before the sales start to fly. When introducing new styles you need to ask yourself how much time you have to design and produce new styles. Try to have some carry-over styles and some new. Once you have a couple of seasons under your belt, you can implement the following collection structure: one-third carry-overs; one-third updated styles; and one-third completely new styles.

Collection structure

It's also a good idea to have a pyramid structure in your collection.

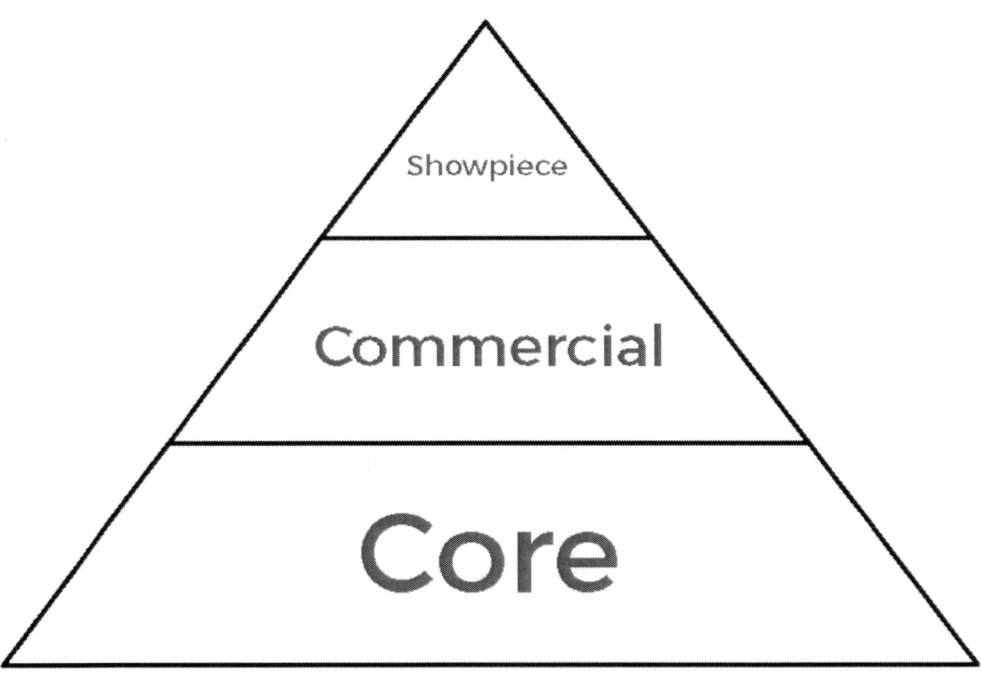

Some iconic showpieces that drive curiosity and the innovative side of your brand, some styles that are pushing it but are a bit more commercial, and then the core where you'll have your volumes and the most sales. Every style in your collection should have its own identity and place within the collection. It needs to have a logical position in the price ladder, pyramid structure, color palette, fit, and materials. The most important factor of all is that you're happy and proud of what you put out there. Sometimes it takes a while for other people to get it, but that's fine. *You* love it, and that's what counts!

21.2 Components Of A Thriving Clothing Company

"Retail is dying; traditional outdoor fairs are not working anymore; sales have stagnated! No one has the success recipe anymore!" says the CEO of one of Scandinavia's biggest outdoor brands. After over 16 years working with numerous apparel brands in the outdoor industry, we must admit that the entire industry feels a bit lost at the moment. It feels as if brands are waiting for some sort of sign from above—direction, guidance, a blueprint; call it whatever you want. They're waiting for someone or something to give them the workbook that will turn this downwards spiral around and hand them success.

The outdoor industry has been leading the sustainability wave for some time. Many brands have been pushing the research, innovating incredible products and implementing extremely rigorous standards in sourcing and manufacturing. But when it comes to running contemporary businesses for the modern customer, nope, sorry, that hasn't happened yet. The old ways of doing business aren't working anymore. Customers are too well-educated and want things faster.

The outdoor industry is a great example of the fact that brands need to take a fresh look at all components of the business to become brands of the future. Through our customers at Apparel Entrepreneurship, we see that, to be able to make it now and to get a flying start, new brands need to stay one step ahead of the fast-paced, constantly changing industry.

Having ourselves gotten inspiration from other industries, and seen some beauty and fashion brands turning traditional business models upside down and killing it in sales figures, we wonder why other brands are so slow to react and implement the changes needed to gain forward momentum. Blaming retail, blaming social media, blaming the millennials and Gen Z doesn't get you anywhere.

We've put together a little list, for both new and established apparel brands, of attributes and approaches that will enable you to stay relevant and thrive.

What your brand must have

Without the attributes listed hereunder, a company will have a hard time attracting the younger generations, and will never gain a trusting customer base in general.

1. Clear marketing positioning
Without spot-on positioning, a clear target customer, a brand will never have space to grow.

2. Have a strong purpose
David Hieatt explains it best: "The most important brands in the world make you feel something. They do that because they have something they want to change. And as customers, we want to be part of that change. These companies have a reason to exist over and above just to make a profit: They have a purpose. Yes, we admire the product they make. But the thing we love the most about them is the change they're making."

3. Modern-thinking leaders
Old-school is old-school and won't work in today's fast-paced world. Leaders need to stay educated, curious, and willing to test and iterate to find new ways of doing business. And it goes without saying, leadership

needs to bring on board the younger generation, a diverse group of people, to be relevant NOW.

4. Unique point of view
Closely monitoring competitor brands and going the same route because it's safe will never pave a winning path for your brand. Setting a clear, unique strategy based on your brand's values, and following it closely will keep the brand unique.

5. Tech and data-driven
Everybody has a phone today. In 2018, 1.79 billion people will have bought something online. For a brand to be digitally visible, it needs a tech team in place who manage the website, e-commerce, and all social media platforms. No—we're not talking about the outdated IT department! A modern tech strategy that drives traffic to your website, and a top-notch e-commerce system are vital for securing recurrent and increasing numbers of customers for your brand.

6. Distinct, cohesive design language
Downtown stores and fashion fairs are awash with apparel brands making very similar products. If you removed the logos, you wouldn't be able to distinguish one brand from the next. By intentionally avoiding similarity in design language, you'll ensure your products and brand stand out.

7. Community, inclusivity, diversity
Brands with a strong, loyal customer base have three factors in common: they've built an extremely strong sense of belonging through *community*, *inclusivity*, and *diversity*.

8. Environmental responsibility; sustainability and fair production
Long-term sustainability strategies are musts for the brands of the future. Environmental responsibility should be on every brand's agenda because today's conscious, educated customers demand it from the brands they wear. Help save the world through your brand and your customers.

9. Lifestyle
Strong apparel brands are not just about a good product. They're a lifestyle! Customers tap into a brand's world, values, and total lifestyle. Brands just need to get better at communicating what that lifestyle is and why customers should want to be part of it.

10. Authenticity and honesty

With the ever-constant flood of information, people have become very aware of BS. In order to build strong, long-term relationships with customers, brands need to be honest in everything they do, tell it as it is, in order to gain trust. A customer who knows your story and trusts you as a brand is a very happy customer. They're your loyal champions and will spread the word about your brand.

11. Communication, information, visibility, and engagement with customers

Customers want to belong. They want to be part of something cool and great. They want to know what's going on; they want to know everything about the products, what goes on behind the scenes, and the process. All you have to do is give them the information and let them participate.

12. Customer service

Tony Hsieh, CEO of Zappos, says, "Customer service shouldn't be a department; it should be the entire company." Satisfied customers will always remember how well they were treated. They'll want to come back for more.

13. Happy employees

There's no well-functioning company with miserable employees. Happy employees are a result of effort, affection, engagement, fairness, and positive guidance. Fulfilled employees will always go the extra mile when they have to because they know they're appreciated and supported.

14. Great product

Without a great product, it'll be hard to enter the market and even harder to succeed and thrive in it. A fantastic product is also the best marketing you can have.

15. Financial security

Successful brands deliver season after season, year after year, consistently. Consistency can only be achieved through a well-oiled strategic machine, with systems in place and rigorous planning. Successful brands *plan* for success—they don't just end up successful. Keeping a close eye on the numbers and efficiency, and constantly tweaking to reach those numbers is what makes brands thrive.

Good to have

Brands with the following "good to have" attributes achieve a deeper level of trust from their customers than regular brands do.

1. Storytelling
People don't always care about facts and numbers, how many pockets a product has, what material it's made of—what they'll remember is the story you tell about that product and collection. Storytelling is at the core of every human being. Tell stories that move people and you'll have a much deeper connection with and dedication from your customers.

2. Test new sales strategies
With traditional sales funnels, brands know what to expect and how to proceed. The sales teams meet their buyers, exhibit at fairs, use the online store, etc. But what if brands were to experiment a bit more in their sales strategies with selective offer drops, collaborations, and limited-number products? The upsides are the obvious increase in marketing, potentially generating new customer groups; increase in sales figures; and tapping into new product areas.

3. Test new business models
Do brands still need to operate on season-based models? Could certain parts of the collection be seasonless, available all year round? Could parts of the collection have a "see now—buy now" model? Could brands have a one-year collection instead of the four seasons? There are many opportunities for trying out new approaches.

One last thought: A lot of what we're saying here will be obsolete in the very near future. For brands to remain relevant, they need to ADAPT to the ever-changing scene. As Charles Darwin said: "It is not the strongest of the species that survives, nor the most intelligent that survives. It is the one that is most adaptable to change." Adapting is learning. The quicker you adapt, the better your future will be. What matters is that you respond!

How many of the above points do *you* tick off, as a brand? If it's less than half, it's time to set a meeting with your team, implement a strategy, and start planning. There are some great opportunities out there!

YOU SNOOZE—YOU LOSE

21.3 After-The-Launch Tasks

1. Reflect on your business.

2. Update your strategy.

3. Update your collection.

It's your brand—Make your own rules

Thank you for reading this book. We hope it has given you valuable tips and information to help you run your apparel business. Remember that it's your business, and you're in full control. No one knows your brand like you do, or what's best for it. Travel your own path and don't base your decisions on other people's opinions. Learn, watch, and absorb, and then steer your business in the direction you feel is best.

> If you're not passionate enough from the start, you'll never stick it out.
>
> *–Steve Jobs*

Take good care of your team and your partners. Your company is the total sum of all the people in it. Grow together; make and create a winning brand.

Stay honest. Be honest in all your business relationships. Work *with* people, not against them. Be honest to your vision and stick to what you believe in.
Enjoy the process and the hustle. Keep your passion and be ruthlessly driven. Do it 100 percent your way, as long as you do *something*, and keep the momentum.

Join the Member Zone for apparel entrepreneurs

Your business is dynamic, and new challenges will arise along the way. Some are generic; some are specific to your business. If you want continuous support from apparel entrepreneurs around the globe and from Apparel Entrepreneurship, the Member Zone is something you should take a look at.

You'll find templates, cheat sheets, tech packs, a worldwide community, new content, and more.

Gain instant access to templates and databases with hundreds of manufacturers and suppliers.

Speed up your business process, get help with your daily hustle, and save valuable time.

Visit: apparelentrepreneurship.com

If you are not willing to risk the unusual,
you will have to settle for the ordinary.

-Jim Rohn

Appendix

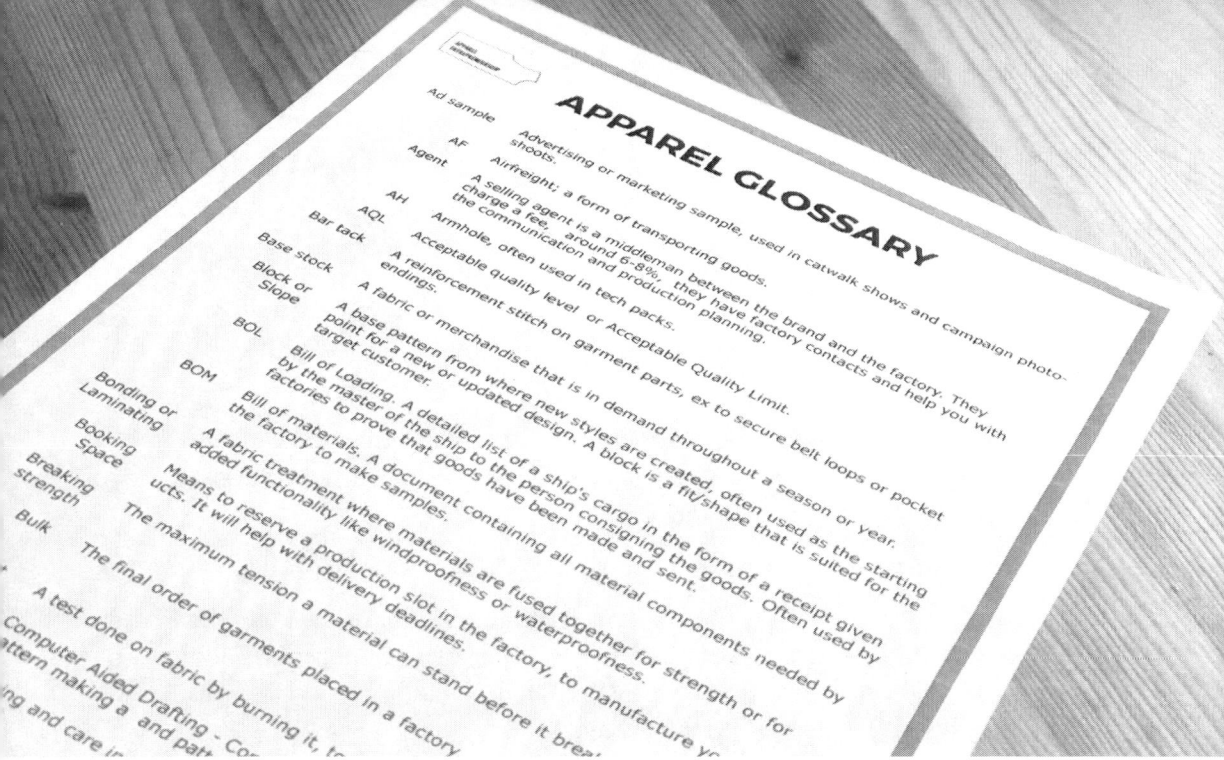

Apparel Glossary

Glossary, terms, and vocabulary

Understanding the glossary and terms used in the apparel business will be an important part of your day-to-day business. Understanding these words, phrases, and abbreviations will help you communicate with suppliers, buyers, and the rest of the teams involved in and around your brand.

Ad sample	Advertising or marketing sample, used in catwalk shows and campaign photo shoots.
AF	Airfreight: a form of transporting goods.
Agent	A selling agent is a middleman between the brand and the factory. They charge a fee, around 6-8 percent; they have factory contacts and help you with the communication and production planning.
AH	Armhole, often used in tech packs.

AQL	Acceptable quality level or Acceptable Quality Limit.
Bar tack	A reinforcement stitch on garment parts; e.g., to secure belt loops or pocket endings.
Base stock	A fabric or merchandise that's in demand throughout a season or year.
Block	A base pattern, often used as the starting point for a new or updated design. A block is a fit/shape that is suited for the target customer.
Block or Slope	A base pattern from which new styles are created.
BOL	Bill of Loading. A detailed list of a ship's cargo in the form of a receipt given by the shipmaster to the person consigning the goods. Often used by factories to prove that goods have been made and sent.
BOM	Bill of materials. A document containing all material components needed by the factory to make samples.
Bonding or Laminating	A fabric treatment where materials are fused together for strength or for added functionality like windproofness or waterproofness.
Booking space	Means to reserve a production slot in the factory, to manufacture your products. It'll help with delivery deadlines.
Breaking strength	The maximum tension a material can stand before it breaks.
Bulk	The final order of garments placed in a factory, made in line with your specifications.
Burn test	A test done on fabric by burning it, to determine the fiber content.
CAD	Computer-aided drafting—Computer software programs that are used for pattern-making and pattern grading.
Care labels or Care instructions	Washing and care instruction label inside of garments. Also states origin of product.

Carryover	A style that's repeated in the next season's collection.
Cartons	Packaging used to transport the bulk stock.
CB	Centre back of a garment.
CF	Centre front of a garment.
CMT	Cut, make, and trim. Refers to a factory's capabilities to cut the fabric, make the garments and provide the trims.
CNY	Chinese New Year. Factories in China close for up to 8 weeks, in January and/or February—no production or sampling will happen during this time. Plan accordingly!
Color standard	A color reference number like Pantone 19-3245TCX or a color swatch, provided by you to the fabric/dye mill. It'll be used to make your exact color.
Colorfastness	A material's ability to keep its color in all stages: manufacturing, storage, usage.
Colorway	Different color options in one single design.
COO	Country of origin. Should be indicated on the care label or somewhere else inside of the garment.
Cost sheet	A document used to calculate the total cost of a product, including all the materials and manufacturing.
Critical path	A document used to check the production process and keep a record of samples received.
CS	Coverstitch. A stitching technique used on stretch materials, often placed at the sleeve ends and hem of a garment.
Cuttable width	The usable width of a fabric. The wider the fabric, the more pattern pieces you can fit on it for cutting. A narrow fabric is therefore more expensive.

DDP	Delivered duty paid. It means that the price includes the garments, fabric, and trims, and the goods will be delivered to you, with the import tax paid by the factory. You'll probably encounter this when receiving quotes for production.
Distributor	Middle person or agency between the brand and the retailer.
DNTS	Double-needle topstitch.
Draping	A 3-dimensional process where a person creates the design on a draping form, in material. The drape is later made into a pattern.
DTM	Dye to match. An indication in a tech pack or spec, to match the trims to the garment color, for example.
Duty	A form of tax, charged by the country the goods are being transported to and from. The amount depends on the country and the number of goods.
Ease	This refers to the extra room in a worn garment. Ease is added for extra comfort, freedom of movement and styling.
EBITDA	Earnings Before Interest, Taxes, Depreciation, and Amortization. This is one of the most important numbers for you as a business. It's the amount of profit or loss your company has made, before taxes. Calculated at the end of the year.
Estimated yardage	The estimated material yardage for a garment.
Ex-factory	The date the goods are leaving the factory. This is different from the shipping date. Shipping date refers to the date your goods are shipped from the port.
Facing	A piece of extra fabric, used to reinforce, for example, the inside of the waistband, pocket entries, sleeve cuffs, and hems.

FCL	Full container load. When dealing with a shipping agent, you can request a full shipping container if you have a lot of goods to ship, which usually means you get a better price.
FF	Freight forwarder. A company who can arrange transport for your goods and customs clearance on your behalf.
Fit model	An employee or freelancer who has the same body measurements as your target customer. The fit model will try on any fit prototypes and samples, so you can achieve the intended fit for that garment.
Fit model	The live model used in your fit sessions, when you try on your prototypes for checking and adjusting.
Fit sample, Sample or Prototype	A garment sent from the factory so you can check the fit, details, solutions, artworks, and trims. This will be fitted on a model and tested. Normally there are 2-3 samples before the salesman sample and bulk production. You'll fit and comment each sample so the factory can perfect the design until it's approved by you.
Fits or Fit sessions	A fit session with a fit model, designer, and product developer. The purpose of the meeting is for the model to try on the garments and improve the fit of any samples. The designer will make the changes needed and the product developer will communicate the changes to the factory for amendments.
FOB	Free on Board or Freight on Board. It means that the cost of delivering goods to the nearest port are included, as well as the costs to manufacture the clothes. It does not include shipping or any other fees such as taxes, duty, and insurance.
Forward cover	To buy foreign currency in advance to lock in the exchange rate. Garment Dye—A process where color is applied to a garment after it has been made, rather than dying the fabric before it's cut out.

Fully fashioned	The shaping points on a knitted garment, like shoulders and elbows.
F u s i b l e , Interlining or Interfacing	Material used to give a certain area of a garment more body, like a collar or waistband.
Garment dyed	White or raw material colored garments that are dyed in the finished process.
Garment twist or Torquing	When a garment is twisting after washing, because of tension in the pattern pieces.
GG	Gauge. It refers to a knitted material's number of needles per inch.
GP	Gross profit. This means the price the customer paid for the product, minus tax and production/shipping costs. It doesn't take into account other expenses such as wages or the cost of running a shop.
Grading	Size grading in between each size in a garment. This step is done to ensure a great fit in all sizes.
Grading or grade rules	Grading means the difference of measurements between sizes in one garment. This is indicated in the spec sheets or measurement lists.
Greige	Fabric that has not yet been dyed. The fabric is later dyed in several colors depending on your needs.
GSM	Grams per square meter. This indicates the weight of a fabric. The weight of a fabric is usually stated on the fabric swatches you receive from suppliers.
Gusset	A piece of extra fabric inserted in, for example, the crotch area, or under the arm to give better movement.
GWR	Garment worksheet. This can mean a tech pack, but could also mean a one-page document with basic information such as the fabric, trims, delivery date and size range.
Hand	The hand feel of a fabric.

Handloom	A fabric sample made by hand to show an example of the finished fabric design or a sample made by an actual handloom. These samples are sent so you can approve the design and color.
Header	This refers to a fabric swatch, sent as a reference from a fabric supplier to a designer, to show the offer.
HSP	High shoulder point. This is a point of measure often referred to on a spec sheet or a measurement list.
Hue	A color tone.
Inventory	All stocked goods, fabric, trims, finished products.
KD	Knitdown. A knit fabric that the factory sends you for approval of knit structure, design and layout.
Knock-off	A copy of someone else's design.
Landed	The cost of a garment after everything has been paid for—all materials, the production, delivery and duty/taxes. This is later used to calculate the gross profit to ensure you get the right margins and profit targets.
LCL	Less than a container load. If you only have a small number of goods to ship, it'll be too expensive to buy a whole shipping container. Therefore, your freight forwarder will combine your goods with another customer's to fill a container and your portion of the goods will be less than a container load.
LD	Lab dip. A small piece of fabric or trim that the factory sends for color approval on dye-to-match colors. The lab dip is matched with your color standard and either you approve it or comment on what changes need to be made to achieve the correct color.
Lead time	The amount of time required for a supplier or manufacturer to complete a product, from the date you placed the order.

Line Plan	A framework for designers and the product-development team, that outlines the entire product range, with SKUs.
Lining	The second layer of fabric, on the inside of a garment, to hide the interior.
LS	Lockstitch. The most common stitch, created with a single needle.
LSP	Low shoulder point. This is a point of measure often referred to on a spec sheet or measurement list.
Man-made fibers	Synthetic fibers.
Markup	The difference between cost price and selling price.
Mill	Where textiles are woven or knitted.
MOQ	Minimum order quantity—the minimum-amount order placed to a supplier or a manufacturer on a material or a product.
MOQ	Minimum order quantity. This is the minimum amount of garments per style a factory is prepared to manufacture, or the minimum amount of fabric trims or labels you're allowed to buy. You can get around MOQs by paying a surcharge.
Natural fibers	All fibers that are produced or grown naturally like cotton, silk, wool, hemp.
Option	Refers to different color options in a single style.
Piece dyed	The process of dying a material after it has been knitted or woven.
POM	Point of measure. Specific measurement points for specing a garment.
Preproduction sample	PP—This is the last sample to be reviewed before the bulk production. This sample has all the correct materials and trims. After approving a PP, bulk production starts.
Production schedule	The schedule to make sure a garment bulk production runs on time.

Re-Order	Products that are reordered by customers.
Registration number (RN#)	A specific number that brands are required to display in each garment.
Retail price	The wholesale price plus the markup that the retailers add to make a profit and cover their costs.
SA	Seam allowance. The amount of fabric left between the edge of the fabric and the stitch line.
Sample	A garment prototype.
Sample cut	Sample yardage/meter (3-5) sent from the fabric supplier to the brand for making the first sample.
Sample room	A place in a factory where protos and salesman samples are made.
SF	Sea freight. A method of transporting the bulk goods.
Size break	The ratio of each size that has been ordered. The final order quantity split over all sizes in a single style.
Size run or Size set	A sample of each size that the style is available in.
Size specification	Garment measurements at a specific part of a garment, decided by the brand.
SKU	Stock Keeping Unit number—a product in a specific size and color.
SMS	Salesman sample—A sample used by the sales team to show buyers. Salesman samples are made before the bulk production and therefore changes can still be made for the bulk.
SN	Single needle. A stitch created with only one needle.
SNTS	Single needle topstitch. A finishing stitch that's done with one needle. It can often be a decorative stitch in a contrast color.

SO	Strike off—A sample of printed fabric that has been sent for approval. It's to check the quality of the print, the size, and the colors. You can either approve the print and bulk will go ahead, or you can give the factory improvements to make and they'll send another SO.
Specs	A document with detailed indications on measurements, detail instructions, material, and colors used to produce a garment.
SPI/SPC	Stitches per inch/stitches per centimeter. The number of stitches per inch/cm can be specified in the tech pack.
SS	Shipping sample. The last fit sample to be received before all garments are finished and shipped to your warehouse. An SS is required to make sure the garments have been produced as expected.
SS	SS can also mean side seam. Both uses of SS will be found in tech packs—make sure you're clear about which one you mean.
Stock fabrics	Fabric that already exists in a supplier's range; this does not include custom fabrics made specifically for you.
Stock market	An industry market that manufacturers go to. Fabric suppliers display their offers and manufacturers order directly from them. Common in Asia.
Stock turnover	The number of times a store's product stock is sold and replaced.
Style	A particular design in your range.
Tech pack	A working document the factory uses to make the garments. It contains detailed information about measurements, fabrics and construction techniques. These are updated by you after your fit sessions to communicate any updates or improvements required of the factory.
Tech sketch/ technical drawing	A detailed drawing of the garment laid out flat, front and back, with details.

Technical drawing or Flats	A drawing drawn flat, front and back, with details. Used in production to make a garment.
Tolerance	The measurements discrepancy of a particular part of a garment that is tolerated in a produced style. For example, if a measurement is 20 and the tolerance is 1, a garment measuring 19 or 21 would be accepted.
Unit control	System to record and control product status. Garments bought, sold, in stock or on order.
UOM	Unit of measure.
Usage	The amount of fabric used to manufacture a garment.
Vertical integration	Joint companies that produce and manufacture different things; for example, a fabric mill with a garment manufacturer.
Warp	The lengthwise thread in a woven fabric.
Wash	A finishing applied to a fabric or an entire garment to achieve a particular look or performance feature.
Weft	The crosswise thread in woven fabrics.
Wholesale price	The price at which stores buy companies' goods. These products are later sold to the end consumer at a retail price.
Wicking	The ability of a fiber or material to transport moisture away from your body.
WIP	Work in progress. A document that varies from company to company, but often includes all of the styles currently going through production and the stage they're at.
YD	Yarn dye. A coloring method where the yarn is dyed before weaving or knitting a material, resulting in much richer color.
Yoke	A shaped pattern piece that forms a part of a garment, usually fitting around the neck and shoulders.

Fabric Descriptions

Fiber

A fiber is a fine hair-like thread or strand and is considered the raw material of textiles. Fiber is extracted from various sources and later woven or knitted into fabrics. As well as being obtained from animals, plants, and minerals, many fibers are made artificially into synthetic fabrics. Below is a list of the most commonly used textile fibers.

Fabrics in the apparel industry are made of natural or artificial fibers and can be produced using three different techniques: weaving, knitting, and felting.

There are two types of textile fibers: Staple and filament. Staple fibers are pretty short, measured in millimeters or inches; filament fibers are quite long and are measured in meters or yards. Most of the natural fibers are staple fibers, except one—silk, which is reeled from a silkworm cocoon. Man-made fibers can be staple or filament, depending on the fabric it's intended for. Man-made fibers are always first produced as filament then cut down to resemble staple fibers.

Based on the source of the fiber, it's classified as natural or man-made:

Natural fibers:
  Animal fibers
  • Animal hair fibers
  • Animal secretion fibers
  Plant Fibers
  • Plant leaf fibers
  • Plant bast fibers
  • Plant seed fibers
  • Plant wood fibers
  Mineral Fibers

Man-Made Fibers:
  Synthetic Fibers

Fabrics

2-LAYER

A 2-layer fabric means that a protective inner coating is bonded to a face fabric, such as polyester or nylon. The inner layer is usually some kind of polyurethane (PU) or expanded polytetrafluoroethylene (ePTFE), which acts as a membrane that allows moisture from the inside to go through the material, but prevents water from the outside getting in. When using a 2L fabric in a jacket, for example, there needs to be a lining on the inside, to protect the membrane and to give the wearer more comfort from the plastic film against the skin.

A 2L material is often waterproof, windproof and breathable. For a garment to be fully waterproof it needs to have taped seams.

2.5-LAYER

A 2.5-layer fabric is a face fabric with a laminated or coated membrane that has an added print on the backside. The print on the membrane protects the membrane from damage and makes the product much more comfortable on the skin. A 2.5L product does not need a lining on the inside to protect the membrane; it can be used as is. This means that 2.5L products are very lightweight and packable. A 2.5L material is often waterproof, windproof and breathable. For a garment to be fully waterproof it needs to have taped seams.

3-LAYER

A 3-layer material has an outer fabric, a coated or laminated membrane in the middle, and a thin protective inner layer. The membrane in the middle is what actually makes the fabric waterproof and windproof. The backer, which is the inner layer, is a thin material that protects the membrane against abrasion from the inside. A 3L is a much more durable fabric than a 2L and a 2.5L and is often used in outdoor wear and sportswear. A 3L material is often waterproof, windproof and breathable. For a garment to be fully waterproof it needs to have taped seams.

ACRYLIC
Acrylic is a synthetic fiber, warm, strong, and light, and is often used in knitted products like sweaters and accessories. It's quite often used mixed with, for example, wool.

BAMBOO
Bamboo is a man-made fiber fabricated from wood pulp. Bamboo material is breathable, durable, very absorbent, and feels soft next to the skin. Bamboo fabric is also biodegradable. Because of the comfort offered by its softness and breathability, this material is well suited for garments worn next to the skin and sportswear.

BONDING
Adhesive bonding is used to fasten two surfaces together, usually producing a smooth bond. This technique involves glues, epoxies, or various plastic agents that bond by evaporation of a solvent, or by curing a bonding agent with heat, pressure, or time.

CALICO
Calico is a plain-woven textile made from unbleached, often not fully processed, cotton. It's less coarse and not as thick or as sturdy as canvas or denim. It's commonly used for toile to construct sample pieces before the actual garment is sent for bulk production.

CASHMERE
Cashmere wool is extremely soft and delicate to the hand. Obtained from cashmere goats, it doesn't have the itchy feel of regular wool. It's lightweight and very warm. Cashmere can be used for any type of product, from sweaters, shawls, and gloves, to coats and summer jackets.

CHIFFON
Chiffon is a lightweight woven sheer fabric. It can be made of silk, polyester, nylon, cotton, or rayon. Most commonly used in evening wear, especially as an overlay, for giving an elegant and floating

appearance to a gown. It's also a popular fabric used in blouses, ribbons, scarves, and lingerie. It's an elegant, floaty, sheer fabric perfect for bridal gowns and evening dresses.

CORDUROY
Corduroy is a heavyweight durable textile composed of twisted fibers similar to twill. Usually, it's made of cotton or cotton blend. It's a rigid form of velvet and looks as if it's made from multiple cords laid parallel to each other then stitched together. The number of ribs varies. Mostly used for trousers, jackets, and shirts.

COTTON
Cotton is a natural vegetable fiber, known to be comfortable and soft. It offers good absorbency, color retention, and strength, and it drapes well. Cotton is a versatile fiber and can be used to make many different woven or knitted fabrics.

CREPE FABRIC
Crepe fabrics are without prominent weave effects but have a crinkled or pebble surface. It's a plain woven fabric made of very high-twist yarns, either in one direction or both warp and weft hence, giving the pebble effect. It may be manufactured in the range of light to medium weight. The fabric has a silk-like texture and drapes well. It's used for making dresses, blouses, linings, and scarves.

CROCHET
Crochet is a process of creating fabric by interlocking loops of yarn, thread, or strands of other materials using a crochet hook. The name is taken from the French word "crochet," meaning "small hook." Commonly used for light, summer sweaters, other kinds of tops, shorts, dresses, and skirts.

DENIM
Denim is a fabric made mostly of the natural fiber cotton, in a twill structure. Denim is most commonly associated with jeans fabric. Depending on the weight, denim can be used for shirtings, jeans, dresses, and jackets. The denim fabric is generally colored with indigo dye to create blue jeans, although the term "jeans" formerly denoted a different, lighter, cotton textile.

DOBBY
Dobby is a decorative weave featuring woven small geometric patterns and extra texture in the cloth. Dobby (similar to Jacquard, although

technically different) varies widely. The warp and weft threads may be the same color or different. Satin threads are particularly effective in this kind of weave as their texture will highlight the pattern.

DWR
DWR, or durable water-repellent, is a protective coating used on the outside of a fabric to make it water-resistant. DWR treatment aims to repel water from the outside to prevent the outer layer of fabric from becoming saturated with water. Most factory-applied treatments are fluoropolymer-based. DWR wears off over time, and the fabric needs to be re-treated to maintain its water-repellency.

FELT
Felt is a non-woven fabric made from wool, hair, or fur, and sometimes in combination with certain manufactured fibers, where the fibers are locked together in a process utilizing heat, moisture, and pressure, to form a compact material. While some types of felt are very soft, some are tough enough to form construction materials.

FLANNEL
Flannel is plain or twill woven fabric popular for its softness and coziness. The softness comes from a technique employed by the mills called "double brushing." It may be classified as brushed fabric with soft fibers protruding on one or both of the fabric's surfaces. Originally, flannel was made of wool, but now it's made of cotton, wool, or any other synthetic fiber. Flannel fabrics are ideal for suitings, shirtings, jackets, bedspreads, and pajamas.

FLEECE
Fleece is a fluffy material that resembles the fleece coat on a sheep and is made of synthetic and mixed fibers with a pile face on both sides. It's soft, breathable, and extremely warm yet fairly lightweight. Fleece is also quite durable. It's used for warm products for colder weather like jackets, mid-layers, and accessories.

FRENCH TERRY
French Terry is a knitted fabric most commonly made of cotton, but it can be of a mixture of fibers. It has a knit-like face and soft looped backside. French Terry can be used for apparel like loungewear, hoodies, and activewear. Due to its weight, garments have great structure and shape.

GEORGETTE
Georgette is a sheer, lightweight, dull-finished crêpe fabric, in a plain weave. It's traditionally made from silk or synthetic fibers. Georgette is strong and tear-resistant and it drapes very well. It's distinct due to its crinkly crepe-light texture, which feels slightly rough but gives the fabric a flowing look. The threads are highly twisted, causing them to crinkle as they relax. Mostly used to create blouses, dresses, evening wear, and shirts.

GINGHAM
Gingham is a checkered-pattern fabric, of medium weight. It's yarn-dyed, plain weave cotton fabric. Gingham has no right or wrong side with respect to color. Uses include shirts, dresses, shorts, and handkerchiefs.

GREIGE FABRIC
When no finish is applied to textiles, they're termed as gray fabrics, greige fabrics, or unfinished textiles, which of course does not refer to the color of the fabric. It implies that no finishing treatment has been given to it.

HEMP
Hemp is a natural fiber, obtained from stalks of hemp plants. Hemp is antimicrobial, has great moisture absorbance and dries fairly quickly. It's a strong fiber that's considered sustainable because it doesn't need much water to grow.

LACE
Lace can be made both from natural and synthetic fibers. It's a decorative openwork fabric consisting of a network of yarns formed into intricate designs. Lace may be hand- or machine-made. Lace is used as trimming on parts of garments and in evening wear, lingerie, dresses and skirts, bridal veils and more. Lace is a very delicate fabric.

LAMINATION
A laminated material is composed of two or more layers, at least one of which is a textile fabric, bonded closely together with a polymer film. The layers are bonded by means of an added adhesive, or by the adhesive properties of one or more of the component layers. Lamination is widely used where fabrics are required to be waterproof and breathable at the same time.

LINEN
Linen fiber is a natural fiber derived from the stems of flax plants. Linen fibers are cooling, quick-drying, have great moisture absorbance and are twice as strong as cotton. Linen fabric can be used for products such as dresses, shirts, pants, jackets, and suits. Great to wear in hot and humid weather.

MOHAIR
Mohair is a long, smooth fiber used in knitwear like sweaters, suits and coats, and accessories. The fiber is obtained from angora goats (not to be confused with angora wool from angora rabbits). It's a durable, soft fiber that's warm in winter thanks to its insulating properties, yet cool in summer.

MUSLIN
Muslin fabrics are plain cotton fabrics produced in a wide range of thickness, from light to heavy. Unfinished muslin is widely used for designer sample garments and interfacing. Muslin fabrics are referred to as book, mull, swiss, and sheeting, based on the grades.

NEOPRENE
Neoprene is a synthetic rubber and is used in weather-resistant products. It's resistant to oil and aging and is used in waterproof products such as wetsuits and diving suits. It's stretchable and can vary in thickness.

NYLON/POLYAMIDE
Nylon is a synthetic fiber. It's lightweight, extremely strong, resistant to abrasion, and easy to wash and dry. Fabrics made from nylon fibers can be used for a very wide variety of products, like blouses, dresses, sportswear, activewear, lingerie, swimwear, underwear, raincoats, ski apparel, windbreakers and cycle wear.

ORGANZA
Organza is a crisp, sheer, lightweight plain weave fabric, with a medium to high yarn count, made of silk, rayon, nylon, or polyester. It's transparent and woven with very fine, tightly twisted yarns in an open, plain weave. Organza is commonly used for bridal wear and evening wear.

OXFORD
Oxford is a type of woven dress-shirt fabric, a particular casual-to-formal cloth in Oxford shirts. The Oxford weave has a basket-weave

structure and a lustrous aspect, making it a popular fabric for a dress shirt. Some other types are the plain, Pinpoint and the more formal Royal Oxfords. They're typically versatile options for dress shirts.

PIQUE
Piqué refers to a weaving style normally used with cotton yarn and recognizable by its waffle weave texture. A knit fabric with a similar texture is used in polo shirts. Piqués may be constructed in patterns such as cord, waffle, honeycomb, and birdseye piqués.

POLYESTER
Polyester is a synthetic fiber that makes strong, quick-drying fabrics. They're shrink- and wrinkle-resistant. The fibers are strong yet lightweight. Commonly used on most garments and usually blended with other fibers such as elastane, spandex, and cotton. It's a quick-drying fabric and well suited for outdoor clothing and sportswear.

POLYPROPYLENE
Polypropylene is a synthetic fiber with excellent durability and moisture-transportation properties. Polypropylene is used in, for example, base layers for sports, where the polypropylene knitting transfers the moisture away from the skin to the next layer of clothing and the wearer feels dry. It's also very light.

POPLIN
Poplin is a durable cotton, cotton blend, or synthetic fiber material with a distinctive ribbed texture. The fabric also has a tightly closed weave texture that gives it a light luster. Poplin fabrics are extremely strong and versatile and can be used for many types of garments including jackets, raincoats, shirts, etc.

RAMIE
Ramie is one of the strongest natural fibers. It has high natural luster, is quick-drying and an absorbent fiber. Ramie fiber holds its shape very well, with minimal wrinkling. It's usually used mixed with other fibers for durability.

SATIN
Satin is a sleek and glossy fabric that has a great drape. Fibers commonly woven to create satin are silk, cotton, and also less-expensive synthetic materials like polyester. Satin is used in apparel such as lingerie, nightgowns, blouses, and evening gowns, but also in some shirts and neckties.

SEERSUCKER
Seersucker is a fairly thin, woven, puckered fabric made in cotton, mixed or synthetic fibers. Often used in garments for spring and summer, like shirts, casual wear, and children's wear.

SILK
Silk is a natural fiber, produced by silkworms when making cocoons. Mainly used in woven fabrics, silk is a very luxurious material. It has a great drape, luster, and good absorbing capabilities. The fabric is also cooling in summer. Silk fiber is the strongest natural fiber, with a slight stretch that makes garments very comfortable. It's used for making scarves, dresses, blouses, and lighter garments.

SLUB
Slub is a special effect, adding character to the fabric. It's a small, thick spot in the twist of a yarn that gives texture to the surface of a knitted or woven fabric. Commonly used for T-shirts and known for its comfort.

SPANDEX
Spandex is a synthetic fiber with extremely stretchy capabilities. It's mostly used in a small percentage, mixed with other fibers to give a bit of stretch for comfort and fit. Used in tight garments like activewear and sportswear.

TAFFETA
Taffeta fabric is a crisp, soft and smooth plain woven fabric with a slight sheen. It's manufactured out of different fibers like rayon, silk, or nylon. It's generally made with a plain weave, fine warp yarns, and heavier filling yarns.

TERRY CLOTH
A little different from French Terry, terry cloth is a fabric that has loops on both sides of the fabric, and can absorb large amounts of water. Made of natural or synthetic fibers, it can be manufactured by weaving or knitting. This absorbent fabric is perfect for making towels and robes because of its softness. Terry cloth can also be used for apparel like streetwear, loungewear, activewear, and casual wear.

VELOUR

Velour fabrics are velvety, soft, plush, and slightly stretchy. Velour is a knitted fabric and can be made from synthetic fibers like polyester or cotton. Common uses are loungewear, sportswear, and casual wear.

VELVET

Velvet is a very smooth and soft fabric with a short, dense pile on one side that gives a smooth hand feel. It can be made of synthetic or natural fibers. It can be used in all sorts of garments, such as dresses, sweaters, and eveningwear.

VISCOSE/RAYON

Viscose is a man-made fiber derived from wood pulp from trees like pine, fir, and birch. Viscose is quite absorbent and has a good abrasion resistance. It's breathable, drapes well, and is soft, comfortable, and relatively light. There's one downside with viscose, though: it can shrink. Viscose fabric is highly versatile and can be used in many different products.

WATERPROOF and BREATHABLE

A material can generally be rendered waterproof and breathable via a physical or chemical process. The physical method uses a basic microporous membrane with holes that are too small for water droplets to seep in, but large enough for vapor to transit out. The chemical method uses a hydrophilic membrane allowing vapor to transit out. The membrane is negatively charged, and the vapor, being positive charged, can transit out through intermolecular gaps. The membrane needs to be applied to supporting fabrics. The breathability also depends on the humidity, the supporting fabrics, and the temperature.

WOOL

Wool is a natural fiber, obtained from sheep. Wool is a wicking fiber, extremely comfortable to wear in warm and cold weather because of the fiber's built-in climate control. It's naturally stain- and wrinkle-resistant. Wool fiber can be strengthened by mixing it with other synthetic fibers for a more durable fabric. Because of its comfort, it's highly versatile and used for formal wear, activewear, sportswear, and casual wear.

Fabric Consumption

In order to know how much fabric is needed to make your style, you have to first make a prototype. Before that, you can only estimate the consumption. To determine the accurate fabric consumption per style, you need your final design and the right materials (the same as for the bulk production). You also want the sample made by the same factory that's going to handle your bulk production, since different factories can cut fabric pieces in different ways. Remember that fabric consumption varies according to sizes.

When planning, making price calculations and strategic decisions, you can estimate fabric usage even before you've made the first prototype. The following list shows typical fabric usage per garment style. It's based on size M for women, and size L for men. The numbers are based on a fabric roll of around 145 cm or 57 inches.

These numbers are only indicative, aimed at high-level planning.

Garment	Fabric usage (meter)	Fabric usage (yard)
Bathing suit	0,8	0,9
Bikini	0,5	0,5
Panties	0,3	0,3
Top	0,8	0,9
W's blazer	2	2,2
Tank top	0,8	0,9
M's board shorts	1,2	1,3
Long M's coat	3,2	3,5
Long W's coat	3	3,3
M's suit	1,8	2,0
Short-sleeve shirt	1,3	1,4
Skirt	1,5	1,6
Hoodie	1,5	1,6
Sweatshirt	1,3	1,4
Jeans M's	1,5	1,6
Pants W's	1,4	1,5
W's leggings	1,2	1,3
Long-sleeve dress	1,7	1,9
M's LS tee	1,1	1,2
W's LS tee	1	1,1
Long dress	3	3,3
M's pants	1,9	2,1
M's polo shirt	1,2	1,3

Garment	Fabric usage (meter)	Fabric usage (yard)
W's shorts	0,5	0,5
M's shorts	1	1,1
Jacket	1,8	2,0
T-shirt	1	1,1
Varsity jacket	1,8	2,0
W's jacket	1,7	1,9

About The Authors

Ana is a former national athlete who has honed her skills at cutting and tailoring school, art school, and Parsons School of Art and Design in Paris and New York. She has over 15 years' experience working in the apparel industry. She has designed and product-developed award-winning technical products for international brands. She has also launched and run two own brands.

Klas is an IT engineer with a Master of Science degree from The Royal Institute of Technology in Stockholm and ENST in Paris. He has over 15 years' experience in project management, business development, tech, e-commerce, and running startups in an international environment. His background includes working as senior project manager for Europe's largest workwear company, as well as starting up two clothing brands.

Ana and Klas also run a technical apparel design agency: Ana Kristiansson Design Agency; anakristiansson.com. They've lived in Los Angeles and New York in the US, Paris and Annecy in France, Gothenburg and Stockholm in Sweden, and Romania. Their studio is now located in an old porcelain factory in the archipelago outside of Stockholm, Sweden. They work online, and the world is their workspace.

Template Examples

The following pages contain examples of some of the most common and useful documents you need in an apparel business. These templates, cheat sheets and checklists can be downloaded in the Member Zone when you're a registered member of Apparel Entrepreneurship.

The following downloadables are currently available. Others are added continuously.

- Line Sheet Template
- Label and Hangtag Template
- Product Price Matrix
- Male Croquis Template
- Female Croquis Template
- Men's Tee Tech Pack Template
- Women's Tee Tech Pack Template
- Men's Hoodie Tech Pack Template
- Women's Hoodie Tech Pack Template
- Men's Softshell Tech Pack Template
- Women's Softshell Tech Pack Template
- Men's Tights Tech Pack Template
- Women's Tights Tech Pack Template

- Order Form
- Costing Sheet
- How To Brief A Designer
- Apparel Glossary
- Expenses/Budget/Cash flow Template
- Business Plan Template
- Business Startup Checklist
- Manufacturing Checklist
- Bootstrapping List
- Style-Number Guide
- Check Points For Commenting A Garment and Tools Needed
- Customer Profile Template
- Online Store Checklist
- Terms Of Agreement
- Bill Of Materials
- Product-Range Plan
- Project Design Brief
- Product Design Brief

BUDGET TEMPLATE EXAMPLE

APPAREL ENTREPRENEURSHIP BASIC EXPENSES / BUDGET /CASHFLOW SPREADSHEET

TOTALS	JAN	FEB	MAR	APR	MAY	JUN	JUL	AUG	SEP	OCT	NOV	DEC	YLY TOTAL
OVERHEADS													
ADMINISTRATION													
SAMPLES													
PRODUCTION													
SALES & MARKETING													
TOTAL PER MONTH													

OVERHEADS	JAN	FEB	MAR	APR	MAY	JUN	JUL	AUG	SEP	OCT	NOV	DEC	YLY TOTAL
Rent													
Service Charges													
Electricity													
Telephone													
Insurance													
Internet													
Bank charges													
Registration costs													
Total overheads													

ADMINISTRATION	JAN	FEB	MAR	APR	MAY	JUN	JUL	AUG	SEP	OCT	NOV	DEC	YLY TOTAL
Accountant													
Courier													
Lawyer													
Office supply													
Postage													
Travel - production													
Travel - sales													
Travel - trending													
Total administration													

SAMPLES	JAN	FEB	MAR	APR	MAY	JUN	JUL	AUG	SEP	OCT	NOV	DEC	YLY TOTAL
Design & tech packs													
Pattern													
Fabric													
Accessories													
Trims													
Fitting													
Sample production													
Shipping													
Total sample costs													

PRODUCTION	JAN	FEB	MAR	APR	MAY	JUN	JUL	AUG	SEP	OCT	NOV	DEC	YLY TOTAL
Fabric													
Accessories													
Trims													
Labels													
Pattern grading													
Bulk production													
Shipping													
Total production costs													

SALES & MARKETING	JAN	FEB	MAR	APR	MAY	JUN	JUL	AUG	SEP	OCT	NOV	DEC	YLY TOTAL
Advertising													
Events & shows													
Sales material													
Photo													
Events													
Website													
Total sales & marketing costs													

PRODUCT PRICE MATRIX EXAMPLE

APPAREL ENTREPRENEURSHIP PRODUCT / PRICE /MATERIAL MATRIX

PRODUCT STYLE NAME	MATERIAL 1	2	3	4	5	6	7	8	TOTAL NO OF MATERIALS IN EACH STYLE	PRODUCT RETAIL PRICE
TOPS										
Top 1	1					1			2	50
Top 2		1					1		2	75
Top 3			1					1	2	100
Top 4				1					1	125
Top 5					1				1	150
MIDLAYERS										
Midlayer 1	1					1			2	
Midlayer 2		1					1		2	
Midlayer 3			1					1	2	
Midlayer 4				1					1	
Midlayer 5					1				1	
OUTERWEAR										
Outerwear 1	1					1			2	
Outerwear 2		1					1		2	
Outerwear 3			1					1	2	
Outerwear 4				1					1	
Outerwear 5					1				1	
BOTTOMS										
Bottom 1	1					1			2	
Bottom 2		1					1		2	
Bottom 3			1					1	2	
Bottom 4				1					1	
Bottom 5					1				1	
TOTALS NO OF STYLES IN EACH MATERIAL	4	4	4	4	4	4	4	4		

COSTING SHEET EXAMPLE

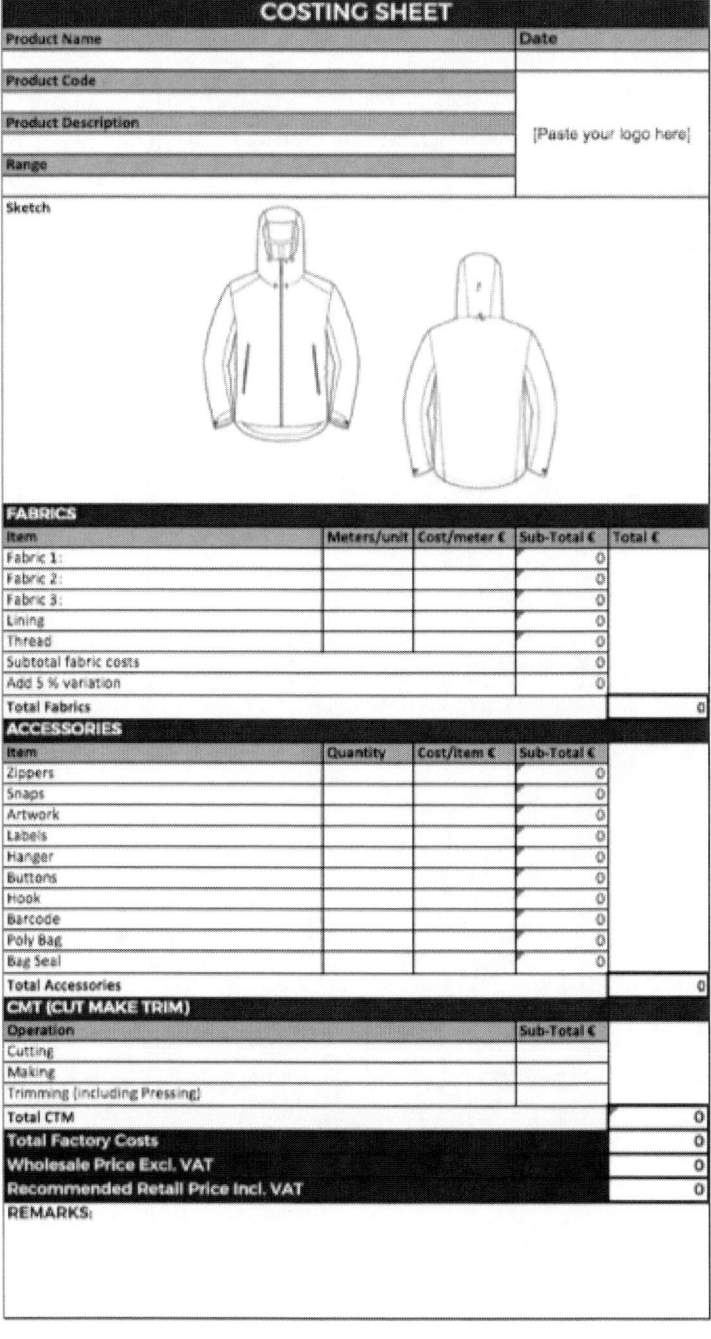

COSTING SHEET

Product Name				Date	
Product Code					
Product Description				[Paste your logo here]	
Range					

Sketch

FABRICS

Item	Meters/unit	Cost/meter €	Sub-Total €	Total €
Fabric 1:			0	
Fabric 2:			0	
Fabric 3:			0	
Lining			0	
Thread			0	
Subtotal fabric costs			0	
Add 5 % variation			0	
Total Fabrics				0

ACCESSORIES

Item	Quantity	Cost/item €	Sub-Total €	Total €
Zippers			0	
Snaps			0	
Artwork			0	
Labels			0	
Hanger			0	
Buttons			0	
Hook			0	
Barcode			0	
Poly Bag			0	
Bag Seal			0	
Total Accessories				0

CMT (CUT MAKE TRIM)

Operation	Sub-Total €	
Cutting		
Making		
Trimming (including Pressing)		
Total CTM		0
Total Factory Costs		0
Wholesale Price Excl. VAT		0
Recommended Retail Price Incl. VAT		0

REMARKS:

LINE SHEET EXAMPLE

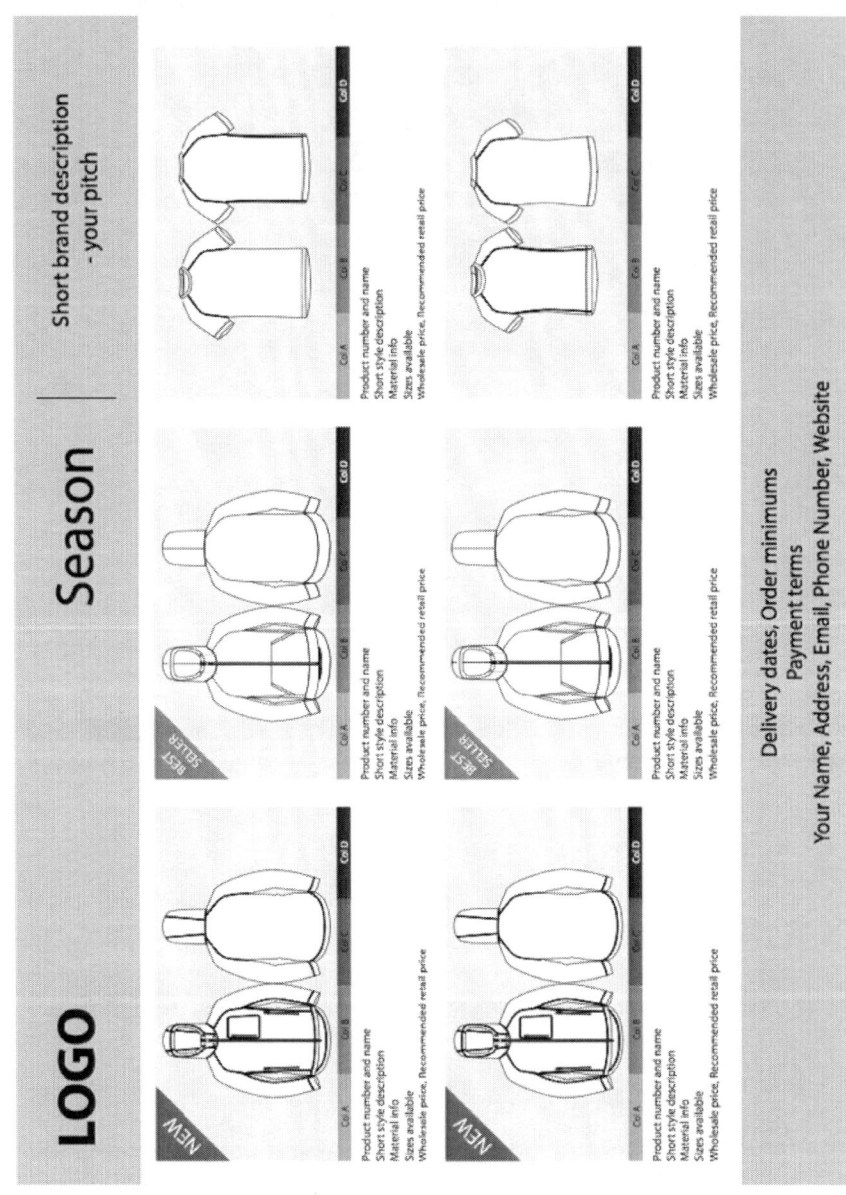

ORDER FORM EXAMPLE

ORDER FORM

CUSTOMER   **Date:**

[Company]
[Contact Person]
[Address]
[Org.no]
[VAT no]   [Paste your logo here]
[Phone]
[Email]

SHIPPING ADDRESS (IF DIFFERENT)
[Shipping Address]

PRODUCT	PRICE	QUANTITY			TOTAL QTY	TOTAL PRICE SEK
Women's Styles		S	M	L		
001 Wstyle 1					0	0
002 Wstyle 2					0	0
003 Wstyle 3					0	0
004 Wstyle 4					0	0
005 Wstyle 5					0	0
006 Wstyle 6					0	0
Men's Styles		M	L	XL		
011 Mstyle1					0	0
012 Mstyle 2					0	0
013 Mstyle 3					0	0
014 Mstyle 4					0	0
015 Mstyle 5					0	0
016 Mstyle 6					0	0

Total Excl. VAT	0 SEK
VAT 25 %	0 SEK
Total Incl. VAT	0 SEK

Customer's Approval. This is a binding order.

Date	Authorized signature

Your company name	Your phone no
Your address line 1	Your email address
Your address line 2	PlusYour bank details
Registration no. XXXXXX	Payment Terms 30 days net
VAT No. SEXXXXXX01	

FEMALE CROQUIS EXAMPLE

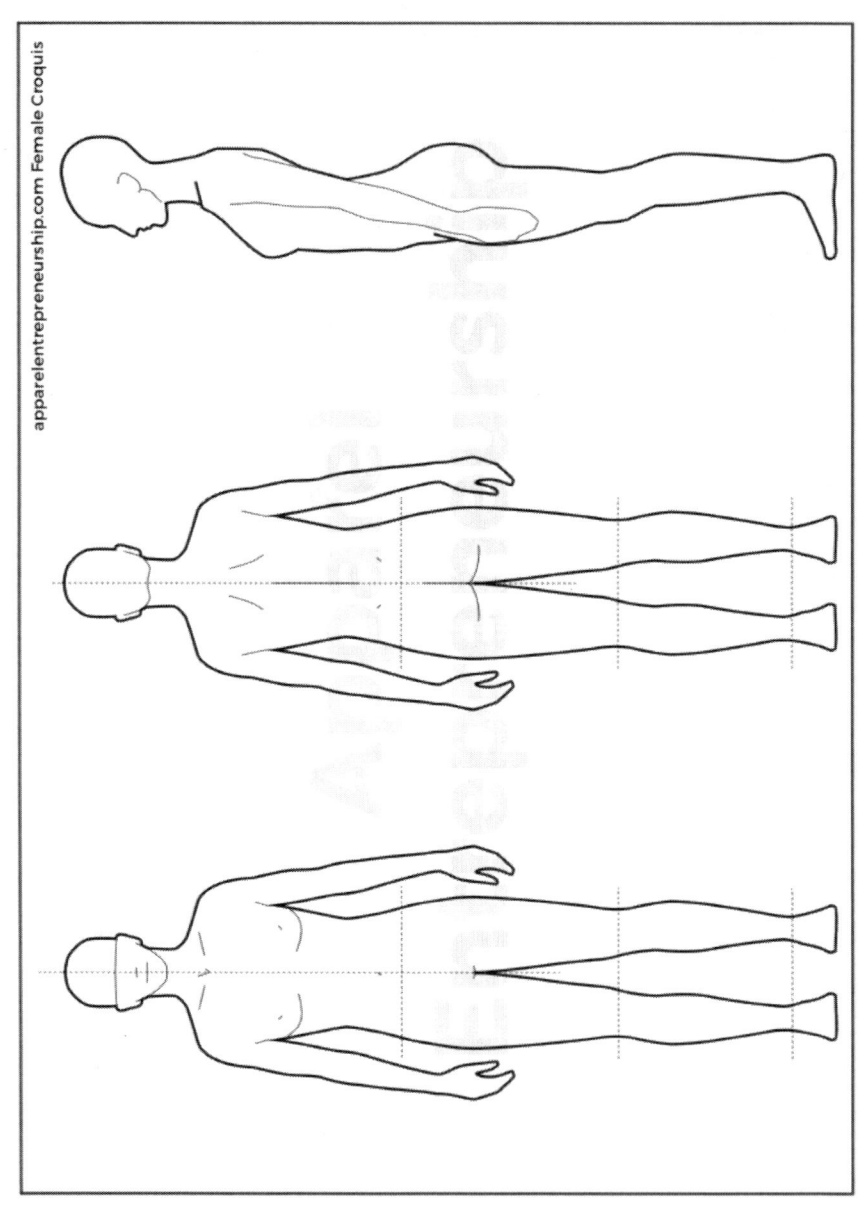

MALE CROQUIS EXAMPLE

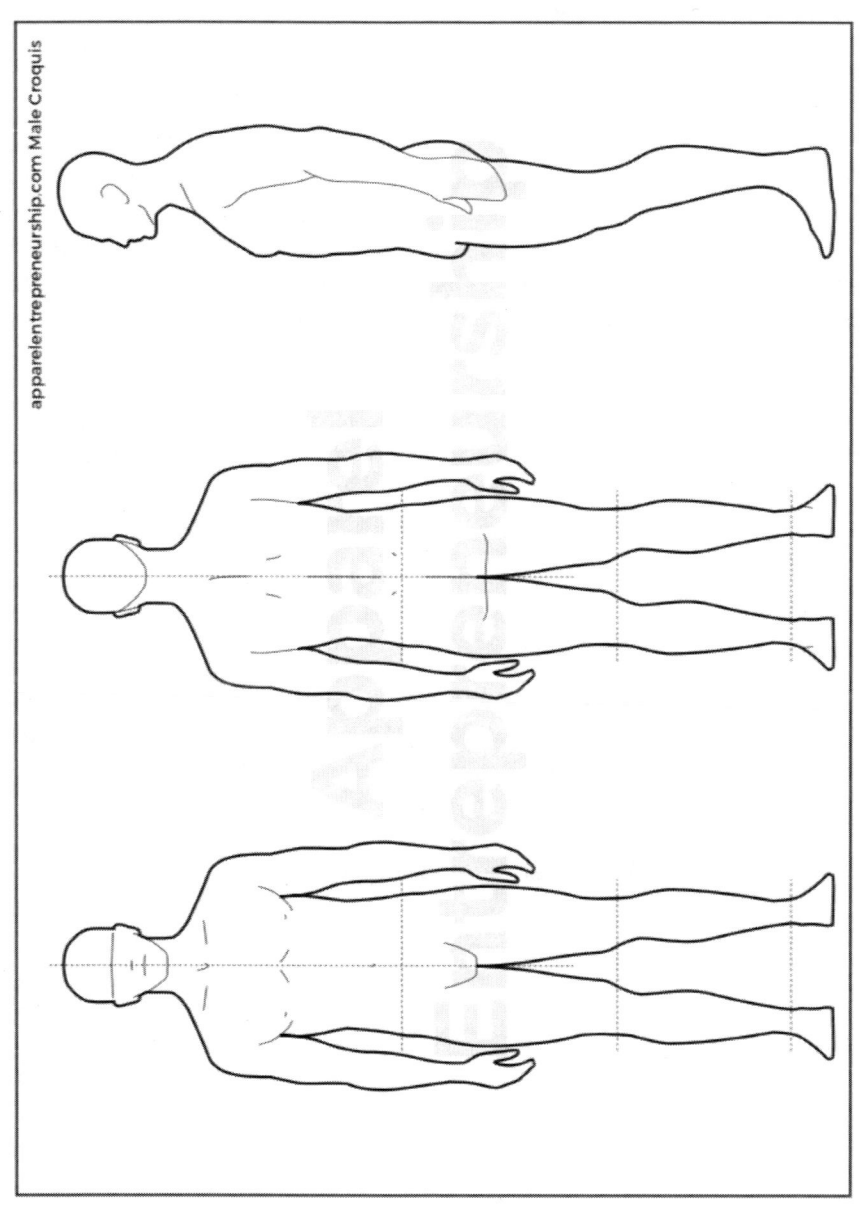

Disclaimer

The information contained in this book is for informational purposes only. We're not lawyers or accountants. Any legal or financial advice that we give is our opinion, based on our own experiences. You should always seek the advice of a professional before acting on something that we have published or recommended.

It's up to *you* how you run your apparel brand and entrepreneurial endeavors. Actual costs may vary depending on how you decide to work, whom you pick as your partners and suppliers, and whether you involve consultants or have employees who alter the costs. Also, your agreement with your suppliers, your choice of shipping partners and materials will differ from business to business.

Users of this book are advised to do their own due diligence when it comes to making business decisions, and all information, products, and services that have been provided should be independently verified by your own qualified professionals. By reading this book, you agree that we and our company are not responsible for the success or failure of your business decisions relating to any information presented in this book.

Made in United States
North Haven, CT
07 June 2024

53338201R00221